SNAKES AND LADDERS

INTRODUCTION

'Dad, can I have a guitar, please?'

It was a simple request, but it turned out to be an important one. Thankfully, I didn't ask him for a spanner. Since that day, over fifty years ago, a guitar of some description has never been far from my side: Gibson, Fender, Martin, ESP, Dobro, Ibanez, Takamine, Flying Finn, National, Tokai, Washburn, Gretsch, Hagstrom, Supro, Coral, Zematis, Ovation and lesser-known brands such as Harmony, Kalamazoo, Heritage, Vox and Ozark. Been there, done that and worn the strings.

The instrument he bought me was purchased at a second-hand shop, and was only in there because the local charity shop refused to take it on the grounds that it could damage a twelve-year-old's fingers. Thankfully, my fingers survived for a couple of months before I managed to cajole good old Dad into buying me something a little more user friendly. And I've never looked back.

SNAKES AND LADDERS

The guitar has been an undeviating force in my life and has accompanied me to places I could only dream of, places I shouldn't have been and, on a couple of occasions, places I was lucky to get out of alive. Well, I'm still here and I'm still playing the guitar with as much uninhibited fervour as I'm allowed. For the moment, join me on a twenty-year musical journey, which took place between 1963 and 1983. From humble beginnings to rock-star status. Enjoy!

Micky Moody
London, 2016

CHAPTER 1

A PLECTRUM TOO FAR

My father was a very practical man whose way of thinking implied that anything bought must prove to be value for money. The idea of another instrument standing idly in the corner like 'that bloody piano' may have evoked memories of his tough childhood, when such instruments may have served a better purpose by being chopped up into firewood. Due to a lack of interest, the aforementioned piano was eventually wheeled off to the scrapheap, while my sister, for whom the device of doom had originally been targeted, looked on dispassionately. I regarded it as the way now being clear for me to make my first step towards a much more interesting replacement: a guitar.

My curiosity towards the phenomenon known as pop music was stirred by the radio, and it was on one Saturday afternoon in Woolworth's record department that I first heard 'Red River Rock' by Johnny and the Hurricanes. I found their raw brand of rocking instrumentals very appealing, especially the guitar solos. And, like a lot of people, I loved the Shadows and had become one of the legion of early air guitarists miming along to 'Apache'. Prior to the production of those blow-up plastic replicas they use now, we employed a cricket bat to mime along to Hank Marvin and the exciting sounds he produced via his Fender Stratocaster. Some aspiring guitar heroes were lucky enough to have older brothers who'd bought the latest Stateside recordings by Elvis Presley, Little Richard, Chuck Berry and a host of first-generation rockers. Alas, with no elder brother to rely on, I had to make do with an elder sister's choice of Cliff Richard and Lonnie Donegan, and my mother's prized record – 'Little Donkey' by the Beverly Sisters.

It was tough at the bottom.

I was inspired enough to acquire a used four-string plastic guitar with a picture of Elvis Presley on the headstock. Brushing aside the image of a fading icon, the neck had a nasty crack in it, though this had no bearing on my inability to play it. Years later, it came to my attention that this instrument came with a 'push-button auto-chord' attachment which, in this case, had been forcibly removed from the neck, resulting in said fissure. Within a week, I could almost play 'Apache' on one string, which was a start, with or without the auto-chord. However, the Shadows just weren't cool anymore. They still had greasy hair, unlike those new kids on the block, the Beatles, who majored in shampoo and hairdryers. The 'Fab Four' were 'the tops', as they used to say.

Within a week, I'd arrived at a justifiable conclusion: the Presley guitar was just a toy, a broken piece of junk. Drastic measures were required to quell my frustration, so I took it upon myself to reply to an advertisement in a popular music paper. The offer promised a catalogue of guitars that were: 'Genuine models of both imported and English production, made of specially selected seasoned woods chosen for their tonal qualities and prepared by craftsmen who have spent their lives in the manufacture of fretted instruments.'

Today, as a cynical old pro, I'd describe them as: 'Genuine crap aimed at the elementary student or beginner.'

However, to an impressionable twelve-year-old, the Bell Musical Instruments catalogue contained the sexiest bodies I'd cast eyes on since seeing Kim Novak's latest film. Black-and-white shots of the Watkins Rapier 33, the Burns Vista Sonic and the Levin Goliath filled me with feelings of excitement and otherworldly anticipation, though the prices soon brought me back down to earth. The aforementioned Vista Sonic, priced at ninety-five guineas, was never going to form an alliance with my under-funded piggy bank, so the cheapest electric guitar in the brochure – the Rosetti Lucky Seven, at fourteen guineas – became the object of my desires.

The now-legendary triangular Watkins Dominator amplifier was available for a reasonable thirty-eight pounds and ten shillings, though the Bird Golden Eagle fifteen-watt model with reverb, tremolo and optional set of screw-on legs (thirty shillings for a set of four) came in at thirty-nine guineas. Guitarists earning a low wage must have spent many a sleepless night worrying about the extra pound notes, which, in those days, featured a very young-looking Queen Elizabeth.

Any thoughts I'd harboured of acquiring a second-hand guitar from Hamilton's music store were soon dispelled as we came to a halt under the three brass balls of Greenwood's pawn shop. My father had finally succumbed to my constant requests for a guitar and agreed to help me find a cheap one, providing, of course, that I mastered the instrument sufficiently to give Andrés Segovia a run for his pesetas. My imagination began to run wild: just what would I be holding close to my chest later that evening? Would I look like a member of a beat group? Would it match my new Beatle jacket? Or would I be stuck with that plastic Presley thing?

As we entered Greenwood's, the sheer volume of articles packed into one room was overwhelming. Accordions hung breathlessly among radio sets, vacuum cleaners, treasures of taxidermy, furniture, clocks (which all seemed to strike the hour every minute) and complete sets of *Encyclopaedia Britannica*. Against the back wall loomed a ceiling-high pile of clothes; some were no doubt recently procured from the houses of recently deceased pensioners. Judging by the general disarray, there was a possibility that one or two of the poor sods were still in there. I half-expected to see Albert Steptoe and Private Frazer from *Dad's Army* arguing the toss over some fingerless gloves. The gloomy atmosphere suddenly brightened as I spied a couple of acoustic guitars hanging side by side from the ceiling, like a couple of dead Mexicans in a Sergio Leone spaghetti western. A slinky-looking electric model that hung nearby cost an impossible fifteen guineas.

I chose the one with the butterfly motif, naïvely ignoring the fact that the strings stood roughly one-and-a-half inches above the fingerboard, thus rendering the instrument more suitable for slicing cheese or garrotting hamsters and ensuring that my novice fingers were to suffer for some time to come.

Dad lowered the instrument from its gallows and studied it like a man who knew even less about guitars than his son did.

''Ow much?' he enquired, holding up the object of my desire like a dead rabbit.

'Three quid, mate,' responded the shifty-looking assistant. Dad winced, then, scratching his chin, took a sharp intake of breath.

'Two pounds ten – I'm not daft, y' know,' he announced. The shifty sod behind the counter looked as though he'd just been offered five bob for the pleasure of his sister.

'Oh, I don't know, first-class instrument that,' he remonstrated. 'Tommy Steele played one just like it. 'E went from rags to riches and 'e even went to sea when 'e was fifteen.'

My heart began to beat a little faster as the visions of me sitting at home that night caressing the guitar of my dreams began to fade. Dad scratched his cloth cap and stared out of the window. He was not going to yield.

'All right, all right,' conceded Shifty, muttering obscenities under his breath.

He prised the money from my benefactor, took one look at the inch-and-a-half-high string action, bit his bottom lip and gave out a nasal snort. The sadistic bastard. My love for guitars endures, but I'm pleased to report that the quality has seriously improved.

Lacking any domestic musical influence, apart from my sister's short-lived musical career and my dad's one-fingered stabs at 'that bloody piano', it soon became apparent that some sort of tutelage would be appropriate. What was required was the *Dick Sadler Complete Guitar Method*, although it looked about as interesting as a book on nuclear physics. I have never been a particularly enthusiastic scholar, and as there were no threats of admonishment – e.g. lines or the dreaded cane – the publication was respectfully ignored. Still, the images of the Beatles and the Rolling Stones stood foremost in my mind and I decided to persevere to the point where I was able to pick out the odd melody, though chords were a bit of a mystery. A little voice, possibly influenced by my French teacher Mr Hughes, said, 'Stick at it, laddie – don't be a daftie.'

In June 1963, the Beatles played at the Astoria Ballroom in my home town of Middlesbrough and I managed to get hold of a ticket. The place was, as expected, full to capacity. An entry in my notebook of the time described the event:

> Before the Beatles came on to the stage there were two local groups who were quite good, but when the Beatles came on the place went mad. There was a barrier of two rows of chairs and one row of settees, but that did not stop the crowd from surging over. if it had not been for the officials, they would have climbed onto the stage.
>
> Because of the pandemonium around the stage, and fearful of physical injury, I beat a hasty retreat to the balcony where I found a safer spot amid some older fans.

The notebook entry summed up my feelings at the end of the evening:

> Although I was nearly squashed at the Astoria, I still managed to see the Beatles and still think they are the best band out.

They were to remain the 'best band out' for many years to come.

One of my closest schoolmates was John Rowney, an amiable, pasty-looking lad, who lived with his folks on the same council estate as me. A friendship blossomed through shared tastes: pop music, obviously, but also humour and limited fashion-wear. He'd managed to acquire a cap from the C&A department store that bore a striking resemblance to the one worn by John Lennon on the Beatles's conquest of the United States. It offset my round-collared Beatle jacket to a tee.

His parents, succumbing to continuous demands for a six-string accomplice, had treated their loved one to a guitar not dissimilar to mine. After a few schoolyard enquiries, we discovered that our classmate, Paul Rodgers, possessed a budget-priced acoustic guitar and that Dennis Minchella and Ray McConnell would be willing to help out our humble band on improvised 'percussion'.

I suggested that we should gather at my house to begin a musical journey, and together we entered the world of music with typical schoolboy ineptitude, while persuading the other members of the Moody family to retire to the remaining rooms to suffer the ensuing melee.

Oh to have been a fly on the wall of our dining room that evening, as the clueless fingers of Masters Moody, Rodgers and Rowney, spurred on by a percussive accompaniment (yes, Dennis and Ray hammering the crap out of my mother's pots and pans), strove to put musical progression back by at least three thousand years. Those squeaky, monotone voices battling against a wall of tonal ignorance during a particularly destructive version of 'She Loves You' must have given the neighbours some serious thoughts of upheaval.

My parents always visited the working men's club at weekends. It gave my father a chance to down pints at subsidised prices, while my mother could enjoy a 'snowball' and watch the evening's entertainment, otherwise known as 'the turn'. One particular Sunday, they returned home extolling the talents of Johnny Goffin, the guitar-playing half of that night's act. Apparently he gave lessons, and, aware of my eagerness to progress as a musician, they had arranged for me to visit him the following Thursday. Thanks!

Lying in bed that night, my ambivalent feelings towards the impending lesson left me tossing and turning to the faint sounds transmitted from a small studio in Luxembourg. I could never figure out why the studio of the coolest radio station on our sets was so far away. Where the hell was Luxembourg and why, for that matter, did it stay up so late? Didn't its residents have to get up early and work down mines and in steelworks like everybody else? Who was Horace Batchelor and what was the Infra-Draw Method, and why did it all happen at Keynsham (spelt K-E-Y-N-S-H-A-M), near Bristol?

Johnny Goffin was a middle-aged man of middle-aged proportions who exuded a seemingly working-class snobbery. You know the type: smoked a pipe and read books. Probably had a back yard and owned a lawnmower. Then again, he may have been a decent, intelligent man who was being given the once-over by a twelve-year-old council-house kid with a limited outlook.

Having failed to impress my mother with a feigned bilious attack, I insisted that she accompany me to my inaugural lesson and, on arrival at Chez Goffin, we were beckoned into his living room through a haze of St Bruno pipe smoke. There were items lounging in the lounge – furniture, a television, a bookcase, a stuffed hippopotamus etc. – but it was the presence of a music stand centre stage that made me want to turn and run out of there. It may well have been a dentist's chair or an alien from the planet Zlonk as far as I was concerned.

There it was, gazing at me with chromium-plated intensity, hell-bent on my destruction. Somewhere on the periphery of this paranoid state, I could hear Mr Goffin suggesting to my mother that she should come back in forty minutes.

Once I'd removed my starter guitar from the large brown parcel-bag which acted as a carrying case, I could tell by Mr Goffin's expression that he was far from impressed.

'Hmm,' was his only response, apart from sucking on his pipe.

He then allowed himself a knowing smile before producing something known as a tutor – an instruction book containing what appeared to be diagrams of tadpoles climbing up and down telegraph wires. This, he informed me, was music, and by learning to read it, I could do better than 'all that long-haired lot.' As I happened to be a fan of 'all that long-haired lot', this remark was not appreciated, but I remained passive and let him press on. He then informed me that the *Mel Bay Modern Guitar Method* was the most up-to-date and progressive of all graded guitar courses. By now, I was completely lost and was seriously considering a swift exit, when a voice broke through the silence.

'Right, Michael, take hold of your plectrum,' insisted Puffing Billy. Without moving, I shot him a sideways glance.

'You have got a plectrum, haven't you?' he enquired.

I patted each of my pockets in turn, hoping to give him the impression that I may have mislaid one somewhere. He must have fallen for my bluff because he started to pat his own pockets.

'Here, try mine,' he said, handing me something that looked like a big toenail shed by someone involved in an industrial accident. I, in turn, held it like one would hold dead body tissue.

'Between the thumb and forefinger, lad, between the thumb and forefinger,' instructed the cognisant one.

I gave my hand a studious look, then came to the conclusion that the forefinger must, indeed, be the fourth or smallest digit, inspiring me to adopt the pose of some arthritic castanet player. He gave me such a despairing look that I could do nothing but smile inanely before dropping the plectrum on the carpet.

For the remaining thirty minutes, Mr Goffin tried valiantly to persuade one or two of my fingers to press down on the lower registers of the bottom string – an exercise not unfamiliar to him, as he no doubt went through the same motions with other virginal wannabes. I did try, and at one point almost sounded the note of G, but the intensity of the movement caused me to lose my grip on the plectrum and it fell into the sound hole of the guitar. Johnny sat back and scratched around for his weed as the sound of a doorbell ended the first round.

'That'll be your mother,' said Goff the Cough as he hurried towards the door.

'Bloody hell,' I thought. 'The man's psychic!' Maybe if he conducted these lessons by ESP it would cut the travelling costs and insure me against the passive inhalation of Ogden's Nut Ground Shag.

'He's got potential,' enthused Mr Goffin as he prised six shillings out of my mother's wash-day hands. 'Oh, and another eight for the tutor book. Same time next week?'

I stepped out from that house like a man who'd just completed a ten-year stretch at Wormwood Scrubs, breathing in the freedom of life on the outside. In actual fact, I was inhaling some of the most noxious fumes that the ICI chemical plant at nearby Wilton could produce.

'How was it, son?' enquired the woman who'd just trudged the streets for forty-five minutes on my behalf.

'Never again,' I hissed before going into a sulk.

'It'll be all right,' she assured me.

How the heck did she know? The only thing she played was Bingo.

Once home, I fondled my security football while watching *Crackerjack* (Crackerjack!). Five minutes later, my father entered the room and bollocked me in no uncertain terms.

'I didn't spend all that money on that guitar for nothing, you know. Get practising and be there next week for your next lesson – and you're going on your own too, I'm flamin' starvin'. Dragging your mother down there with you when she could be at home cooking my dinner. You don't know you're born!'

Honourable though my intentions were, the thought of sitting down for half an hour each day, striking a note and counting to four then repeating it, was not what I'd had in mind when posing in front of the bedroom mirror a week before. Still, I'd made the commitment, practising for the allotted half an hour until I could pick out the three lowest notes with incredibly boring precision.

I readied myself for a brief musical encounter of the second kind.

Friday arrived and I cycled back from school, secure in the knowledge that, due to a few hours of finger-slicing fret abuse, I could now face my arbiter with newfound confidence. Even the brown parcel-bag had bitten the dust, thanks to a valiant effort by my mother. Her tailoring talents had produced a made-to-measure carrying bag from material not dissimilar to a nun's habit. There was every chance that it had been, considering that she was an enthusiastic member of the

Catholic Women's League. The absence of a handle meant that I had to carry it under my arm. From a distance, it must have looked as though I was assisting some inebriated sister, bereft of limbs, with a two-foot-long neck and no head.

On the long walk to the bus stop I attracted the odd inquisitive glance. Twelve-year-old boys do suffer from a certain lack of confidence – some more than others – and the bus stop was a welcome oasis in a desert of self-consciousness.

'What you got in that bag?' a voice interrupted my train of thought. A couple of scruffy lads stood nearby.

I gave the young inquisitor a steely glance and, turning away, mumbled something about a guitar. Either my muffled response was inaudible or the boy was aurally challenged, because he turned to his mate and informed him that I had a 'bucket o' tar' in the bag. I told him to bugger off or I'd kick him in the shins.

'Oh, you will, will ya? Dad, come 'ere.'

A seven-foot-tall brute wearing a singlet and boxing shorts stuck his head out of a local pub doorway. I suddenly felt insecure, speechless and erm . . . shit scared. Luckily, the bus arrived and I leaped aboard, clutching my mutilated nun, while Neanderthal and son took it in turns to shout abuse.

During my lesson, their faces suddenly appeared on the music stave, superimposed on a pair of quavers. I shivered momentarily. It was the first time I'd quivered over a quaver. Maybe they'd still be there on my return, snacking on raw meat and shooting at cats with an air rifle. On the journey back, I hopped off the bus a stop earlier and sneaked home by an alternative route, carrying my 'nun's torso', and looking over my shoulder every couple of seconds.

CHAPTER 2

CLASS OF 1964

The classroom band started to take shape and we had some enjoyable evenings demolishing a selection of current hits. However, it soon became apparent that my private musical education, coupled with an inner yearning to be part of a 'proper' group, was leaving Dennis and Ray well and truly with the pots and pans. Even though John had persuaded his parents to buy him a second-hand Hofner Colorama electric, the 'front-room band' was about to murder its last tune.

As my confidence grew, I was able to convince Mr Goffin that applying myself to elementary guitar was easily within my grasp. Having mastered such musical landmarks as 'Old Black Joe' and 'The Caissons Go Rolling Along', I began to take pride in my ability to 'play properly' and persevered with Mel Bay's carefully graded, melodious and distinctive method. This, I was assured, would enable me to perform solos, duets and études. Yes, but would it give me the 'beat', like the blokes in groups had? My ever-helpful dad almost came to the rescue when a drinking buddy from his local pub – the caretaker from a local school – offered to coach Paul Rodgers, John Rowney and myself, as he'd apparently done with local band Del and the Falcons. However, learning to play Shadows tunes from sheet music wasn't exactly what we had in mind, and we kicked him into touch after two sessions. It was time for some kind of stimulation.

As luck would have it, it wouldn't be too long in the waiting.

Colin Bradley came from an 'elder brother' background, enjoying the shared upbringing of two music enthusiasts, including one who'd shown him some basic chords. He also possessed a Hofner Congress cello-bodied guitar, an instrument of respected vintage on the semi-pro circuit. He'd attended primary school with Paul and, though we'd been classmates for a couple of years, it wasn't until our shared musical interests collided that we became good friends. Following an invitation to Paul and myself to his house to have a 'strum' and strip the family larder of anything digestible, we decided to pursue our common ground – beat music. Colin's limited yet impressive repertoire of skiffle hits, Peter, Paul and Mary songs and Buddy Holly covers would need no updating, but with my input and recently acquired musical knowledge, and Paul's enthusiasm and self-confidence, there was every possibility of us forming a group.

My primary objective was to upgrade my instrument, and, having impressed my father with my musical endeavours, I had little trouble persuading him to cough up the necessary 'readies'.

'No more than forty pounds though,' he insisted. It sounded like a reasonable offer.

The next few weeks were spent scouring the 'for sale' ads for a suitable replacement guitar – a tedious pastime but satisfying in the knowledge that soon I'd be plugging in my new electric guitar with grown-up confidence. Then, one evening, the following advert appeared in the local newspaper, the *Evening Gazette*:

67. Musical Instruments Etc.
For Sale, Harmony Roy Smeck electric guitar,
v.g.c. £42.00 Tel: M'bro 56843

Persuading my dad to increase his investment by two pounds was a hurdle I didn't even attempt to jump. Optimism would be the key word. Soon I found myself in a phone box pressing Button A, nervously enquiring about this 'Roy Smeck' thing.

'Oh, it's still 'ere,' uttered the voice at the other end, inspiring me to memorise his address before leaping onto the nearest bus.

Many guitar players, when becoming nostalgic about their instruments, often refer to 'the smell' on opening a mysterious-looking guitar case: that exotic blend of mature wood lacquer and felt, with a hint of passive smoke and steel. I experienced it myself on that evening over five decades ago, and it's something you never really forget. The instrument looked gorgeous to my impressionable eyes: a creamy butter colour with knobs and chromed grills. I assumed the grills were for the electric sound. After a brief musical grope, I nodded my approval and proffered the contents of my trouser pocket as payment, while being shrewd enough to leave the pocket lining hanging loose. It hid no more than a few biscuit crumbs and a bent comb.

'Erm, it's forty-two actually,' said the man, looking a little hurt by the offer.

'Oh, I've only got this much,' I replied, and gave him a look that a baby spaniel would have been proud of.

Well, he must have been a dog lover because he let me have it! I barked my appreciation but decided to draw the line at licking his face. The journey home seemed timeless and blissful, like walking on air. I was one happy lad.

Over the next few months, I started to get together on a regular basis with Colin and Paul. Mums, dads, brothers, sisters and family pets gave up living-room space, often sacrificing their favourite television programmes to support our gallant cause. To make things easier, we'd sometimes treat ourselves to the sheet music of current hits. For two shillings and sixpence, schoolboys with a limited knowledge of pop music could scrape through such up-to-the-minute hits as 'Can't Buy Me Love' and 'Things We Said Today' (the Beatles), 'Shout' (Lulu), 'I Think of You' (the Merseybeats) and 'Not Fade Away' (the Rolling Stones).

I continued with my weekly visits to Johnny Goffin, convinced that his tuition would stand me in good stead, even though the Mel Bay method was a slow, tedious process. The sole requirement was the ability to learn one short piece of music a week, which gave me plenty of time to pursue my pop-music interests, undeterred by dotted quarter notes and scale studies in the key of G Major. As for Mr Bay's arrangement of Hayden's 'Austrian Hymn', it was as interesting to me as potholing.

However, Colin, Paul and me forged ahead, ignoring not only hymns but also symphonies, oratorios and a selection of masses also attributed to the great Austrian composer. We'd stick to Mersey Beat, thank you.

A neighbourhood friend, Alan Morris, joined up as bass guitarist but, after one or two sessions, it was quite obvious that he wasn't cutting it. He was having difficulty getting the notes in the right order. (Paul would eventually buy his bass and Alan went on to become a very successful tour manager.)

What we desperately needed now was a drummer.

Q: What is a beat group without a drummer?

A: A bloody folk group, that's what!

Percussionists were definitely in short supply at my school that year – not one person with a drum kit! Just as we were starting to consider the possibilities of a downward spiral into the world of Peter, Paul and Mary, the horrors of 'Puff the Magic Dragon' and 'Stewball' were suddenly dispelled due to the timely intervention of Barry Usher. He was the proud custodian of a plastic Ringo Starr snare drum – fantastic, now we could be the Beatles! Unfortunately, Barry's snare drum gained more respect than his ability to play it, so he followed Alan Morris into the Museum of Never Were (maybe he became a tour manager as well). Once again, the spectre of Peter, Paul and Mary loomed ominously.

Music shops have, somewhat unsurprisingly, always played an important part in the lives of musicians, supplying instruments, accessories, recorded works and necessary advice. They've also functioned as meeting places for local band members to meet and discuss a whole range of subjects – notably music and girls. Hamilton's had formed an integral part of the town's shopping centre for as long as I could remember: a two-storey building housing both records and musical instruments. The downstairs section offered a comprehensive selection of vinyl records, with small airless cubicles containing a basic turntable and small speaker for listening to the goods prior to purchase. Fine, of course, unless the previous occupant was a cigarette-smoking bath-dodger who picked his nose. Wall-bogies at eye level can be pretty disconcerting. Still, we took it all in our stride and added to the ambience by dropping the occasional fart for good measure.

The upstairs department dealt with instruments, amplifiers, sheet music etc. – a veritable Aladdin's Cave to the young and impressionable. By now, we'd managed to upgrade and had entered the world of amplification. Colin had acquired a pickup for his Hofner, plus a Watkins Westminster amplifier in a nice shade of blue and cream. Paul sported the Vox bass guitar he'd bought off Alan Morris, though an amplifier was still in the pipeline. In the meantime, he plugged into my recent purchase – a Harmony amplifier (thanks, Dad!).

Things were starting to come together.

The focal point at Hamilton's was the display window, where local groups pinned their business cards. Weird, wonderful and soon-to-be forgotten collectives like the Fly-By-Nights, the Hafta Darks, and Del and the Falcons offered up their services. It also served for advertising people's rather odd requirements, such as:

Wanted. Blonde-haired rhythm guitarist. Neither mod nor rocker.
Must be rhythmic. Own equipment essential.

This actually fitted Colin's description but he remained loyal to Paul and me, probably because he was unsure of his fashion status.

We did, however, observe one postcard of interest, declaring the talents of Malcolm Cairns, a drummer seeking employment within a young musical environment. Colin made contact and a rehearsal was arranged at a pub near the town centre, which was managed by a friend of my dad. The Class of 1964 was about to enter the big wide world of show business, in an age when the Western world had been presented with the freedom of choice the 'optimistic fifties' promised. Liberation from post-war attitudes had come of age and the younger generation were starting to dive headfirst into an unchartered sea of temerity. The Pill encouraged people to adopt an open mind towards sex, and the music of the day, inspired by the earthy rhythm and blues drifting in from the United States, provided a raunchy accompaniment. Now that the barber's suggestion of 'Something for the weekend, sir?' had become passé, men grew their hair long. In the midst of this orgy of indulgence stood Freddie and the Dreamers, a beat group from Manchester whose singer resembled a chromosomally-challenged Buddy Holly. Granted, they'd produced a few pop hits, but their image was strictly appalling.

Now, you may be wondering why I've singled out this particular partnership for personal criticism, considering that a few of the older bands had only recently dispensed with Brylcreem, but there is a valid point. Malcolm Cairns looked like bloody Freddie – *quelle horreur!*

'This is Malcolm,' announced my dad. 'He says he's an experienced drummer.' Judging by the buxom girl by his side, there was no doubt about it – he was certainly experienced. We shot sideways glances without moving our heads, which is not easy, then said nothing until the ever-courteous Colin responded with a polite 'Hello.'

Malcolm studied the virginal trio and smiled. He must have thought that, in the event of musical inertia, he wouldn't have to worry about dragging us out of pubs and brothels. It made us cringe to think we were in the same group as this 'bloke', though, to be fair, he hadn't said anything about our cheap schoolboy jeans. Furthermore, he had to be an improvement on Barry Usher and his plastic snare drum. And his bird had tits!

We set up our tiny amps in the room upstairs from the bar and waited awkwardly while Malcolm began to assemble his drum kit. Soon we began to gaze in wonderment at his 'proper drums'. Compared to Master Usher's plaything, it looked like the Taj Mahal standing there proudly in a poky room in a rough-and-tumble building in downtown Middlesbrough.

Our living-room sessions had stood us in good stead and we were confident enough to suggest the Rolling Stones' 'What a Shame' to kick off the evening's events. As soon as the opening four bars were under our belts, we were off into the unknown, carefully avoiding eye-to-horn-rimmed-glasses contact with our first real drummer. It soon became evident that Malcolm was no Charlie Watts, but we were no Keith, Brian and Bill either. We self-consciously tore through a few more tunes before diving into the ham and pickle sandwiches, allowing ourselves a few moments of rumination before a respectful, albeit rather naïve rendition of 'If You Need Me'. Ironically, we needed Malcolm, dodgy image or not, to help launch the musical careers of Mick, Colin and Paul, known collectively as... ah, yes, we'd need a name before we could venture any further.

Oh, and a manager too.

Joe Bradley was a short-distance lorry driver by profession, and Colin's eldest brother.

Though there was an age gap of twenty-one years between

the two siblings, they had much in common, especially when it came to music. His easy-going, confident personality commanded respect from his male counterparts and exuded a natural charm towards female company – he was definitely a good man to have on board. At Colin's request, he attended the next session, and after listening to a few songs offered to help us in any way possible. We all knew right away that Joe was the one to help us establish some sort of direction.

What's in a name? Influence, fantasy, ego, fashion or just plain desperation? Speaking as one who has pondered on the subject over the years, I'd say a little of each. Though we'd considered calling ourselves the Premiers, Colin suggested the Intrepids. However, taking the piss out of weak-natured teachers and working with a drummer who looked like Freddie Garrity hardly gave us the authority to be judged intrepid. In the end, we settled for the Titans, yet another contradiction in terms. This decision may have been influenced by the front skin on Malcolm's bass drum, which already had the chosen moniker emblazoned across it – a reminder of his previous set-up.

I retired that night secure in the knowledge that I was now a member of a fully-fledged beat group who would rise as late as possible to go to boring old school.

CHAPTER 3

I'M A ROAD RUNNER, HONEY!!

As 1964 drew to a close, I gave my first public performance as a member of the Titans, at St Mary's Cathedral hall, Middlesbrough. Our English teacher, Mr Early, helped set up the venue, while Paul's elder sister printed up some tickets on her office typewriter. I seem to recall that the admission was a modest two shillings but we couldn't have cared less – money was not the prime objective. My memory eludes me from that cold December night, but I assume that Malcolm drove himself, his kit and his ever-present girlfriend to the gig, while Joe took care of the schoolboy three and their equipment. The expression 'PA system' meant nothing to us; we would simply plug two cheap microphones (recently acquired) into our guitar amplifiers and hope for the best. As it turned out, the stage area yielded only one plug socket and, in the absence of any kind of adaptor, two of the amplifiers had to be connected to the mains supply via the overhead light socket, thus impeding stage visibility to those in the audience. Thankfully, we were all wearing white shirts.

The ticket sales had fared well and even Dennis and Ray from the 'pots and pans' band lent their support, chatting excitedly with Mr Early, or 'Sir', as he was habitually referred to. Joe helped us out where he could before retiring to the nearest boozer for a quick pint, no doubt enthusing to anybody within earshot about the lads in the hall next door. We busied ourselves by tuning up and parting our hair in the right place until the time came for us to take to the stage. I struck a Chuck Berry riff and we were into 'Around and Around'.

It was a successful night. In fact, we were treated to lemonade when we finally ran out of songs. Yep, it was that good.

Once the New Year had sobered up, Joe and his lovely wife Gladys let us use their living room to rehearse and, as a bonus, we could listen to records on their stereo radiogram – a thrill to anybody raised on mono. To satisfy our teenage appetites, Gladys would prepare great snacks and, very soon, a real family atmosphere prevailed.

Joe pointed out that a PA was of paramount importance, and contacted various pubs and working men's clubs, hard-selling us as 'the youngest beat group around', or 'R&B at its best'. His self-confident and sociable disposition often persuaded landlords and club secretaries to give us a chance. We started to build up our repertoire, which drew heavily on the songs of the Beatles, the Stones, Chuck Berry and other current favourites, as well as Colin's folk, skiffle and Buddy Holly influences.

I still made weekly appearances at the court of Johnny

Goffin, though the pipe-smoking one was, by now, approaching his sell-by date. He'd become as boring as school.

It was 1965 and the times they were a-changing. This involved a rapidly maturing testosterone level. Adolescence can be a difficult time of life, and it often helps to share these transitional years with others. While Colin, Paul and myself were undergoing a parallel experience, Malcolm, being a few years older, was going off on a different tangent: that of courtship and musical indifference. Joe rallied on, and his persistent visits to local youth clubs and pubs helped secure some initial bookings and introduced our nasal senses to the aroma of stale beer, cheap perfume and second-hand cigarette smoke.

On one of our earlier shows, at the local British Legion club, we followed a comedian, who finished his set with, 'Oh, you grow your own rhubarb, do you? What do you put on it? Manure? Oh, I usually put custard on mine!'

We decided that the band's name was, perhaps, a little old-fashioned, so it was back on with the thinking caps. Turning to the *New Musical Express* for inspiration, we noted that the pages were full of Bob Dylan, who was coming to Britain for a sell-out tour. I'd read that the Beatles liked him, which I thought was a bit odd. He was a folk singer, wasn't he? Elsewhere, Eric Clapton had left the Yardbirds and was to be replaced by somebody called Jeff Beck. Gene Pitney had recorded an album of country duets with George Jones. No inspiration there.

Eventually, we looked to the blues masters at Chess recordings before deciding on the Road Runners, a progression on the song 'Road Runner' by Bo Diddley. Building up our repertoire was both educational and enjoyable. Our set list soon boasted such gems as 'Farmer John' by the Searchers, 'What a Shame' and 'Off the Hook' by the Stones, 'I'm a Loser' by the Beatles, plus a selection of hits from the songbook of my favourite artist at the time, Chuck Berry.

Our decision to include a drum solo in the set backfired, as Malcolm's percussive poundings were less than impressive. He was certainly no Ginger Baker. Or Hilda Baker for that matter. Continuing with a drum solo was out of the question. In fact, after a few gigs, continuing with the same drummer was out of the question. We plucked up enough courage to ask Joe to pluck up enough courage to inform Malcolm of our wishes, before slinking off into the night. Once the dirty deed was done, we sat with Joe over a Gladys 'special' of sandwiches and chocolate biscuits to discuss plans for a replacement.

Malcolm was understandably gutted by our decision to let him go, though he did have those big knockers waiting to help soothe his soul.

Local drummer Ian Naisbit helped us out on a couple of gigs, then recommended a friend of his, Dave Usher. As usual, Joe and Gladys gave us the run of their living room to audition our second drumming Usher. We arrived that evening to find Joe sporting a rather amused expression, apparently brought on by his earlier introduction to the somewhat eccentric Dave.

'Well, lads,' he started. 'He's a bit of a character, this one.'

The conversation suddenly came to a halt as the doorbell chimed. Enter Dave – exit gasps of disbelief. He looked nothing like his namesake, Barry. In fact, he looked like nothing I'd ever clapped eyes on before. His bright ginger hair flowed over his shoulders and down most of his back and most of his face, offsetting his rust-coloured Sloppy Joe jumper with almost surreal effect. Grubby jeans and winkle-picker boots completed a picture of absolute sartorial failure.

'This is Dave,' announced Joe. Muttered responses of 'All right?' greeted the oddball as we fidgeted with our instruments. The conversation continued in the 'slightly embarrassed' mode, as Joe prompted the proceedings by giving Dave a hand to set up his drum kit. In no time at all, we were off into beat-groupdom, sounding like we'd never sounded before.

Dave was on board and the ship was ready to sail.

It soon became clear that we'd need to work on a regular basis to update our equipment. Dave's genuine commitment became immediately apparent when he decided to trade in a seemingly perfect Shaftsbury drum kit for a super-deluxe red sparkle Trixon set-up. In retrospect, I'd say the reasons for this were purely artistic, but one could have mistaken it for a ruse to detract some of the attention away from his rather bizarre appearance.

Not wishing to be outdone, I took steps to update my rather sad-looking backline of amplification, and, aided by heartfelt pleas and part-exchange, managed to acquire a Watkins Pick-A-Back amplifier, which looked pretty cool to me. The bookings eventually started to trickle in, and, as we weren't in a position to invest in a van (like the big lads), Joe advanced us eight pounds and negotiated a deal on a small trailer. When hooked onto his Ford Consul, it served us well for the time being.

One thing I've learned over the years is that if you try too hard, you'll almost always fail to get the desired result. So, with regard to image, the age of adolescence is often a period of confusion and inspired individualism, which some adapt to better than others. We didn't do too badly, I suppose, though it didn't stop us being envious of the older lads who could afford to travel to Newcastle and purchase (or steal) the latest London styles. This sometimes led us to sport some rather sad combinations. I remember being impressed by a pair of yellow dogtooth-check 'hipster' pants, as worn by the Who's Roger Daltrey, and pestered my mother until she promised to buy me a pair on her Saturday shopping expedition. The excitement rose as I rushed home to try on my new 'duds', but subsided depressingly when I glanced at the mirror. The reflection showed the top half of a skinny youth, whose bottom half was enveloped by what appeared to be the hindquarters of a jaundiced pantomime horse.

I haven't worn yellow since.

Joe organized the printing of some business cards and soon the Road Runners were pinned up alongside our peers in Hamilton's window. A proud moment indeed, but I really had to update my old-fashioned Harmony Roy Smeck guitar to something a little more 'hip'. Choosing it was a very simple and straightforward exercise. All that was required was a dad with some money and a limited knowledge of mid-priced electric guitars.

The shape of the thing was of the utmost importance, and, as Keith Richards played an Epiphone Casino model, my preference lay in that direction. Burdon's in Stockton had in their display window a Harmony H77 model, similar in shape to the revered Mr Richards' instrument but in red as opposed to sunburst. The Teesside area seemed to be bestowed with Harmony equipment. Anyway, I accepted the alternative tint and was offered a part-exchange value of twenty-seven pounds on the Roy Smeck model – an offer which did not impress my father, as he had to fork out sixty-five pounds to complete the deal.

'There's nothing wrong with that one. What do you want to change it for?'

'Because this one looks like Keith Richards' guitar. It'll improve my standard of playing.'

'Well, I hope so. I'm not a bloomin' millionaire, you know.'

Two days later, the guitar, held proudly by its new owner, made its Road Runners debut at a local church hall, where we played non-stop for two and a half hours. By the time we reached the final song, our fingertips were almost bleeding. Joe took pity on us and took to lugging around a large Truvox reel-to-reel tape machine of pre-recorded music, to ensure that the kids would be occupied during breaks. This, he assured us, would 'prevent boredom and fights breaking out'.

Our bookings at the time were secured by our newly elected 'mentor', courtesy of a type-copied circular, which went as follows:

THE ROAD RUNNERS

Dear Sirs,

It gives me great pleasure to convey to you the following information.

'The Road Runners' Rhythm Group is comprised of Lead, Rhythm and Bass guitar, Vocals and Harmonica and Drums.

We have recently played, with success in most local Youth Clubs, also a number of Social Clubs and Institutes on Tees Side and in the South Durham area.

We have a number of bookings on Tees Side, but at the moment we are 'not busy'. It would give our group pleasure to be considered for a booking at your establishment.

Our fee is negotiable, depending on the distance to travel and the type and length of performance required and whether a weekday or weekend.

Enclosed is a stamped addressed envelope, but if you wish to telephone, a call to the above- mentioned number, between 6.30. and 9.00pm will receive our prompt attention.

I am Sir,

Yours respectfully

J. Bradley. (Manager)

Rhythm group – what a lovely expression! I suppose we'd have been happier with rhythm and blues, a burgeoning influence attributable mainly to Dave Usher. He'd acquired a handful of EPs (a record comprising of four tracks) on the Chess-Pye International label featuring Howlin' Wolf, Tommy Tucker, Buddy Guy and Little Walter. We were duly impressed. Chuck Berry obviously didn't have the monopoly on the label, even though our set list soon gave us the option on no less than seventeen of his compositions. However, we were unable to approach the Howlin' Wolf tunes with the required enthusiasm, as our powers of emulation regarding huge black men from Mississippi were rather limited. Instead, we persevered with our Hollies, Kinks, Stones and Merseybeat, realising, correctly, that we'd have plenty of time to get the blues when we were older.

If I was asked to name two people who created the greatest impression on me as a teenager, I'd have no hesitation in citing

Spike Milligan and Jeff Beck. And not necessarily in that order. As my dad was not a fan of *The Goon Show*, I was never really aware of their radio series in the late 1950s and early 1960s. I had to wait for *The Telegoons* before I would succumb to Milligan's devastating sense of humour. I was a lot luckier with Beck, who I got to see at the KD Club in Billingham just after he'd joined the Yardbirds. Now, here was a man who was more than a mere guitar virtuoso – he was also a showman to boot. Stepping into Eric Clapton's shoes had to be a daunting task, not literally as I'm sure the pioneering Mr Clapton's taste in footwear stopped somewhat short of desert boots! However, from the ankles up, Beck's playing and onstage presence was truly remarkable. An influential night and a great source of inspiration to an impressionable youth.

Back in the real world, the school-leavers department arranged for me to be interviewed by British Steel in the vain hope of acquiring a position in their technical drawing department. No chance, young man – not enough CSEs. In fact, no CSEs! In the end, I was offered an apprenticeship in motor mechanics at a local garage and decided to accept it. My parents were pleased. I had a 'job with a future, lad'. So in July 1965, at the ripe old age of fourteen years and eleven months, I gave my final performances as a schoolboy, entertaining the patrons of such high-profile establishments as the Acklam Steelworks Club, Joe Walton's Youth Club, St Mary's College and the Catcote Hotel. We were well-received at most venues or, at worst, lived to play another day, apart from at the Acklam Steelworks Club, where we were paid off for being too loud. Loud? We only had 25-watt amplifiers, for God's sake!

The Road Runners set list continued to expand to

incorporate a folk spot, inspired initially by Colin's folk and skiffle roots. We added a few trendy Bob Dylan tunes, plus Donovan's 'Catch the Wind', to become an outfit specialising in the ability to slip into 'versatile' mode. This inspired Joe to have some business cards printed bearing the slogan: 'YOU CALL IT – WE'LL PLAY IT!'

Thanks, Joe. When some of the local piss-takers got wind of our confident boast, they responded with shouts of '"Take Five" by Dave Brubeck!' and '"Dominique" by the Singing Nun!' Even Bach's 'Gavotte in D Minor' got thrown at us one night, but we managed to escape by claiming that we only recognised the original version in C Major, and that Bach never played any of our tunes so why should we play any of his? Sometimes the audiences were hard and unresponsive, other times warm and encouraging; you learned to take the rough with the smooth, though when they were rough, man, were they rough!

The summer months saw bookings in pretty Yorkshire market towns, such as Brompton and Richmond, where we performed in the grounds of the old castle. On one of these gigs, an older lad from the headline act complimented me on my playing but suggested that the task would be made a lot easier if I fitted my guitar with lighter-gauge strings. Ah, now he tells me! The secret, apparently, was to dispose of the wound third and replace it with the second string, which was made of plain steel, then to simply add another first string in place of the relocated second. *Voila!* Suddenly, my fingers were on a holiday of a lifetime, for a lifetime.

This enlightened state led me to an intense period of 'bending madness', where the continual pushing up and down of guitar strings caused my calluses to develop calluses of their

31

own. The novelty wore off eventually, allowing familiarity to add some method to the madness. I'm still indebted to that fellow, whoever he was.

It didn't take me long to realise that working in a dirty garage for a paltry wage was not the way forward, so I jacked it in and took on another proposed apprenticeship, as a heating engineer for a small company specialising in installing central heating. I began to regret leaving school at such an early age when I could have stayed on to gain certificates in education. Still, bollocks to them. Apart from playing in the school football team, there was very little about formal education that stirred my interests and emotions. I cheered myself up by purchasing my favourite magazine, *Beat Instrumental* – the only monthly magazine to gain the respect of both professional and amateur musicians. It featured articles on all the latest 'beat' sensations, news on all the top gear, and regular columns such as Player of the Month.

In the autumn of 1965, I finally bade farewell to Johnny Goffin's weekly guitar lessons and celebrated by treating myself to a second-hand Vox AC30 amplifier, while Joe found us an old Bedford Dormobile van. We started to attract a small fan base: just a few local lasses who thought we were cute. As one or two of them were quite passable in the looks department, we would often exchange small talk and flirtatious banter. A few of them even made up a banner from a small sheet, which expressed their love for us in red paint: 'PAUL, MICK, COLIN, DAVE – WE LOVE YOU!!'

Though it did wonders for the self-esteem, it failed to make an impression on the judges at the Darlington Civic Theatre's annual talent contest. A blind piano player beat us into third place – and it wasn't Ray Charles. We played 'Get Off My Cloud', the Stones' latest hit, and in the front row were these two girls from Stockton who we'd always try to avoid. They would follow us around like hyenas, waiting to pounce at any opportune moment. Fortunately, their possessiveness was to be their undoing one night, when the two flew into a rage and attacked a rather attractive new fan, reducing her to tears. They were warned to keep their distance at future gigs and we never saw them again.

Unfortunately, we never saw the attractive new fan again either.

CHAPTER 4

RUNNING OUT OF ROAD AND TRAMLINES

A slight yet pertinent digression: in 1979, as a member of the popular beat combo Whitesnake, I flew to Los Angeles to meet the band's record company, attend press conferences and perform at UCLA (or the University of California, as it's better known). We spent most of our nights at the notorious Rainbow Bar and Grill, a late-night venue for rock 'n' rollers on the Sunset Strip. The Deep Purple half of the band (or the Brass Section, as they'd been christened) had virtually lived in the place during their heyday and introduced the rest of us to some serious nightlife. Which leads me to my original encounter with its namesake – and a far cry from L.A.'s nightlife – the Rainbow Room at Seaton Carew, County Durham.

Situated on the north-east coast of England, close to Hartlepool, this shabby seaside resort was used mainly as a daytime source of entertainment by the local workers and their families, whose hardiness pointed two fingers at the often-blustery North Sea. A character named Ken Tyzak ran a promenade café, which, during the day, offered tea, coffee, ice cream and candy floss, while reserving a back room for evening gigs or jukebox sessions. The Road Runners made their debut there on a cold January evening, entertaining a small yet appreciative crowd.

Sitting in that L.A. establishment nearly fourteen years later – and living the rock 'n' roll dream – my thoughts drifted back to that chilly winter's evening early in 1966 and, to be honest, I felt quite pleased with myself.

I also felt pleased with myself one summer's day in 1966 when I offloaded my entire savings (bequeathed to me by my recently deceased nana) on a new guitar – a beautiful-looking sunburst Gibson ES345 Stereo model. I should have known better. The vendor – a local businessman from a dodgy part of town – had a reputation for shady dealings and keeping nefarious company. I knew that my dad would never agree to me owning two guitars, which he would have regarded as an act of extravagance, so I took to smuggling it into the house under the complete delusion that it would go unnoticed.

A couple of months later, the former owner of the guitar turned up at our house and demanded to know why, as the new owner of the guitar, I hadn't kept up the monthly payments. I'd been conned: the bastard hadn't mentioned anything about hire purchase, only a cash deal. My dad hit the roof and showed true bottle by marching me to the rogue's house and demanding the money back.

He got it without incurring any sort of injury and I was seriously in the doghouse for some time after that.

As the amount of gigs increased, so did the wear and tear

on the already vintage Bedford van. Once again, Joe Bradley came to the rescue and found us a replacement. This time, we were presented with a fibreglass-bodied Thames, a former mobile food truck, which may have failed not just the MOT but also the Food Safety Act. Still, it was roomy and, due to its opaque shell, somewhat light inside.

Paul Rodgers' voice had, by now, matured to such an extent that it was obvious to everybody that he should progress to out-front vocalist. His transition from bass player to out-front was boosted by the inauguration of Bruce Thomas, a graphic artist in the advertising department at the *Evening Gazette* newspaper. Bruce was hip and a fine bass player, with much in common with the rest of us. Sadly, Colin's contribution was much less valued than Bruce's and the role of rhythm guitar was, by now, surplus to requirements, so we had no alternative but to relieve him of his duties. Joe was bitterly disappointed by our actions and resigned in protest. His actions were of course justified, but it was an inevitable conclusion.

By now, we'd progressed from R&B into a cool form of rock-soul, which inspired us to colour our repertoire with versions of such classics as 'Ride Your Pony', 'See-Saw', 'Mustang Sally' and 'Ain't Too Proud to Beg'. The obligatory drum solo was still in evidence, though some of the comments were often less than complimentary.

'Sounds like a bloody train crash,' was a popular one, followed closely by, 'Oo does 'e think 'e is, Ginger fuckin' Baker?'

These cultured observations were not lost on us, and, once back on stage, readying ourselves for the conclusive 'kerrang', we'd pass on these comments to our perspiring percussionist. His response was to reciprocate in his own inimitable style.

'Fuck off, yer little bastads, or I'll ploat yer.' Ah, yes, a man all too familiar with the Bard's work.

Some of us went to see John Mayall's Bluesbreakers, featuring Eric Clapton, at the KD Club, and arrived early, just as the band's van was pulling up. And there he was, Eric Clapton – or God to his burgeoning army of guitar fans – dressed, somewhat individually, in a fur coat and Levis, wearing spats over his black patent leather shoes. We were to behold that unusual sartorial concoction a few months later on the cover of Mayall's legendary 'Beano' album.

With a little financial help from my dad, I acquired a Fender Telecaster guitar and traded in my Vox amplifier for a Gibson Vari-Tone model. We began to work hard on our musical direction and, utilising the influences of Cream, the Paul Butterfield Blues Band and newly discovered Jimi Hendrix as a benchmark, approached our soul-blues covers with renewed inspiration. Paul was coming into his own as a frontman and the band's confidence was growing by the gig. Some of our rather unexpected behaviour began to worry some people: I suppose you could say we had 'attitude'. Onstage posturing was sometimes combined with silly stunts, such as wielding a bamboo cane with a sock on the end, and then dousing it with petrol and setting it alight. Interestingly, Jimi Hendrix would adopt an almost identical routine the following year at the Monterey Pop Festival, though his chosen weapon of attack was the Fender Stratocaster – a wiser choice if you ask me.

Apart from such cockiness, a driving ambition to inhabit the same time and space as Clapton, Beck, Hendrix and Baker had become our *raison d'être*.

The Road Runners left their homes and families on a sunny spring morning to make their mark on the London scene. We were just a bunch of north-country teenagers with high hopes of attaining a bit more in life than a future in an industrial hotspot for steel and chemical products. And as we now considered ourselves to be rather cool young men, it had become apparent that our chosen name was no longer in tune with the times. We were aware of the psychedelic culture over in the U.S., and the hip musical trends seemed to be leaning in that direction. So, on Bruce's recommendation, we became the Wild Flowers, and motored off in our Thames van, full of optimism and fish paste sandwiches. The van, now customised to house two sets of bunk beds, would be our home from home until... well, we'd just have to wait and see. We'd exercised enough foresight to contact a number of booking agencies, one being Cana Variety Agency, a well-established set-up which kindly offered us an audition at the Refectory in north London. We performed well enough to impress them into offering us an agency contract, found a bedsit just big enough to house four beds, a table, a sink and a gas ring for cooking, and settled in.

Someone over at Cana organised a short tour of the Scottish Highlands, which wasn't quite what we'd had in mind after perusing the *Melody Maker*'s gig guide week after week. However, it was a start, and we could now proudly state that we were professional musicians, with camaraderie to match. And we certainly needed the latter. London to Elgin is almost six hundred miles – a mammoth trek in a well-used former mobile shop, or any vehicle come to that. Luckily, we all had families who lived approximately halfway there, so we were able to renew our acquaintance with our former bedrooms *and* be provided with a slap-up meal or two.

We arrived in Elgin slightly disorientated. Dave, as the only driver, looked as though he'd been interrogated – mad staring eyes, drained features and shaking hands. Mind you, that's pretty much how he looked anyway. We stayed for a week, to savour the delights of Elgin Town Hall, where we entertained a stiff-necked crowd from our vantage point on the balcony. A room of stony-faced airmen looked on, unimpressed with our brand of blues and soul-tinged rock at RAF Lossiemouth (referred to thereafter as Mount Rushmore). It made Hades look lively. Then there was Aberdeen, where a large percentage of the audience at the Beach Ballroom spent the night walking around in a large circle. Strange.

After a few days, we were actually looking forward to the long haul back to London, aka civilisation.

Work was slack, like the waist of my Levis, and although I was in a state of semi-starvation, I still managed to persuade my dad to take out a hire-purchase agreement on a Marshall 50-watt amplifier and a four-twelve speaker cabinet, bless him.

Then, on the way to a gig in Great Yarmouth, the van's big end went, along with Dave, who, roused by his initial determination to go home and return with helping hands, never did. The rest of us managed to hitch-hike back to London, where we summoned help to get the gear back to safety.

Once back, we gave our saviours the broken-down van as payment for services rendered before abating our gloom with a shared packet of crisps and a tin of beans.

The following day, we attempted to stave off the boredom of 'resting between engagements' by journeying into the West End to browse the music shops. In Selmers, we chatted to a young shop assistant who, it transpired, shared similar musical tastes and, apparently, owned a 1959 Gibson Les Paul. The lucky sod. His name was Paul Kossoff, son of the famous TV actor David, and after hearing of our woes, he recommended a drumming friend of his. Not only that: he arranged a rehearsal for us to try him out and brought his little tape recorder to review the results. He even brought his Les Paul for me to drool over. I couldn't compete with this as far as status was concerned, though it did impel me to go out and swap my new Telecaster for an older, customised model.

We ended up hiring a man with a van, and the new drummer worked out. Sadly, the Wild Flowers didn't, and as 1967's Summer of Love morphed into the usual Autumn of Shitty Weather, I left Paul and Bruce to ponder the divide that had gradually appeared to distance us. They didn't, although I kept in touch with Bruce for a number of years afterwards, by which time he'd progressed from the Sutherland Brothers to being an Attraction for Elvis Costello.

The sound of the nylon-strung classical guitar had entranced me for some time, and I possessed an LP by Andrés Segovia, the master of the instrument. Although I harboured no secret desire to implement the kind of dedication needed to achieve even a modicum of success in that particular style, I still fancied having a go out of interest. On my return to Middlesbrough, I found a teacher in – of all places – Stockton, and within days I'd purchased a modestly priced instrument. However, my trusty Telecaster was never far from my side, and my restless fingers were itching to plug it in and let rip when local singer/entrepreneur John McCoy contacted me regarding the formation of a blues-based, west-coast-themed four-piece. John's business threads had unravelled themselves at the door of Chris Blackwell, head of the burgeoning Island

Records label, where his powers of persuasion led to a two-album deal for John's new band Tramline.

Ironically, Paul Rodgers and Paul Kossoff's friendship had blossomed into a musical partnership – Free – which was also signed to the same label. 'Twas, indeed, a small world.

My dedication to music meant that anything serious regarding the opposite sex was (apart from the odd dalliance) secondary, though I did have a fling with a renowned vamp whose experience was obviously superior to mine. In fact, it was rumoured that she even had her own pheromone made by the local chemist. I found myself leading a musical double-life: a natural rock-and-blues personality existing side by side with an alter ego of amateur classical guitarist. A night of Telecaster-bashing sometimes preceded a calm morning in my tutor's sitting room, where I could furrow my brow to the works of Sor, Giuliani or Bach.

Although Tramline was, in essence, a 'local' band – i.e. familiar to Middlesbrough and surrounding areas – owing to John McCoy's business connections we were able to venture further afield, finding support spots at such nationally known rock venues as Mother's in Birmingham, the Cellar Club in South Shields (where we headlined) and, of course, the legendary Marquee Club in London, where we opened for some of the biggest names on the blues scene, including Ten Years After and Jethro Tull.

We travelled to London to record *Somewhere Down the Line* in the allocated three days and, believe me, it sounds like we recorded it in three days. Hindsight is a marvellous thing; at the time I just plugged in and played, and when the engineer started verbalising about the merits of overdubs, drop-ins and individual monitor foldback, my eyes just glazed over.

Retrospection is a marvellous thing too – I just wish I'd known about it then.

On 11 August 1968 we were booked to play on the third and final day of the eighth National Jazz and Blues Festival, which, at the time, was probably the biggest date in the festival calendar. Granted, we were bottom of a rather large bill, but it was still an achievement in anybody's eyes and John's powers of persuasion may well have held sway. The line-up was very 1960s, in as much as it was an eclectic mix: not only jazz and blues but folk too. And what a line-up! Over the weekend, the three-day ticket holders could rock to the likes of Jerry Lee Lewis, Deep Purple, Joe Cocker, the Nice, Jeff Beck, Traffic, Jethro Tull, the Crazy World of Arthur Brown, John Mayall's Bluesbreakers, Ten Years After and Taste. Those with a predilection for jazz could stroke their goatees to the Ronnie Scott Quintet, the Alan Haven Trio, the Don Rendell & Ian Carr Quartet, the Mike Westbrook Band and Jon Hendricks. The folkies had Fairport Convention, the Incredible String Band, Fotheringay, Al Stewart and Eclection. And if your tastes were limited to mere pop, there was always the Herd, Marmalade and a relative unknown called Marc Bolan with his Tyrannosaurus Rex.

Of course, there were many more lesser-known names – Tramline being one of them – who enjoyed their day out with the big names, then retired late to dream of fame and fortune in the cut-throat world of rock 'n' roll.

The release of *Somewhere Down the Line* created little impression. Legendary rhythm and blues pundit Mike Raven played 'Statesboro Blues' on his Sunday evening radio show and was less than enthusiastic. He described our rendition as somewhat inferior to Taj Mahal's version. He was correct.

As a teenager with it all before me, I lost little sleep over his critique. This would stand me in good stead for the future – I put it down to experience, and then endeavoured to improve by effort. Years later, I added 'and try to keep sober whenever possible'.

Somewhere down the line, Tramline ran out of creative fuel and rolled quietly towards the great terminus of failed deliveries. However, we were contracted to make one more album for Island Records before we called it a day. Chris Blackwell had hired a loose cannon called Guy Stevens to, hopefully, do a better job in the production chair than he'd done on the first one and, though the latter had scored some success with Spooky Tooth and Mott the Hoople, he may already have had his work cut out by trying to produce a band that was about to split up.

Stevens was definitely 'out there' and the evidence was plain to see. First, he brought into his particular workplace a strange, cabaret-suited piano player called Norman – a man who held a singular liking for Jerry Lee Lewis-style glissandos. And second, judging by his deranged style of production, he also brought a highly possible misuse of various substances, which may or may not have influenced the energised endeavours of our Norman.

'Hey, man, get a bigger sound on the guitar. That will really make the track rock so the listener will go, "Yeh, baby," then wanna hear more and feel good as the drums go badum badum behind the vocals that stretch over the thud of the bass and Norman can sail like a liner through unchartered seas. Yeh?'

He even came up with the title of the album, the unsurpassed *Moves of Vegetable Centuries*. Spinal Tap would have loved him. Unfortunately, his excessive lifestyle got the better of him and he was dead and buried long before the Tap's rise to infamy.

The recording of *Moves of Vegetable Centuries* was, to me, a notable improvement on its predecessor. Once again, we were in and out of the studio within a few days, blissfully ignoring the fact that studio technique and a modicum of foresight were required, just to add that extra touch. One lives and learns.

We were joined this time by a couple of great musicians – Colin Hodgkinson on bass, and Middlesbrough-born saxophone virtuoso, Ron Aspery – which, to be honest, added a real sense of progression. Their tasteful deliveries were often at odds with Norman's personal quest to fill every space he could with rock 'n' roll histrionics, but sometimes you just have to take the glut with the smooth.

The end result was a kind of organised jam session: a direction I felt at ease with, though Island Records may have found the product a little indulgent.

There was no ill-feeling or resentment regarding the demise of Tramline, and we were even included in *Disc and Music Echo*'s article on the British blues scene, where we were praised as an up-and-coming name alongside the likes of Led Zeppelin, Taste, Savoy Brown, Duster Bennet, Bakerloo Line, Love Sculpture and Free. '...The list is virtually endless and all are good, solid blues groups, each with that essential ingredient of musical honesty.'

It was a shame that this line-up didn't go any further, but somewhere down the line I was destined to link up with Messrs Popple, Hodgkinson and Aspery, and savour some real moments of musical delight.

David O'List had made a name for himself as the guitarist with the original Nice line-up, though it soon became apparent that the awesome talents of keyboard-player extraordinaire Keith Emerson expressed little mercy for stragglers. He appeared nervous and unsure of himself. Recent press reports had stated that he was now a member of a new outfit called Roxy Music, so I was quite surprised to see him at the audition. A quick mental deduction suggested that he'd been relieved of his duties. The third and final competitor was a nerdy-looking individual called Jim Roach, who'd played in the original line-up of Jon Hiseman's Coliseum. He was obviously a good player, but his ability to soul-stir seemed suspect. I weighed up the odds and concluded that a move to London was on the cards.

Our inevitable jury were a good bunch of guys. Trumpeter Mike Cotton had headed the youngest professional jazz band of the early 1960s trad-jazz revival before going into R&B. This had progressed to follow the trend for soul music, and was now fronted by Lucas McPherson, an Ohio-born ex-GI, a natural singer and showman. He entered the room amid wafts of aftershave, offered a raised palm and requested 'Gimme five!' from anybody in close proximity. A definite character.

The band's choice of audition material centred, as expected, around standard soul hits like 'Cold Sweat' and 'Dance to the Music', which demanded a disciplined rhythmic approach.

Sensitive to David's unease, Mike decided to alleviate the poor lad's apprehension by allowing him to bat first, leaving Jim Roach and myself to avoid eye contact. David didn't seem to be on the same wavelength – or even the same planet – and his wah-wah-induced raga variations were an unfortunate choice that lent nothing to the melodies and grooves peculiar to James Brown or Sly and the Family Stone. Consequently, he was sent for an early bath after two songs and was never seen again.

Jim went next and did well, but my confidence in my ability remained undaunted. I did my bit, and after a brief interlude, where they assessed the merits of Messrs Roach and Moody, was voted in on a five-to-one decision.

Memo: Have entered the fast lane – buy a diary and some Old Spice aftershave.

Life in the conventional lanes for Lucas and the Mike Cotton Sound was undertaken by two particular modes of transport: namely a Ford Zephyr Six car and a Commer van. As the band's line-up consisted of tenor sax, trumpet, bass, drums, guitar and Lucas, two of the members were usually required to accompany the band's roadie Martin and the equipment. To my recollection, there was some kind of rota system employed to keep everybody happy, though whoever adopted the 'middleman' position in the Commer had drawn the short straw. The location of the vehicle's engine, housed between the driver and passenger seats, meant the unlucky one was required to perch on its rubber casing for the duration. This could be uncomfortable and somewhat warm around the nether regions but we never complained. These guys were real pros and I was pleased to be among them. Soon I began to understand what being 'on the road' was all about.

The club scene was thriving and the band had built up a pretty good fan base over the years, working most days of the week. Lucas's stage wear was something else. He wore two-piece satin suits, of which he had three: red, gold and silver. Their appearance would be described as garish. And to complement these spectacular creations, he chose a pair of

Chelsea boots. Though they'd walked off the cobbler's bench a dark shade of brown, they were soon rendered chalky white by their new owner, whose prowess with a brush and a tin of emulsion paint was, to be honest, limited. Prior to every performance, Lucas would spend a considerable amount of time arranging his processed hair into a splendid pompadour, which was then kept in situ with a small silk scarf, or 'do-rag'. This little act of ritualistic vanity proved to be counter-productive, for as soon as he let out his first James Brown-inspired 'Oowwww!' the whole thing collapsed into an untidy plumage, which required constant attention.

Within a month of joining the band, I was taking part in one of those now-legendary 1960s package tours backing the American singing star Gene Pitney. I was familiar with his hits, which were often semi-dramatic dirges about hurt and heartache. Even the odd sprightly tune somehow sounded ominous. However, he still commanded respect and attracted large audiences. To help achieve Pitney's recorded sound, ex-Zombie Rod Argent joined us on keyboards – a sophisticated player and all-round nice chap. He and the band's bass player, Jim Rodford, had already made future plans, and after the final show would be leaving to explore new horizons with the newly formed Argent.

The line-up for the tour was interesting, to say the least. Scottish lads, the cheerful albeit naughty Marmalade, shared the pop songs with new Apple Records signing the Ivys, who would eventually change their name to Badfinger before tragedy struck with devastating consequences. Having scored a massive hit with Harry Nilsson's 'Without You', the band's chief songwriters – Pete Ham and Tom Evans – eventually took their own lives, due, allegedly, to misappropriation of their royalty payments. Much to my delight, the special guests were Joe Cocker and the Grease Band. Tramline had supported them a couple of times and I really dug their music. Their guitarist, an amiable Irishman named Henry McCulloch, had a lovely, lazy style and a warm tone that seemed to reflect his personality. Also, they gave a whole new meaning to the word stoned. What a bunch! After their set, they'd glide back to their dressing room for more spliffs.

I occasionally joined them, spectacularly mistiming my leisure time one evening and ending up out of my crust on stage, trying to make sense of Gene's string of hits. Thankfully, the shouts and screams from his adoring fans masked the minimal sounds coming, somewhat erratically, from my amplifier.

On another occasion, Cocker and his band had procured a rather large amount of marijuana, which was wrapped up in a newspaper like fish and chips. Within minutes of arriving at their dressing room, the first of what was to be many joints was being rolled. Meanwhile, in the room next door, Marmalade took to throwing handfuls of their publicity photos out of the window to fans and autograph hunters below. It was a gesture appreciated by everyone except a couple of local cops, who regarded it, somewhat impetuously, as an irresponsible act. Their immediate reaction was to dash upstairs, burst into the dressing room and admonish the perpetrators for their reckless behaviour. This little manoeuvre was carried out with flawless professionalism. However, they fell at the last hurdle and entered Cocker's dressing room by mistake. 'Right, whoever's chucking photos out of the window, pack it in now!' commanded the taller of the two.

Through a haze of sweet-smelling smoke, a bunch of guys froze, hearts beating hard, paranoia building up inside. They could already see the headlines in the following morning's papers.

PoP Stars in Drugs Bust
Hemp Smokers Caught in the Act
Liverpool Empire Shamed By Hash-Heads

The room became deathly quiet as the guilty-faced deviants awaited their fate. You could have heard a cigarette paper drop.

'I don't care who you are. One more photograph through that window and you'll be arrested!' warned the fatter officer. Then, giving the stunned 'heads' a stern look, they left, slamming the door behind them. There were some very relieved young men in that room. I know – I was one of them.

The north-east was rife with cabaret clubs and I'd prided myself on managing to avoid them. However, at the end of the theatre tour, Gene was booked to appear for a week at the Showboat in my home town of Middlesbrough, followed by a week at the world-famous Batley Variety Club. Pitney was obviously big in Middlesbrough and we played to packed houses every night. My dad even came to watch the show and ended up giving me the thumbs-up. 'You've made it now son, all right,' he said, nodding towards the stage. 'Playing with trumpets!'

He'd not only given me his approval, he'd also given me his blessing. I didn't really mind that he'd misapprehended the true roles of saxophonist Nick Newall and trombone player John 'Boat' Beecham. I'm sure they'd have had a chuckle on hearing that little gem.

Now that Jim and Rod had left to concentrate on Argent,

Lem Lubin joined as a permanent replacement on bass and an overweight John Steed lookalike called Peter was taken on as pianist for the two weeks of cabaret. Lem had been the guitarist for Unit 4 + 2, who'd scored a hit a few years earlier with the catchy 'Concrete and Clay', and was part of the Hertfordshire musical mafia that included Jim, Rod, Russ Ballard and Bob Henrit, now collectively known as Argent. Yes, it's an incestuous business! Peter the pianist was an archetypal session musician of the old school, which meant that he could read fly shit and always performed in an evening suit. Onstage, he stood out like a sore thumb among our all-black-and-chiffon-scarf creations. And he was old enough to be my dad! He also found it difficult to hang on to money, losing most of it in the club casino after the performance. If Lemmy from Motörhead acquired his assumed title due to repeated requests to 'Lemmy a quid 'til Friday', Peter the pianist should have been rechristened Ernie, as in 'Ernie chance of a sub?' Poor old sod.

Batley Variety Club was opened in March 1967 and quickly established itself as Britain's premier cabaret club. It epitomised all that was expected of glamour and entertainment by presenting the biggest names from the world of showbiz – a world a million miles away from the harsh realities of Batley and its surroundings. It was an ugly area, blighted by its industrial heritage of mines and mills. God, even the soil had a layer of grime on it.

It was packed every night, of course, and on the way in, the audience were treated to a novel experience in the form of questionnaires, on which they could ask the illustrious Mr Pitney trivial albeit friendly questions such as 'How's the family?' or write comments such as 'I love your new record!'

etc. Gene would read these out during the set, and would then reciprocate on a one-to-one basis, making a fuss of the questioner and bringing an element of participation into the act. Once collected, the questionnaires would be placed on a stool at the side of the stage, to be brought on by his tour manager at an arranged time. This entertaining little interlude went well until the third night, when Gene read out the first item on the pile.

'Gene, we think you are a fine-looking man but who is that hunk on bass guitar?' Laughs all round.

'Oh, that's Lem,' he replied cheerfully before picking up the next piece of paper.

'Dear Gene, which side do you dress on?' Pitney wasn't so cheerful now.

I looked around at the other band members. Some of them didn't look particularly surprised. Gene looked at the next questionnaire then put it back on the stool before beckoning his aide to take it away.

After the show, I heard raised voices in Gene's dressing room. Soon after, the door opened and a couple of the band exited with serious faces. The tour manager shouted after them, 'And if it ever happens again, you'll be sacked. Naughty boys!'

CHAPTER 6

EURO
TRAVELLER

One thing I'd discovered about being a professional musician was the total lack of continuity. How about this: finish at Batley Variety Club on the Saturday night, travel to Bexley in Kent on the Sunday for a gig at the Black Prince, then have two days off in London. Travel to Belgium on the Wednesday for a gig at Shape Military Base in Mons, then on to Rome via Bologna for a fortnight's residency at the Titan Club. This kind of itinerary wouldn't suit everybody but, when you're only eighteen, you're not fazed at all. Crossing the Alps into Italy was a memorable experience and the drive through the Brenner Pass was breathtaking.

Our new roadie Geoff remained at the wheel throughout and, to assist him in yielding to the lures of the Sandman, had popped a couple of 'uppers'.

When I asked him how he was feeling, he smiled broadly

and answered with wide-eyed sincerity, 'I feel great! I love everyone!' Right on, Hannibal.

We arrived in Rome and, within minutes, someone had broken into our car and stolen my green full-length leather coat. Not a good start but on with the show. Prior to our epic journey, I'd treated myself to a Cry Baby 'wah-wah' pedal *à la* Eric Clapton and Jimi Hendrix, and had incorporated it into a couple of songs. After one of the sets at the Titan Club, a middle-aged guy, who, judging by his general appearance, could easily have been a member of the Cosa Nostra or a lawyer, approached me.

'Hey, dat'a pedal you usin' reminda me ofa de trumpet players when deya use a mute.' I think he may have been Italian.

I toyed with the idea of asking him if he was in 'the mob', and saying that if any of his friends or associates came across some twat wearing a dark green, full-length leather coat, they had my permission to cement him into the next motorway bridge. I didn't, of course, but eased the pain by buying a nice pair of Italian leather ankle boots that offset my new pedal with matching laces.

Our next European jaunt was to the liberal-minded (nudge-nudge, wink-wink) Sweden, where we spent almost four weeks backing former Manfred Mann singer Paul Jones. Flying to Stockholm via Copenhagen was my first time on a plane. I was nervous – if we were meant to fly, God would have given us Valium.

All the shows took place in 'folkparks', popular summer locations and ideal for outdoor gigs. As usual, Lucas had the easiest job: get changed, sing two or three songs, get unchanged, head back to the hotel bar, then search for the nearest half-cut salesman to blag drinks from. And judging by the price of the drinks, he was going to have his work cut out. Mugging them might have been a better option.

Paul travelled separately with his tour manager, an ex-boxer called Billy, who had the nose to prove it. Our driver and tour manager was an aging Swede called Jay Elwing, who looked like a cross between Aristotle Onassis and Mister Pastry and seemed a bit too old for this lark. He would often become agitated, spitting out odd curses like 'Shit on my arsehole!' or 'Fuck at the car!' He told us he was an ex-jazz musician who'd turned to tour managing to supplement his income, found steady work and never returned to his chosen profession.

Our mode of transport was an American four-wheel drive, which dragged our equipment around in a trailer and had a couple of small roof windows placed about three feet apart. We soon discovered that, if you judged the air flow correctly, you could release your cigarette butt from the forward opening and have it sail back in through the rear one, much to the alarm of the person sitting three rows back. Shouts of 'Fuckin' hell!' or 'Who did that, you bastard?' would get Jay going, 'Stop the bollocks, wanker nuts!'

The perpetrator would never admit to their deliberate actions, citing strong breezes over the lakes as an excuse.

I was aware of the 'Sexy Sweden' tag before we arrived. Any country with openly sold pornography and a large ratio of stunning-looking women could hardly be ignored, and therefore wasn't. The porn was hardly tactfully placed, and often appeared in newsagents' windows on the lower shelves between *Auto Trader* and *Fishing World*. A shock for us British, but nothing to the indigenous, who seemed blasé about it.

Although I wasn't particularly interested in 'pulling', a week or two into the tour I found myself in the company of a young beauty, and the mutual attraction was becoming too much to bear. We were just about to head for the hotel when she admitted that she was only fourteen. Now, I was still only eighteen myself, but I was old enough to go to jail for the next five years and I didn't fancy spending them with a bunch of psychotic Vikings. I'd leave that kind of gamble to Jerry Lee Lewis when he passed through town.

'Goodnight, little Anifrid. Get yourself straight home now!'

Paul Jones had chosen an interesting selection of songs to perform, including the obvious Manfred Mann hits like 'Pretty Flamingo' and 'If You Gotta Go, Go Now', his own hits 'High Time' and 'I've Been a Bad Bad Boy' and a rather dramatic rendition of Country Joe and the Fish's anti-Vietnam War song, 'Fixin' to Die Rag'. At its climax, Paul would drop to the floor, apparently having been shot. This little bit of theatre stayed in the set until one night when, resplendent in a pair of brand new, expensively cut grey velvet trousers, he 'died' atop a rather large patch of wet paint, which some careless stagehand had hurriedly overlooked. It left a huge stain down one leg. Given that the offending pigment was deep red, the effect was stunningly realistic. Paul was neither convinced, impressed nor amused, and from then on the song was performed without the death scene. It just wasn't the same after that.

I persuaded him to perform a B-side from another one of his singles – an off-the-wall track called 'The Dog Presides', which had Jeff Beck on guitar. As the original had no brass section, the lads could have a breather while I attempted my Beck licks – a bit of expression in a set now devoid of death scenes. I'd hoped that Paul would invent another dramatic exit: one which didn't require him to hit the deck, such as being turned into a pillar of salt or getting vaporised in an atomic bomb explosion, but alas, it never materialised.

Having been formally educated of the fact that 'We beat them three times – two wars and a World Cup final,' I looked forward to my first visit to Germany (then only the Western half) with time-honoured feelings of excitement and trepidation. Two weeks at the PN Club in Munich, performing three sets a night and staying on the other side of Leopold Strasse at the two-bedroom apartment provided by the club's owner, Peter Neumann. Now, eight into two doesn't really go, even if the bedrooms are quite spacious. A power trio without a roadie would have been extremely happy with this arrangement and one-hit-wonder busker Don Partridge would have had room to spare. We just mucked in; as I mentioned before, when you're only eighteen nothing really bothers you – apart from spots. Or crabs.

Sitting in the back of the band's Ford Granada somewhere in Belgium, I felt a natural urge to scratch one of my hairy legs. Well, if I'd have scratched somebody else's I would have looked a right prat, wouldn't I? And apart from that, nobody else knew where the itch was. Soon the irritation became more intense and, ominously, more widespread. Sitting in a crowded car with one trouser leg rolled up like some sort of disorientated freemason dispelled any thoughts I'd had on concealing my quandary. It didn't take long for the others to become aware of my obvious discomfort and about a nanosecond more to establish the cause.

'You've got crabs!' exclaimed a voice, as drummer Bernie Higgins almost lost control of the car.

'Is that bad then?' I enquired in a pathetic semi-apologetic way.

Silly question: they may as well have handed me a bell and a sign proclaiming 'UNCLEAN' if their expressions were anything to go by.

'Just bloody roll your trousers down and tuck them into your socks. And stay that way until we get to Munich.'

Now, the subject of body lice usually crops up in conversations about social diseases, but I can honestly say that I'd had absolutely no contact with unfamiliar women in the time leading up to our departure. However, a few days earlier, we'd played a gig in Cornwall where we'd spent the night at a less than salubrious hotel. In fact, it was a lorry driver's hostel at the back of a petrol station. Limited as I was in the field of overnight accommodation, it had soon became apparent that the fare on offer was not going to win any awards for comfort, cleanliness or modern appliances, though it did have a 'shilling a go' gas fire. And the bed seemed to have been made but not changed... hmmm. The next morning, I'd passed on the breakfast – which looked like it had been cooked in boiling tar and regurgitated by a demented skunk – and headed home.

As I scratched my way through the remainder of Belgium and into Germany, I mulled over the newfound knowledge that a local chemist would supply me with the mother of all ointments. 'It'll burn your bollocks off!' the others informed me with more than a touch of sadistic glee. What a start. Still, sod it – it couldn't get any worse. Oh, yes it could – oh, yes it did!

We arrived in Munich mid-evening and, due to my position as host to the ugly ball-clingers, I was awarded pariah status in the shared bedroom – a position that required me to move my bed as far away from the other three sharers as possible. Once settled into Outcast's Corner, I resisted the urge to pacify my multitude of itches and joined the rest of the guys in search of food. This was the band's second residency at the PN, so they were on familiar turf and knew the local eating places, in particular the Wienerwald. This popular chain of restaurants offered quality food at reasonable prices, with a lively atmosphere created, to a certain extent, by the waitresses – busty *fräuleins* carrying armfuls of beer. Of course, the menu was in German so I didn't have a clue what to ask for.

'Try the *Hühnerbrust*,' suggested Boat Beecham. 'It's chicken breast in a curry sauce with rice.'

'Sounds good to me,' I replied, scratching my groin. The others moved away as one in the opposite direction to where I was sitting. Bernie, at least, offered some sympathy. 'Tomorrow I'll take you to the chemist – they call it the *apotheke* here – and we'll get you sorted out.'

I woke up in the middle of the night and knew immediately that something was wrong. An overwhelming sense of nausea had gripped my insides, like a maelstrom of army boots trying to kick their way out of my gut. Surprise soon gave way to realisation as neon letters blinked in my mind's eye... *food poisoning*.

I somehow managed to negotiate a successful path to the bathroom without walking over my slumbering roommates, and made it just in time. After the deluge, I sat back, spent and dispirited on that unfamiliar bathroom floor, engulfed in a wave of melancholy: that sad, desolate emotion I'd experienced in Finsbury with the Wild Flowers. From homesick to 'badly cooked chicken' sick. Eventually, I managed to drag myself to bed, with only my body lice for company.

I awoke un-refreshed and full of *joie de mort*. My head ached, my stomach felt as though I'd been punched repeatedly by Henry Cooper, I had a taste in my mouth like I'd been French-kissing a camel and the parasites were digging in like Tommies at Ypres. The rest of the guys, unaware of my toilet trauma, urged me to visit the chemist pronto or face banishment to Crab Island. Bernie, true to his word, led me across the road to the *apotheke*, creating in me a sense of reassurance.

'I know a couple of words in German – leave it to me,' he said.

Good bloke. He headed straight for the counter, while I surveyed the hairbrush rack.

'*Mittel für lousen, bitte?*' he asked the stern-looking lady assistant. She gave him a slightly horrified look, which prompted Bernie to turn round and point his finger directly at me. 'For him,' he proclaimed.

The bastard! A woman near to me gave out what I can only describe as a suppressed scream, then hurried out of the shop. The Brunhilde behind the counter, still taken aback by the original request, now directed her attention to the spineless outcast by the brush collection.

'Ze lotion is to be applied twice,' she said as she eyed me contemptuously. 'No, four times a day, until ze scourge is eliminated.'

I settled for three and, let me tell you, it was painful. The pests weren't just killed off: more like incinerated.

The clientele at the PN Club was the usual mix of regulars and in-town-for-the-night merchants, and as the audience for the first of the three sets was usually a bit on the sparse side, this time could be used to try out new songs. The band's repertoire of cover versions guaranteed that the portable record player back at the apartment could be put to good use. Lucas would come in with a new soul album, the other guys would put on the latest Chicago Transit Authority or Buddy Miles Express and I turned up with Jeff Beck's new release, *Beck Ola*, and Joe Cocker's latest. Lucas or the others would win hands down, but it didn't worry me – it was all good stuff. I loved – in fact, still love – soul music. There's just nothing like James Brown's grooves, Tamla Motown's songs or the instrumental prowess of Booker T. & the M.G.'s.

This was great experience and fun, especially as I was now totally in control of my motions, and my pubic areas were once more free from unwanted visitors.

CHAPTER 7

MADMAN WADING THROUGH A SEA OF MARS BARS

Anybody who claims to have been party to the club scene of the mid-1960s but can't recall Zoot Money wasn't there at all. The expression 'character' could almost have been defined for George Bruno 'Zoot' Money. Though he would be the first to admit to being influenced by Ray Charles, his own madcap personality broke new grounds. A true 'raver', as they used to say, he didn't give a damn about convention and, I'm pleased to say, still doesn't. His Big Roll Band were a talented bunch and featured a young blond guitarist who was playing an original Gibson Les Paul before Eric Clapton – Andy Summers, way before he helped form the Police.

Zoot progressed to psychedelia in 1967 and formed Dantalion's Chariot with Andy Summers and Big Roll Band drummer Colin Allen. They performed in white robes, used white instruments and amplifiers, and released a single entitled 'Madman Running Through the Fields'. Audiences soon came to the conclusion that real ale was not their prime creative influence. Shortly afterwards, Zoot moved to California to join his partner in crime Eric Burdon in the New Animals. Here endeth the history lesson.

Zoot returned to Britain in the autumn of 1969, a mellower man raring to go, and spoke to Nick Newall, who, in turn, spoke to Mike Cotton. Our leader then informed us that the band needed to progress, and that the progression was going to be Zoot Money and the Mike Cotton Sound. We all agreed that it was, with great respect to Lucas, a move in the right direction. It transpired that Lucas was very philosophical about the whole thing and no bad blood was spilt. The guy was a trooper; he just got on with it. Nick was back with his old boss, who was full of musical ideas: the brass section could stretch out into the realm of Blood, Sweat and Tears, Bernie and Lem could chill out on some new rhythms and I could do a bit more in the solo department. Unfortunately, it didn't work out in the end. Maybe people still expected Zoot to act the goat and fool around within the music, but people change.

The 'old looner' was still in there somewhere but the man had moved on.

There was now a deeper aspect to his character, especially when he performed pieces like Judy Collins' 'Both Sides Now' and Leonard Cohen's 'Story of Isaac'. However, just as people were readying themselves to adopt the cross-legged 'sitting-and-listening position', he'd launch into an exhilarating version of the Beatles's 'Blackbird', complete with simultaneous manic soloing from the brass players. Then, once the unprompted witticisms started, it was into 'Big Time Operator' and vintage Zoot at the Flamingo Club circa 1965.

I loved Zoot and got on well with him; he had a musical outlook and a strength of character that had to be admired. So, early in 1970, when Mike announced plans to transform the Mike Cotton Sound into Satisfaction, I decided to stay with Zoot in his new, pared-down line-up.

To coincide with Zoot's new phase, his publicist issued a new press release. Under the heading 'All hope abandon, ye who enter the head of Money,' he was described thus:

> That thick thatch of flaming ginger frizz that sprang from that head. And the cherubic-demonic face grew in front of it, too. But the stuff inside the head of money remains a black, festering secret. The man himself is one of those complexities you find cackling away under the tables at four in the morning; the one in the black cape and evil laugh when you're stoned.

Though I'd only known Zoot for a short time, it's fair to say that the writer had presented a fairly accurate profile, apart from his preoccupation with the colour black. To my knowledge, none of his festering secrets were black – and neither was his cape. It was a striking shade of burgundy, in crushed velvet.

The new band was a four-piece, featuring Zoot, Barry Dean on bass, Barry Wilson on drums and yours truly on the trusty Telecaster. Zoot was playing what he described as 'the only travelling Fender Rhodes electric piano in the country'. It was a beautiful-looking instrument with a gorgeous, warm tone, and the lower half housed two large speakers which could 'pan' the tremolo into a stereo effect. The equipment travelled in a short-wheelbase Ford Transit van commandeered by

Johnny Mac, a relative of Zoot and a very sound bloke to boot. It seemed that Zoot was the only driver in the band, so he was lumbered with the task of getting us from gig to gig – on a Californian driving licence. If the police had stopped him, he'd have had to adopt a West Coast twang. Luckily, they didn't and we were spared the Venice Beach boy / Malibu Beach bum impersonations.

Zoot was very funny. During one conversation about the effects of drugs, he offered, 'It depends on whether you want to go up, go down, or sort of wobble about in the middle.' And on the subject of downers, 'It was like wading through a sea of Mars bars.'

After a few days' rehearsal above a pub on Chiswick High Road, the cool little combo set off on its travels. The musical direction was pioneered by Zoot alone (as opposed to Zoot alors!), though the three musketeers were encouraged to put forward any ideas that might avail the 'black festering secret' that lurked in the corridors of Zoot's head. He decided to keep 'Blackbird', 'Both Sides Now' and 'Story of Isaac' from the previous set-up, and added the Band's 'Up on Cripple Creek', plus some Zoot originals. On one particular song, I was inspired to adopt the second movement (the slow one) from the 'Concerto de Aranjuez' by the Spanish composer Rodrigo, which I played on my classical guitar. Nowadays, such a move might be regarded as pretentious. In general, the set was a musical hybrid of melodic, down-home and out-there songs performed by an eccentric, ever-so-slightly manic bandleader and three keen, trouble-free young chaps.

Ah, the nostalgia of it all.

I reserve very little of that nostalgia for one of the band's first gigs, at a small basement club in Whitley Bay, a seaside resort near Newcastle. For a start, there was no stage. This presented us with the disadvantage of having to stand eyeball to eyeball with the people standing directly in front of us, who were mainly disinterested young men out on the piss. Hovering directly above their heads was a thick pall of cigarette smoke, which gradually descended upon them like a Victorian fog, giving them the appearance of an inquisitive crowd at a Jack the Ripper murder scene. Everybody in the place seemed to be smoking at least two cigarettes each, including the industrious bar staff.

Years later, I came across a quote from one Samuel de Sorbiere. It read, 'The English are naturally lazy, and spend half their time in taking tobacco.' He obviously didn't visit Whitley Bay, where they seemed to spend all their time in taking it. They should have had caged beagles playing there. One ignorant sod, standing directly in front of Zoot, turned around, sat on the piano and started chatting to his mates, seemingly completely unaware that he was doing so on 'the only travelling Fender Rhodes electric piano in the country.' And in Whitley Bay. Zoot reacted immediately and pushed the cretin away. He disappeared into the nicotine haze like a dejected Heathcliffe.

After the gig, I didn't even bother to have a fag; after two hours in that place, I could almost feel the first twinges of emphysema. A girl with calluses on her knees started chatting to me then pulled me into a nearby cupboard. What a bloody place! I left with a satisfied smile and an irritating cough.

A few weeks later, we embarked on a tour with John Mayall's Bluesbreakers, whose line-up was unusual, to say the least: just keyboards, bass, nylon-strung guitar and saxophone. No drums! Most unusual. Also on the bill was Duster Bennett –

a brilliant one-man blues band who was signed to the Blue Horizon label and was a good friend of Peter Green. The venues were highly respectable concert halls in major cities.

From the outset, it was plain to see that, apart from Mayall, the Bluesbreakers were a little frayed round the edges or, to put it more politely, tired and emotional. At the start of one performance, the stage was bereft of bass player until the man in question, Alex Dmchowski, came dashing on, plugged in and started to adjust his amplifier settings. This prompted the somewhat unimpressed Mayall to announce, 'That's Alex Dmchowski, who has adopted the professional habit of always being late on stage.' Oooh! A couple of nights later, in the communal dressing room, guitarist Jon Mark blasted sax player Johnny Almond for playing an upright piano. Unaware of the condition known as stress, I looked on, somewhat perplexed as they continued to overstretch their obviously frayed nerves.

The next step for Zoot was to record an album, and I was pleased to be asked to participate in the proceedings. With a bit of luck, he might come up with a hit single and help rid the Top 10 of novelty records like 'Two Little Boys' and 'Wanderin' Star', not to mention the mind-numbing 'Yellow River'. His manager had secured a deal with Polydor that nominated Alan Price as producer and modern-jazz musician Keith Tippett as arranger for the brass and string parts.

The musical and artistic direction was obvious from the first two tracks. In 'When Will You Know', we were given some straight insight into Zoot's way of thinking:

Running and fighting for ever
And writing my life into a script

> Trying to please the people I love
> So there will be no rift

Then, in 'When Tomorrow Comes':

> But when tomorrow comes
> And I will see you cross the threshold
> And your voice is not the echo of yesterday

Mmm, well, it was 1970 after all. In 'Leaving It All Behind', Zoot balanced precariously on the precipice of the deep and meaningful/meaningless:

> I have changed somehow
> Things are different now in me
> Now I think it's time to wake up
> Before I know I'm gonna break up again
> I'm gonna go and see if my mind will mend

This track came complete with an underwater vocal effect that somehow found its way on to my scat-style guitar solo. However, the *pièce de résistance* had to be 'I Need Your Inspiration'.

What started off as a mid-tempo, gospel-tinged pop song was quickly dispelled by Barry Wilson's determination to enter the *Guinness Book of Records* for the most drum fills in the shortest period of time. I followed closely in second place, soloing relentlessly with arguably the smallest guitar sound ever recorded, creating the impression that the instrument could be the size of a small oven glove. After three and a half minutes of laboured rhythms, the violin players launched into

Keith Tippet's arrangement *à la* 'All You Need Is Love', spurred on, no doubt, by Zoot's continuous pleas for inspiration.

Suddenly, taking their cues from Mr Tippett, the brass players began soloing wildly with – and sometimes against – the oven glove. As if this wasn't enough, Zoot started belting it out on piano. At this point, the band broke into a shuffle and Alan Price was seen jumping around in the control room.

'Fuckin' 'ell, man, ye canna whack it!'

'Pardon?' the engineer may have responded.

Then, as if by magic, the tempo broke again and we were into the riff from the Beatles's 'Come Together'. I'd like to think that this was once again a pre-arrangement, rather than an S.O.S from some of the saner people in the room, but, given the circumstances, I'm not sure.

To round it up, Zoot repeatedly suggested that we should come together. Play together might have been a better recommendation. As the song careered towards a frenzied climax, several of the older string players became disorientated, packed up their instruments and fled the building. One re-entered with an invoice. All that was missing was a liquid-light show, highlighting the title of Zoot's press release: 'All hope abandon, ye who enter the head of Money.' Absolute madness!

A few days later, Zoot showed us the proposed album cover. It was a painting of a medieval mother with a child in her lap. The child's head had been replaced by a recent headshot of Zoot gazing into the distance while the mother wept. Who could blame her? A face of innocence had been replaced by a cherubic-demonic face fronting a head that contained a black festering secret. Interestingly, in the background, a futuristic tower headed some kind of fiery jetty, while a couple of naked winged figures seemed to be attempting aerial sex. Other assorted objects included an orange, some sort of melted bauble and a gorilla's shrunken head – nothing unusual there then. The right side of the painting continued on the back cover and closer inspection revealed the possible reason why: another naked winged figure half-kneeled on the head of a huge, limbed penis with smoke billowing from it.

'Will you get away with that?' I asked innocently.

'Get away with what?' replied Zoot characteristically.

'You know, the thingie,' I ventured tactfully. He looked at me enquiringly.

'Ah, if they don't like the orange, bollocks to 'em.'

Contrary to the romantic imagery presented by some rock journalists, the road does not go on forever. It merges into motorways, freeways and autobahns before offering you a huge choice of exits. Most performers choose to stop and refuel; some drive on into oblivion. However, the metaphorical journey does offer opportunity, which is something Leicester Forest East service station cannot boast in its CV.

Zoot and the band ran on for a little while longer, traversing that bygone university/college/club circuit which enabled professional musicians to work regularly and hone their craft. His eponymous solo album was released to, shall we say, tepid reviews, persuading him to halt proceedings and review his prospects.

I still see him from time to time and he's still out there doing what he's always done: making good music with all his heart and soul, and loving every minute of it!

CHAPTER 8

GET YOUR KICKS IN TORQUAY

Juicy Lucy was a band with a recording contract, personal management, a three-man road crew and an appealing brand of blues-tinged rock 'n' roll. Taking a contemporary stance, they were rehearsing at an old farmhouse in the country, which is where I was introduced to the guys in the band. The band's singer, Paul Williams, an ex-bandmate of Zoot's, had been kind enough to recommend me as the replacement for Neil Hubbard, who'd left to join the Grease Band. After a cursory jam, my position was confirmed. Later, on the walk to the village pub, Paul brought up the subject of the Mike Cotton Sound, whose average age was twenty-nine.

'What was it like working with Lucas and the Mike Cotton Sound?' he asked.

'Oh, I enjoyed it but they were all old blokes,' I replied.

Paul, who was also twenty-nine, remained silent for the rest of the journey. Come in, Mr Tact!

This was my induction into a band that had experienced a hit record with 'Who Do You Love', a recording which had reached No.14 in the UK charts earlier that year. It was also the first time I would play in a band with someone I really admired. An ex-member of the Misunderstood, Glenn Campbell was a Californian who played blues-rock on a twin-neck steel guitar and, as my dad would have said, 'could make it talk'. And he could. I would be all ears for a long time to come.

It was July 1970 and I felt like I was going places, and the first place I went to was Torquay, where we played to a large audience of locals, yokels and holidaymakers. During rehearsals, bass player Keith Ellis had struck me as being a decent sort of guy. How wrong can you be? The show wasn't even at the halfway stage when he sought to liven up the proceedings by booting an over-enthusiastic member of the audience in the face. I was just getting over the shock of witnessing such an act when Glenn pulled out a locking knife and proceeded to wave it at the boisterous crowd. This air of decadence continued after the show, with the dressing-room appearance of two pre-Raphaelite-styled groupies who were looking for more than just an art-class modelling fee.

Jesus, it didn't seem that long ago that I was an altar boy.

The following weekend, we were booked to play the Plumpton Festival and arrived early enough to savour the kind of atmosphere that a well-attended festival provides. Although fourth on the bill to Deep Purple, Yes and Jon Hiseman's Coliseum, behind-the-scenes sabre-rattling and an unexpected appearance by Ginger Baker's Airforce saw our early-evening spot stolen, pushed around and stolen again before being kicked unceremoniously into final place. However, due to an overabundance of self-indulgence and the aftermath of Ritchie Blackmore's public display of arson (in which he set fire to his speakers), we never got to play. That night, a decibel-fuelled cloud of positive/negative ions spelling out the word 'EGO' seemed to hover precariously above the stage, though at the time I didn't really understand the underlying causes that resulted in such an uncomfortable ambience. Artistic temperament, self-importance and unbridled braggadocio are all intrinsically linked to the artistic psyche, and many of us have thrown 'the odd wobbler' in order to establish position, or simply to gain attention.

A week later, amid the idyll of the West Riding, the Yorkshire Folk, Blues and Jazz Festival invited people to sample a weekend of delights from Elton John, the Pretty Things, Taste, the Groundhogs, Juicy Lucy, Fairport Convention, Pentangle, Mike Westbrook et al. Unfortunately, what promised to be a musical celebration turned out to be a complete washout, as storms battered the site into glum submission. Juicy Lucy did get to perform, albeit without Glenn, who was too ill to travel. Pushed in at the deep end, I did what I could to fill out the sound in Glenn's absence, even attempting to play his revered lap steel guitar for the 'Robert Johnson Interlude'. Incidentally, during Johnson's 'Come On in My Kitchen', Paul bellowed out part of the original lyric: 'Can you hear the wind howl?' A field full of wet and dispirited people yelled back, 'Yes!'

The following day, we passed through storm-battered areas of Halifax that made L.S. Lowry's paintings look like Palm Beach in July. If there were ever a case for the assisted use of Nembutal, this grim urban landscape would have won hands down.

Juicy Lucy's manager, Nigel Thomas, was an educated man with a ruthless streak. Within weeks of joining the band, I found myself in an office belonging to the band's record company, Bronze Records. Though I'd been advised that the meeting might not be of interest, I went along nevertheless. Within minutes, it became of interest. Without any prompting, Nigel and Keith tore into the managing director, Gerry Bron, with a joint effort that smacked of conspiracy. It seemed that the finer points of the agreement regarding the band's soon-to-be recorded album were, as yet, unresolved, and Messrs Thomas and Ellis were conveying the impression that Bron was trying to concoct some kind of contractual Faustian pact in his company's favour. I was confused: if it's true that the Devil has all the best tunes, why would he want to sign Juicy Lucy? The rest of us shifted uneasily in our seats as the Thomas/Ellis alliance continued to verbally abuse then accuse Bron of unjust demands. He finally yielded to the two-against-one verbal tennis match when, having been referred to as a Svengali once too often, he threw in the towel along with his lawyer's credentials. I surmised by the look on his face and his abrupt exit that he was off to seek refuge from this tie-break with a large Scotch, rather than the time-honoured Robinson's barley water.

After a few gigs of a more a conventional nature – i.e. without bodily assault or knife threats – I settled in and began to enjoy my newfound status. Paul Williams was a great singer and looked out for me in a big-brotherly sort of way. Chris Mercer on saxophone and occasional keyboards had previously played with John Mayall's Bluesbreakers, and Rod Coombes had drummed with an early version of the Jeff Beck Group. With or without the underlying psychotic potentials of Messrs Ellis and Campbell, this was a line-up of impressive pedigree. As it turned out, Glenn was really just an insecure character with a tendency to worry about things – and he had the ulcer to prove it. On the other hand, Keith was already showing signs of drug dependency. During those initial shows, I'd seen him reach up to the top of his amplifier prior to the final number, pick up something small and pop it into his mouth. I soon found out what it was – a bloody Mandrax sleeping tablet. By the time we reached the dressing room after the encore, he was already staggering ashore onto Barbiturate Island, drawn like a helpless sailor by the hypnotic lure of some soporific siren.

I'd only been a member of the band for a matter of weeks when I found myself in a large house in the Surrey countryside. Not only had I joined a top recording band, I was also being primed to direct my talents towards the silver screen. In true early-1970s fashion, the band had been offered a featured role in a film about three young guys who organise a pop festival and have a truly enlightening time.

Or so we were led to believe.

What transpired was a cheaply-made B-movie called *Bread*, which was more scorify than Scorsese and a possible contender for the worst pop film ever. Bereft of make-up and wardrobe and lacking any sort of script, Juicy Lucy were shown 'rehearsing' in the local village hall prior to their bill-topping appearance in a local field. Optimistically edited to give the impression that 50,000 fans were 'really into it', the authentic footage from the recent Isle of White Festival was lacking in just one rather important detail. The sun may have shone in Ryde on that historic weekend in August, but mid-September in Surrey was decidedly overcast. The two hundred and fifty or so genuine punters, who'd been bussed out from London, were totally oblivious to the creative subterfuge taking place and thoroughly enjoyed themselves. Hey, a free day out is a free day out in anyone's language.

Within days of my induction into the world of film stardom, I found myself in the recording studios overdubbing and recording live for Paul Williams's *Tribute to Robert Johnson* album. Bearing in mind the amount of blues tribute albums that came out in the 1990s, Paul was ahead of his time. Mind you, the record companies weren't so enthusiastic about the idea, and it would be almost three years before the album eventually surfaced. When it did, I was miffed to discover that, due to an oversight in administration, my name didn't appear among the credits. I was not impressed. The album's front cover read:

DELTA BLUES SINGER ROBERT JOHNSON WAS
FOUND DEAD IN A HOTEL ROOM AUGUST 1937.
HE WAS AGED 27 YEARS. THIS ALBUM IS IN HIS
MEMORY.

My thought process read:

GUITARIST MICK MOODY WAS FOUND PISSED
OFF IN A HOTEL ROOM APRIL 1973. HE IS AGED
TWENTY TWO YEARS. HIS NAME WAS NOT IN
THE RECORD COMPANY'S MEMORY.

I'm sure that Mr Johnson would have been less than happy too, given that the date of his demise was incorrect. It would be another twenty-five years and a re-release before the king of the delta blues and yours truly were finally awarded some truth in the matter.

It could only have been a matter of days – possibly hours – before I found myself in another studio, keenly anticipating the laying down of tracks for the new Juicy Lucy album. The band had concentrated on writing its own material, though it would occasionally tip its selective cap at an influential blues master. For this particular album, it was Howlin' Wolf, whose version of Willie Dixon's 'Built for Comfort' was captured on tape during the first day's recording. Two more cover versions were to end up on the album: Mac Davis and Delaney Bramlett's 'Hello L.A., Bye Bye Birmingham' and a manic version of Frank Zappa's 'Willie the Pimp'. The latter had proved to be a show-stopper in the band's live set, and included the obligatory drum solo in which Rod sometimes employed the use of his front teeth for that extra . . . er . . . enamel sound – 'It's organic, man!'

So, in the space of a month or so, I'd become a member of a well-known band, appeared in a film, recorded an album and flourished as songwriter. Not a bad career move so far then. To my recollection, there was no bacchanalian atmosphere during the recordings, just the odd sociable beer and joint. And to assist with the band's ambition to make a breakthrough in Glenn's homeland, a short U.S. tour of selected venues was on the cards. America – the home of rock 'n' roll and blues, and all the best TV programmes – how exciting! On 2 September 1970, Concorde had made its inaugural landing at Heathrow airport while Palestinian terrorists were busy blowing up three captured western airliners. Even though the perpetrators were kind enough to allow the passengers to disembark first, it was not good news for 'aerophobics' like me. I tried to make light of it with a little verse: 'Planes there and back, planes to and fro, white-knuckle flyer, oh, here we go!'

Contrary to the recent tragic loss to the music world of the incomparable Jimi Hendrix, over in Juicy Lucy's world things were moving forward at an alarming rate. The album was finished in no time at all, and a single – 'Pretty Woman' (no, not *that* one!), from the rush-released album entitled *Lie Back and Enjoy It* – was premiered on *Top of the Pops*. It was my first experience at miming, on a show I'd been watching since its inception. So that's a member of a well-known band, film star, recording artist, songwriter and TV star. And all for the retained fee of thirty-five quid a week! This wage-structured system was not unusual in those days, when honest managers and music publishers were as rare as Vietnamese comedians.

My personal synopsis is that the music business was – and, in a lot of respects, still is – partly genuine, partly naïve and wholly perfidious.

Roy Carr from *Melody Maker* conducted a half-page interview with Paul and Glenn. Under the heading 'JUICY LUCY - PROBLEMS PAST AND PRESENT', the boys explained that the reason the band worked so much was because they kept their fees down in the medium-price range. From a business perspective, this was probably not a wise statement to have made. They also enthused about the new acoustic set midway through the show, until our record company was mentioned: 'If the agencies, record companies and others did their jobs properly then economically things would be a whole lot better,' opined a dissatisfied Glenn. Another Scotch, Mr Bron?

The Musicians' Union was next for the spit-roast, as a delayed U.S. tour had caused a six-week interruption to the band's economic structure. You could almost see Mr Carr's thought processes fast-tracking to the 'excuses to leave' section.

'To survive you've got to make five hundred pounds a week clear profit. There's six of us in the group, three roadies plus two vans and a heap of equipment that's always in need of some kind of repair,' continued Glenn. 'To be quite honest, we had a bit of a rough time during the summer but this was because we were trying to get our new album out, replenish our stage act and break in our new guitarist Mick Moody. But now everything is hunky-dory.'

Hoorah! Roy's thought processes must have gone to red alert, with a robotic voice intoning, 'Leave now! Leave now! Leave now!'

The missing pieces to the proposed U.S. tour were finally put into place, and we were advised to pack our bags and resort to standby positions. However, photographs with the new band member were an urgent requirement.

We assembled in a small park close to the rehearsal studios and posed, somewhat moodily, for a photographer whose clothes sense and general demeanour were inferior to ours. And believe me, that took some doing. My own personal image was a simple pastiche of past-the-shoulder hair, denim shirt, black knitted waistcoat and a pair of black trousers I'd bought three years previously and whose knees now resembled a vertical version of one of those road signs for a humpback bridge. The rest of the guys were of a similar vintage, give or take the odd shoulder bag. If some of us looked a little glazed round the eyes it was no surprise, as between Keith and one of the roadies – a northern lad called Gerry – there was always a hash joint on the go.

Soon, the U.S. equivalent would be coursing through our lungs with herbaceous fervour.

CHAPTER 9

JAMES BROWN – BIG IN BOSTON

The Fillmore East had officially opened its doors on 3 March 1968 with a programme that featured Big Brother and the Holding Company, Janis Joplin's future partners in crime. The former Village Theatre on Second Avenue and Sixth Street, now firmly under the commanding presence of promoter Bill Graham, had become the hippest and most respected rock venue in town. It boasted an exquisite interior of 1920s vintage, had an in-house staff of over fifty and could service the artists with a choice of two specialist lighting teams: the Joshua Light Show and Pig Light Show. I stood at the back of the stalls and, with mounting realisation, concluded that I'd come a long way since my first gig in a church hall in Middlesbrough.

'Mind your ass, buddy!' bellowed a voice from behind. I turned to face a big guy with waist-length, centre-parted hair, as was *de rigueur*. And he *was* the rigger.

'Oops, sorry!' I responded, as a part of the lighting truss inched past my head.

'Yoo wid de Joocy Loocies from Ingerland?' he enquired.

'Er, yes,' replied a young man struggling to come to terms with a Brooklyn accent.

An educated familiarity with the voices of Top Cat and his gang of homo-felines was one thing, but taking it right in the face from a hairy-arsed truss-erecter was a whole new experience. After wishing the band a good show, he headed for a nearby ladder while we were shown to the dressing room. The friendly and helpful stage crew were a far cry from some of their British counterparts, like the charmers at The Place club in Hanley, Staffordshire, who provided the bands with a list of 'don't-dos' before they'd even unpacked their instruments.

We'd touched down the previous evening and headed for our Manhattan home from home, the Skyway Motel. Due in part to a touch of jet lag, I arose earlier than usual and found myself sharing a buffet-style breakfast with a couple of the entourage, a handful of prematurely obese salesmen and a recently widowed Chinese woman.

'Hey, they've got Kellogg's cereals in this country too,' I observed.

Heads turned and regarded me with eyes that registered both disbelief and dismay.

'They make them over here, son,' said a sympathetic man from Chicago, Illinois.

'Oh, right,' replied a somewhat short-in-the-tooth young man as he gazed out of the window at the incessant activity that was New York City. Oh, the traffic, the traffic! The buildings, the buildings! So much! So tall! This was impressive stuff, and the adrenaline was kicking in and providing us with a natural high. We left the hotel in a fleet of yellow-checkered cabs, each commandeered by a brusque descendant of mid to eastern European stock. As we made our way across the planet's most notorious example of a concrete jungle, the image of an archetypal British army sergeant major appeared in my mind's eye: 'Wits about you – quick, march!'

Back at the Fillmore, where soundchecks were about to start, I glanced at the poster displaying the evening's programme. Top of the bill was Lee Michaels – an organist and singer from California accompanied by Joe Larson on drums. Such a small band – such a roadie's dream! Also on board was Cactus – a four-piece band centred around Carmine Appice and Tim Bogart, the former rhythm section of Vanilla Fudge, and a group credited with being the prime inspiration for Deep Purple. Making up the numbers were former Mitch Rider and the Detroit Wheels and Buddy Miles guitarist Jim McCarty, and singer/harmonica player Rusty Day, another ex-Mitch Rider member who'd also played with the Amboy Dukes. That night, the atmosphere was special, with a good-vibe audience that listened and dug it. The same kind of atmosphere that would be captured the following year on what was to become one of my all-time favourite albums – *Live at the Fillmore* by the Allman Brothers Band. Back at the hotel, somebody gave me a Mogadon – a supposedly potent sleeping tablet. I washed it down with a few beers but it had absolutely no effect on me whatsoever, so I wiled away the next hour or so bouncing off walls draped in a sheet, with a litter bin on my head and a cigarette in each ear. I awoke the next morning in the bath, fully clothed and with a can of beer in my hand. As I said, absolutely no effect.

In the dressing room after the gig, a Vietnam vet came in

and lit up a joint. Somewhat naïvely, I asked him what it was like 'over there'.

'Man, the fungus always grows on death's tendrils.'

'Mmm. That's food for thought,' I mused. Just then, a spaced-out groupie entered the room and announced that she'd lived through a period of solar eclipse which had somehow affected her biochemical make-up. Soon their incomprehensible meanderings began to merge as one.

'Saturn is giving out sonic waves on the cusp of my first house, 5 Leo. . .'

'The gooks, man, they were everywhere. We gave the sons o' bitches a fire in the hole. . .'

'We need to create an awesome mekometer to pick up the love rays from Venus. . .'

'Hey, do you guys know any Indians or Pakingstanleys? I had a Puerto Rican buddy who was blown away in. . .'

'Right, let's go,' signalled the welcome voice of Mick, the band's tour manager. We left them to it, a space cadet and one ever-so-slightly disturbed ex-soldier, conversing in tongues I would no doubt encounter again.

The next day, having skipped breakfast due to a touch of jet lag and a self-conscious awareness as to the origins of breakfast cereals, I set out with a few of the guys and a representative of the band's booking agency to visit Atlantic Records, the mother company of our appointed label, Atco. We hadn't ventured far when we were approached by an individual who looked like he'd spent the night immersed in formaldehyde. His personal greeting was far from convivial: 'Hey, gimme some change.' As his demand was directed at me personally, I responded by way of an unmerited apology, a curious by-product of British social etiquette. His reply was aggressive to say the least and pretty unnerving. It was only the timely intervention of the guy from the agency that saved me from an unpleasant encounter, with a well-directed 'Get the fuck outta here.'

'Right,' I thought. 'I'll make a note of that.'

1970 in New York City was a far cry from the future zero-tolerance era of Mayor Gulliani's reign and, though exciting in its extremities, demanded a certain amount of caution, especially when roaming the streets at night.

After introductions and gifts of complementary albums, we were invited to have a look around their studios. Yes, Atlantic Studios, NYC. Bloody hell – a piece of history or what?! Dizzy Gillespie, Ray Charles, Aretha Franklin, Cream. They'd all poured out their emotions in this very room, creating musical milestones, along with many others too numerous to mention.

'Look at this!' exclaimed Chris Mercer. There, on the windowed screens surrounding the drum kit, were taped A4 size flyers announcing: 'PURDIE – THE FUNK KING; THE GROOVE MAN; PRETTY PURDIE – THE HIT MAKER!'

Of course! Bernard 'Pretty' Purdie *was* the funkiest drummer in town and he had no hesitation in reminding everyone.

Imagine a parallel experience a couple of years later at the infamous, secretly-taped Troggs recording session with singer Reg Presley pasting up A4 size flyers: 'I'M PLAYING IT FACKIN' WRONG; I'LL SPLIT ME 'ANDS; I'LL SPRINKLE SOME FAIRY DUST ON IT; 'OW ABOUT A FACKIN' TWELVE STRING?'

Back in a world far removed from the absurd banter of hayseeds from Hampshire, England, a voluptuous black woman with exquisite teeth had walked into the room and prepared herself for the impending recording session.

'Hi, guys,' she said with a big smile. We returned her greeting.

'Who's that?' I asked Chris innocently.

'Roberta Flack,' he responded, and then reacting to my perplexed expression added, 'Quite a famous singer.'

We flew into Boston on a rainy night aboard a small 'prop' plane that scared the shit out of me. This was only my fourth ever flight, and my maiden voyage on a propelled kite. In retrospect, I could imagine that there were dozens of characters from Stephen King's imaginative mind waiting on the windswept shores of New England far below, eager for a disaster to happen. Luckily, it didn't, though my white-knuckle ride into Massachusetts left me with a distinctly paler hue than when I'd boarded. Glenn was no help and, after I instinctively grabbed his knee during one of the *really* bumpy bits, he reacted like the blasé American frequent flyer he no doubt was.

'Grab yourself a sick bag, man!' he exclaimed.

'I'd rather grab a priest,' I responded.

Getting off that plane was more a case of liberation than disembarkation. I raised my shaking hand to inadvertently light the filtered end of my cigarette, and momentarily considered an alternative lifestyle. Then, gazing around the baggage-collection area at some of the 'straights', I came to the conclusion that I'd made the right decision.

As we approached the Boston Tea Party club, my gaze was alerted to the rather prominent 'JAMES BROWN' on a poster by the main entrance. Excited by the prospect of catching the godfather of soul that night, I took a closer look at the creative work of a truly deluded public relations person:

NOVEMBER 8TH – ONE NIGHT ONLY
Billy Brown, cousin of
JAMES BROWN !!!
Tickets available at the box office

Nice try! Thankfully, Juicy Lucy was advertised as 'from England' and placed third on the bill for two nights to Leon Russell and the Elvin Bishop Band. Leon's set was faultless and his band was an education, while Bishop's band was down-home, funky and infectious. All the bands were serviced with the same communal dressing room, and it was exciting to be able to rub shoulders with such esteemed company. Leon's guitarist, Don Preston, was the proud owner of an original Gibson Explorer – a futuristic-looking guitar that was destined for international recognition. Like most of Leon's band, Don was from Tulsa, Oklahoma; a good ol' boy who was both friendly and approachable. We chatted and he let me have a play on this unusual instrument, which would be purchased a couple of years later by Eric Clapton. Because of their rare status, these guitars can nowadays fetch over a quarter of a million pounds.

Being a Paul Butterfield fan, I was well aware of Elvin Bishop from his time with Butterfield's great blues band. He was also a native of Tulsa and seemed to enjoy playing the rock 'n' roll hayseed to the limit. Lurching around the band room looking like Harpo Marx in a Stetson, he seemed to derive great pleasure from addressing anybody younger than himself as 'Hey, Boyyyy!'

After the show, there was a very lively atmosphere, and standing in the middle of a communal dressing room in the States in 1970 was a bit like being a member of the drug squad burning a field full of marijuana without a protective mask.

Back at the hotel, I was sharing a room with another member of the band and his recently acquired groupie. Thankfully, I was zonked from the passive – and occasionally active – dope smoke, and slept through the predictable grunting and groaning from the adjacent bed.

In Chicago we were joined onstage for a jam session by the excellent fusion violinist Jerry Goodman, late of the band Flock and a soon to be member of John McLaughlin's Mahavishnu Orchestra. He was great, of course, although the overwhelming urge to tell him to 'get the flock outta here' was hard to contain. Later that night, I was given my first toot and was somewhat disappointed by the result – an irritating awareness at the back of my throat. I commented on this . . . in fact, I commented on it quite a few times over the next hour or so.

Back at the hotel, we were met by the night porter – a young black guy – who energetically informed us that he'd dropped some black acid. Whether the substance in question was eponymous in its description or a hallucinogenic familiar only to black people was unclear. Either way, I gratefully stepped into the elevator the second it arrived.

Back in my room, I looked out over the deserted Loop area of this great city and, adhering to the usual advice regarding personal safety, stayed there. I suddenly felt a long way from home; a transatlantic phone call cost a fortune then and the Internet didn't exist. No emails, no texts, no Skype but also, thankfully, no Twitter: that stomping ground for the deluded and desperately insecure. Not all bad then.

After a couple of nights in the cold expanses of Madison, Wisconsin, we were set to round off our U.S. mini-tour in that hotbed of self-indulgence, California.

The former Carousel Ballroom had become the Fillmore

West and was San Francisco's premier rock gig. Unlike its counterpart in New York, it was bereft of seats – an arrangement I've always preferred when it comes to rock music. Why do you think all those Teddy Boys trashed their seats during Bill Haley's performance in the film *Rock Around the Clock*? You can't repress legs! Bill Graham had cornered the market once again, and his initial promotions with the Grateful Dead, Jefferson Airplane and other Haight-Ashbury favourites had given way to some of the biggest names in rock. The blues guys were popular too, especially Albert King, whose searing lead lines were to influence a new generation of white guitarists. Unfortunately, Juicy Lucy didn't get to play alongside the formidable Mr King; we had to settle for a four-night stint with Elton John and the Kinks. Not that that was a bad thing . . . but Albert King! As we mingled in the 'green room' after the first show, a young lady called Debbie picked me out then picked me up. The next night she went through the same procedure with one of the Kinks. Far out!

The next stop on our itinerary was an even crazier place – Los Angeles.

Just after I'd checked into my room at the infamous Tropicana Hotel in Hollywood, the phone rang.

'Hi, this is Barbara the Butter Queen. Is that Mick Moody?'

'Er, Yes.'

'Do you look like Jimmy Page from Led Zeppelin?'

'I suppose there is a resemblance. Why?'

'Because I want to come to your room and do my trick with the butter.'

She then described in intimate detail how she would like to smear my old chap with butter and give me the best popcorn-flavoured sex I'd ever had. It suddenly gave a whole new meaning to the expression 'a knob of butter'. I declined her kind offer, citing a shy disposition and lack of sexual experience involving churned milk fats.

Later that night at the Whisky a Go Go, we changed for the show and I was at once taken by the underlying aroma of Utterly Butterly wafting conspicuously from the direction of Keith Ellis's groin. The Butter Queen had added yet another name to her spread-sheet.

Those with an interest in American rock history would find the Whisky a Go Go and the Tropicana Hotel intrinsically linked. Situated within staggering distance of each other on Sunset Boulevard, they had rock 'n' roll stamped all over their slightly seedy facades. Everybody had played at the Whisky and stayed at the 'Trop'. Jim Morrison had lived there, and some bloke called Alice Cooper was in residence – dressed, thankfully, in his civvies – during our stay. Relaxing in the hotel's Duke's Coffee Shop listening to a bunch of guys perform an impromptu a cappella song, a friendly waitress let it slip that Janis Joplin had died from a heroin overdose in one of the rooms only a few weeks beforehand. Preliminary enquiries failed to reveal the exact location of her expiry, which in turn gave me cause for concern. Was it my room? That night, as I drifted off to sleep, I had visions of being woken in the middle of the night by the restless spirit of Miss Joplin, her primeval screams and machine gun 'm-m-m-m-m-m-m-m's scaring the shit out of me.

'Stop it, Janis. I'll take another little piece of your heart *and* buy you a Mercedes-Benz – honest!'

Jimi Hendrix, Janis Joplin and Canned Heat's Al Wilson all died within weeks of each other from drug overdoses, which, in anybody's estimation, must seem like a tragic trail too far. But were these deaths by misadventure really caused by irresponsibility and insecurities? According to Zeke Madovsky from the Burning Roach Commune in One-Legged Man Falls, Idaho, there may well have been other issues involved: 'Prolonged life has ruined more people than made them happier – why not check out of the Life Hotel on a high, man?' Well, whichever theory you might favour, in Madovsky's eyes, neither Hendrix nor Wilson would succumb to male-pattern baldness or gout, and Joplin would never become the troublesome bag lady whose brain had been frazzled by drink and drugs. Less than a year later, Jim Morrison was dead – an event which led Madovsky to declare that the singer had 'gotten out before he was thirty. He knew that his pubic hair would turn grey and couldn't visualise life in a grey world.' Was there more to these premature demises than we've been led to believe? Maybe they'd all been alerted to George Santayana's belief that 'Music is essentially useless, as life is.'

'What kind of cynical asshole would say something like that, Jimi?'

'Dunno, Janis. Maybe he was the sort of guy that smelled flowers then looked around for a coffin.'

Nigel Thomas accompanied us on the tour and gazed impassively through a window of opportunity that would raise his profile in rock management. Through his dealings with producer Denny Cordell he'd managed to secure European representation for Leon Russell, and it was due to this arrangement that the band found themselves at Skyhill Studios in Leon's house on Skyhill Drive, North Hollywood. We'd been granted a free day's worth of recording time, and from this session emerged one track, an instrumental, which someone in the band entitled 'Big Lil', a derisory swipe at Gerry Bron's wife, Lillian. Things obviously hadn't improved between Juicy Lucy and the Brons! I can't remember why we only recorded one track: either we were short of material or the spliffs were a bit on the strong side. As it turned out, 'Big Lil' would eventually appear on the band's next album. It was the first and probably the last time that I'd be in the same room as a Mellotron – a keyboard that could produce convincing orchestral sounds at the push of a key. All in all, about eight sounds from something that was roughly the same size and weight as a Mini Cooper. The instrument was popular with the Moody Blues, though not necessarily with their road crew.

After our second and final show at the Whisky, a few of us went to a bar for the proverbial nightcap. Later, Rod Coombes and I blagged a lift back to the hotel and were joined by another reveller, who slid into the back of the car beside me.

'Hi, guys, I'm Mickey,' he announced.

'Hello, I'm. . .'

I recognised his face immediately – Mickey Dolenz from the Monkees! He said he'd enjoyed the gig and asked where we were playing next. Before we had time to further our conversation, we were back at the Tropicana and our encounter with a bona-fide pop star was over. We said our farewells and, for my parting shot, I revealed that I remembered him as Corky in *Circus Boy*. His expression begged the question: 'Hasn't *The Monkees* series reached British TV yet, or are you still watching reruns of the late-1950s black-and-white adventures of a travelling circus?'

Back in my room, I switched on the television, where Johnny Cash was singing a song with the Carter Family: 'Where were you when they crucified the Lord?' I don't know, Johnny, but I'll always remember where I was when you crucified that song. Of course, there were many more channels to explore, but the mind-numbing effects of the used-car salesman's pitch became too much for a young man still coming to terms with meeting a Monkee.

The next day, I flew home alone as the others had decided to stay on and soak up a bit more of the sunny West Coast. And who could blame them? The plane was half-empty, so I commandeered a whole row of seats before dropping a Mogadon to relieve the tedium of a very long flight. As I nodded off, I reassessed the comings and goings of the last ten days before arriving at a personal conclusion: California, what a daft place.

Once the full complement had returned from their extended stay, we manoeuvred our often unwilling noses back to the grindstone and set out for the comparatively less-than-attractive nightspots of Bradford, Nelson, Colchester and Western-Super-Mare to pay more dues.

Early in the New Year, Juicy Lucy featured in a couple of TV productions, starting with a trip to Paris to perform live in a programme from La Taverne de l'Olympia. Soon after, we turned up at the BBC television studios to mime (lip-sync, baby) two tracks for *Disco 2*, the forerunner to the *Old Grey Whistle Test*. Pre-Bob Harris and under the gravelly voiced guidance of Tommy Vance, the show sought to present acts not usually featured in the singles charts. Though not as obscure as its predecessor, *Colour Me Pop*, the programme is rarely mentioned these days. So I'd like to mention it again – *Disco 2*. And while I'm back there, I'd also like to mention TV programmes such as *A Family at War*, *Upstairs Downstairs* and *Nearest and Dearest*. How we laughed at Nelly Pledge and her malapropisms, the old codger who rolled his R's and the octogenarian with a weak bladder! The austere black-and-white confines of a pickle factory in east Lancashire was, indeed, a far cry from the sunshine and butter fetishes of colourful Los Angeles.

On 1 February 1971, Nigel Thomas brought Leon Russell to London for a concert at that most prestigious of venues, the Royal Albert Hall. The bill featured Status Quo, Juicy Lucy, the Grease Band, and Leon and the Shelter People. Spot the odd one out? Status Quo had decided that longevity could be attained by developing into a no-nonsense rock 'n' roll band, and had approached Nigel with a view to management, hence the inclusion in the show. It would prove to be a worthless exercise as neither audience nor manager was impressed. Quo, of course, got there in the end. I think I'm right in saying that the Grease Band made their debut that night, playing songs from their forthcoming eponymous album, and, having been an admirer of Henry McCullough's guitar playing since his time with Joe Cocker, I was pleased to get a seat out front. Their set was nicely laid back and, after Status Quo's 'rockin' all over the stage' act, almost delicate, with the odd acoustic-in-the-chair and harmonium thrown in for good effect! These boys could hit a groove and were very well received.

At some point in the evening, one of Leon's band, in need of a narcotic boost, appeared at the door of Status Quo's dressing room and asked if anyone had any coke. Keen and eager to please, a somewhat naïve Francis Rossi allegedly proffered a can of Pepsi Cola. Exit one disappointed American.

Not long after, on returning from a short tour of Germany, Keith Ellis decided to quit the band. I don't recall the exact reasons for his decision to leave, but the poor guy was destined to dissipate his talent and die needlessly before his time.

CHAPTER 10

GET A WHIFF A THIS... AND THIS... AND THIS...

On 19 March 1971, we flew to Zagreb in Yugoslavia for a concert with Mathew's Southern Comfort, a British group that performed country-rock music and included a comparatively old guy, Gordon Huntley, on pedal-steel guitar. This was the year that Josip Tito was re-elected and, with the Cold War still in existence, I felt a touch apprehensive about my first visit to a communist country. I needn't have worried. The Zagreb I saw was relatively calm, and in no time at all our new bass player, Jim Leverton, had scored – twice! No sooner was he rolling up than he was chatting up. This guy didn't hang about!

A few hours before the gig, Jim and yours truly were selected to take part in a TV interview. Having a camera record his every move didn't deter Mr Leverton from rolling a joint, or from sticking bits of cigarette paper to his eyelids and fluttering them like a demented Bambi. The man was mad! It was an enjoyable show and, though the red flag flew close by, we were made to feel welcome.

Tito had made a speech that included the line, 'No one questioned who is a Serb, who is a Croat, who is a Muslim [Bosniak]; we are all one people, that's how it was back then and I still think it is that way today.' Twenty years later, it would all start to go horribly wrong.

Mathew's Southern Comfort performed their hit, Joni Mitchell's 'Woodstock', which included the line, 'By the time we got to Woodstock we were half a million strong.'

Well, by the time Southern Comfort reached their third number, *we* were six strong and gone to chill out at a nearby club.

Winter was melting into spring and we were in Germany (the western part anyway, the east was still *verboten* unless specially invited), moving steadily along the autobahn in our long wheel-base Transit van. I sniggered like a schoolboy at the sign that said *Ausfahrt* and, as the word means 'exit', there were more sniggers until the novelty wore off. Armed with a stage inventory of Gibson guitar, Marshall amplifier and speakers, hat, suede waistcoat and fringed trousers, plus a small case of clothes, I was as happy as Larry – whoever *he* was.

Chris Mercer usually handled the driving duties as the rest of us didn't, couldn't or weren't allowed to – it seemed like a sensible arrangement. On the early-evening ferry across the Channel to Belgium, we'd played a drinking game called Cardinal Puff in which the loser of each round has to down his drink in one and then buy the next round. Thankfully, the stakes were only half-pints of cooking lager, otherwise some of us would have ended up like inoperative cars – piston broke. Then onwards to Hamburg via a rather boring journey through Belgium without the aid of a distracting drinking game or metaphorical road signs, so snoozing soon became the natural antidote.

Jim Leverton was a character, that's for sure. He'd been permanently stoned for a number of years, which made him laugh a lot, and was a fine bass player and backing singer to boot – a good-vibe merchant.

We played the usual round of clubs and halls, and attendance was always good, as they liked their live music in Germany. With a night off in Frankfurt, we made our way to the legendary Zoom Club, where we were booked to play the following evening. It was a wise move, as the legendary blues singer Champion Jack Dupree was performing solo that very night. When we arrived, he was having a break between sets and I was introduced to him by the club's owner, Cooky Dahl. I possessed recordings of Dupree on the Decca label with people like Eric Clapton, Mickey Baker and Tony McPhee as accompanists, so I was blown away when he asked me to get up and play with him that night. Of course, I jumped at the chance. However, I needed my equipment, and the roadies – custodians of the van keys – were nowhere to be found. Of course, there were no mobile phones those days, so a runner was sent out as a solo search party. The thrill of playing with such an authority on the blues started to fade, so I accepted the inevitable, found a seat and watched the man. Towards the end of his set, an out-of-breath roadie appeared with my guitar and amplifier, so I did manage to get on stage for a couple of numbers. Marvellous!

Though there never seemed to be a shortage of dope, there was an unexpected windfall after our gig at the Zoom. During the show – and unbeknown to anyone else – a local dealer had squeezed a rather large slab of hash into the small gap between the stage and the wall for safekeeping. Unfortunately for him – and due possibly to the vibrations caused by the band's boisterous performance – it fell through the aperture and disappeared into the darkness under the stage. As expected, he was not a happy man, and his efforts to prise the stage away from the wall were fruitless. He was hardly in a position to complain to the management, so he retired from the scene defeated, dejected and extremely pissed off. However, Gerry the roadie had other ideas. Once the coast was clear, he produced a small handsaw with which he carefully created a hole big enough to accommodate both his hand and arm, which resulted in the victorious salvage of the wayward dope. It stood the band and crew in good stead and lasted for the remainder of the tour, with Gerry's room suddenly taking a rise in the popularity ratings.

Being a slim, dark, twenty-year-old member of a popular band, with a fine head of hair and a shy disposition, I suppose I held a certain attraction to the opposite sex. This led me into the company of two attractive young ladies. Eva was a dusky teenage beauty from a middle-class background and Anna was a petite blonde who may have dropped one tab of acid too many. Both were a welcome distraction from the hairy-arsed company I usually found myself in. We became friends, and a certain amount of juggling would be required to maintain this relationship on further visits to this rather exciting country.

After the last gig, I decided to head straight home via the ferry with Gerry and the other roadie, Spot. Just before the Belgian border, one of the guys suggested we finish off his small nugget of dope and, as there was too much to smoke, he decided to eat it, knowing full well that the eventual effect would be somewhat more pronounced than the standard procedure of mere inhalation. Halfway through Belgium, it started to take effect. This posed no problem, though as expected the conversations trailed away to nothing. Suddenly, there was a slight lurch and the van began to shudder. We looked at each other with red-eyed anticipation and an overall sense of capitulation.

'Bollocks, that's all we need,' said Gerry.

'No, it's not,' responded Spot.

And in the most futile manner, the best I could come up with was, 'There must be something wrong with the van!'

The van, though lacking in its anticipated horsepower, soldiered on until we reached a roadside garage, which of course was closed. It was 5am and we would have to wait, tired, very stoned and with a mounting sense of being in the wrong place at the wrong time.

We awoke with a collective start. A small man with an agitated expression was knocking on the window and speaking in French.

'*Quel est votre problème? Qu'est-ce que vous faites ici? Est-ce que vous des gitanes?*' he asked.

'*Gitanes?*' answered Gerry. 'You want a cigarette? I've got some Rothmans.'

'*Non, non,*' countered the man. '*Gitanes.* Gypsies!'

'We're not bloody gypsies – we're a music group,' explained Gerry.

'Ah, music. *J'aime* music,' came the reply. He must have been impressed because he pointed to the van and said, '*Est-ce que vous êtes tombe en panne?*'

The question was greeted by three perplexed expressions. What followed next was some sort of condensed vaudeville sketch in which the mechanic, with the aid of gesticulations and over-presented silly noises, tried to act out the question in a non-lingual fashion. The inclusion of a bowler hat, a red nose, a clarinet and a bucket of whitewash would have provided us with a first-rate impersonation of that great circus clown, Charlie Carolli. Considering the state we were in, we could have done with it.

'I think he's asking us if the van's knackered,' droned a still-stoned Spot.

A few minutes later, the van was in the garage being connected at the front end of the chassis to an ancient-looking hoist. Monsieur Carolli appeared at the window with more gesticulations, this time directed towards me and Spot.

'Tirez! Tirez!' My limited French took this to mean 'get out of the van', but the pair of us remained rooted to our very tired and stoned front passenger-seat positions. Then, with a Gallic shrug, he returned to his hoist and, amid grunts and gasps, managed to persuade the front of the van to raise itself to an angle of approximately sixty degrees. That is, the van, Spot and myself.

I'm not sure how Spot felt, but observing a peeling ceiling from a discerning angle at 7.30am in Belgium while trying to fight off an overall sense of nausea was a situation I'd never experienced before, or for that matter, since. I tried thinking of Eva and Anna but it didn't help.

Quite recently – and for some inexplicable reason – the conversation turned to Jimmy Clitheroe, that long-dead midget comedian who was a product of deepest Lancashire. Mention of that particular part of England suddenly evoked memories of the time that some deluded fool came up with the not-so-bright idea of spreading a little culture – via Juicy Lucy – into the limited confines of the cabaret circuit. Blue-sky thinking, 1971 style! Whether the local rock fans had exerted any influence over the manager of their local Bailey's nightclub or he'd come up with the idea himself remains lost in the annals of time, but the good people of Blackburn were offered a change in the usual structure of their nightly fixes of popular entertainment in an atmosphere of subdued lighting, extended bar tariff, chicken-in-a-basket meals and large bouncers. Headlining acts were booked for a week-long engagement, and it was during the period assigned to Billy J. Kramer and the 'new' Dakotas that Juicy Lucy made their groundbreaking appearance, albeit for one night only. And as soon as we entered the Cavendish Club, the clock seemed to rewind three or four years and I suddenly felt like I'd been transported back to my early gigging days 'oop north'.

The atmosphere backstage prior to the show left me with the distinct impression that our Billy was just a tad precious, and that certain members of his band seemed to belong in the 'men with a fine prospect of happiness behind them' category. The motley audience of 1960s pop fans and 1970s rock enthusiasts that leaned into their tables during our one-hour set seemed slightly ill at ease, and the sight of 'hairies' nodding their heads in time to the music alongside the unimpressed 'straights' was off-putting to say the least.

We soldiered on to the end and, once the final steel-guitar screams, vocal hollers and percussive poundings of 'Willy the Pimp' had faded into the plastic and PVC decor, our backline was moved to one side to make way for Billy J.'s entrance – and what an entrance it was! As the Dakotas set the mood with the opening bars of some bygone hit, the commanding voice of the M.C. heralded the great arrival: 'Laydeees and genelmerrrn, here he is – Billy J. Kramer!' Enter stage-right the man himself, spotless, beaming and sporting the whitest suit in the entertainment business. His zestful little bound towards the centre of the stage would have been effective had his foot not made contact with a small puddle of spilled beer. This unfortunate encounter caused the hapless singer to land flat on his back, slide across the remainder of the stage and come to an abrupt halt beneath a table of Juicy Lucy fans. Although he managed to extricate himself from this unfortunate abeyance, his rictus grin fooled nobody and he remained flustered until he got to 'Do You Want to Know a Secret?'

Well, Billy, do *you* want to know a secret? You had a bloody great beer stain on the back of your jacket for the rest of the set!

The 'one-nighters' came and went, and on the college and university circuit we found ourselves sharing stages with an interesting selection of acts such as Wishbone Ash, Van Der Graaf Generator, Stone the Crows and Keef Hartley's Halfbreed. The last was led by Preston-born Hartley, a drummer with a predilection for dressing up as a Native American chief, an image slightly at odds with his thick Lancashire accent. He was alleged to have travelled to the Chelsea flat of a top model, prepared and lit a fire on the pavement outside, then wafted up sexually explicit smoke signals to her boudoir.

'Ey oop, squaw, lass, pass um peace pipe, like, before t'shag.'

Arriving at Lancaster University, I heard the voice of the support band's singer: Aretha Franklin? No, it was Terry Reid. What a voice, so full of passion and vitality, which was more than could be said about Graham Bond, who shuffled into one communal dressing room looking like an obese corpse.

Two or three years later, he jumped in front of a tube train at Finsbury Park station, the victim of serious drug abuse and an unhealthy interest in the dark arts.

Regardless of the fact that new material was thin on the ground and artistic collaboration almost non-existent, it was time to record a new album. Paul seemed to be the only one with any sort of leaning towards lyrics, and, though 'Big Lil' was in the can from our day at Leon Russell's house, musical inspiration was in need of a kick-start. The writing partnership of Williams and Moody produced the wistful 'Jessica', but cover versions were urgently needed. Chris suggested 'Mr Skin' by the Californian band Spirit, Glenn put forward the Allman Brothers Band's 'Midnight Rider' and I came up with the rather obscure 'Harvest', a song written by Bobby Darin during his hippie period. The resulting album – *Get a Whiff a This* – came in at thirty-two minutes and forty-one seconds, arguably one of the shortest albums ever recorded and a possible contender for the contravention of the Trades Descriptions Act. Nigel Thomas 'produced' the album; that is to say, he agreed with most things and spent a lot of time trying to bullshit the engineer.

The album sleeve was designed by Glenn and featured his drawing of the cartoon character and unlikely comic-book hero created by S. Clay Wilson, the Checkered Demon: a portly, shirtless being always seen wearing checked pants. Glenn's initial offering showed the demon releasing a flatulent gust from the back of his famous pants (Johnny Fartpants eat your heart out!) while proudly proclaiming 'Get a whiff a this!' Fortunately for the world at large, the drawing was expurgated and the infamous emission ended up in the trash can.

At a club in Baden-Baden in Germany, we'd just started the third number when there was an almighty crash. I glanced across the stage – which had a small fence around it – and saw the boot-soled lower end of a pair of legs sticking up in the air like some sort of surreal V-sign. They belonged to Jim Leverton, who, in trying to steady his inebriated body by sitting on said fence, had fallen arse over tit and was now lodged at an angle of approximately eighty degrees twixt the stage and the dance floor. Like a true professional, he didn't miss a beat and continued playing.

The band's usual onstage line-up of six had now been reduced to four, as Glenn Campbell, having paired up with Jim at the hotel bar, was now lying comatose in his room back at the hotel. Downing shots of Tequila in the daytime is never a good idea, and Glenn wasn't much of a drinker to start with. Jim was righted by the road crew and finished the gig sitting on a chair. Afterwards, somebody scored a few Mogadons and some of us were seen staggering about with the kind of silly grins that always seem to accompany that 'haven't got a care in the world' expression.

After a short tour of Germany, Jim handed in his notice, though I can't remember the reason why – maybe he banged his head in Baden-Baden. It's more likely that he just wasn't really enjoying it. He was replaced by DeLisle Harper, a friend of Chris and formally of funk band The Gass.

We continued with the usual round of one-nighters, taking in most of the established rock venues across the country, like the Van Dyke Club in Plymouth, Mothers in Birmingham, the Marquee in London, Friars in Aylesbury, the Mayfair Ballroom in Newcastle, Nottingham Boat Club, Wolverhampton's Club Lafayette et al., plus the usual run of universities and colleges. DeLisle's musical prowess and warm personality *did* raise the collective spirits for a while, but the air of uninspired creativity, which had surfaced prior to and during the *Get a Whiff a This* sessions, showed no real signs of abating. In retrospect, it all boiled down to a lack of musical direction, something all too *au fait* in the life of a band. And let's be honest, Juicy Lucy could never have relied on its non-image of untidy long hair, jeans and cowboy boots to boost its popularity, especially when in competition with the new wave of glam rockers. Not that we would have considered it, but dyeing our hair blonde, wearing worryingly camp clothes and performing songs like 'Co-Co' and 'I'm the Leader of the Gang' could have gained us a new audience, but would have destroyed any feelings of cool authenticity and instilled feelings of contempt for all things commercial.

That summer, Juicy Lucy featured in some prime 'happenings', including the now legendary Weeley Festival in Essex. This was a truly awesome event, in which there were so many bands appearing that they had to play continuously, twenty four hours a day, for nearly three days! We took to the stage at three o'clock on the Saturday morning, feeling almost as knackered as those who were still awake. Among the bands appearing that weekend were Rod Stewart and the Faces, T. Rex, Status Quo, Rory Gallagher, the Edgar Broughton Band, King Crimson, the Groundhogs, Barclay James Harvest, Mott the Hoople, Curved Air and Lindisfarne. As with many festivals in those days, some people in the crowd felt the need to liberate themselves by stripping off. I've always found this to be somewhat embarrassing: if God had wanted us to walk around naked, we would have been born that way.

We flew to Finland to play at the Turku Festival on a

weekend that also featured the Jeff Beck Group, the Kinks and Canned Heat. Next in the book was the Speyer Festival in Germany, where I spent time with the lovely Eva. Lesser attractions included Family and Osibisa.

Back home, the band entertained enthusiastic audiences at the Sound 71 Festival in Buxton, once more in the company of the Groundhogs and the Edgar Broughton Band, plus Gentle Giant, Paladin, Brewer's Droop, Harry Hopper, and Tea and Symphony, before heading for the Lyceum in London to share the bill with Man.

Recreational time between travelling? I stayed at home, rolled a joint and listened to sounds, man!

My tastes were beginning to widen and I started listening to all kinds of music, with the exception of opera, which I regarded as overemotional and with a lyrical content that I didn't understand. And believe me, I had no intention of studying Italian just to find out what I wasn't missing! American comedian Ed Gardner may have got it right when he said that opera is when a guy gets stabbed in the back, and instead of bleeding, he sings. 'Nessun Dorma' just about sums it up – you've got no chance of sleeping with that bloody racket going on. The incomparable Ambrose Bierce was a little more astute: 'Henry Krehbiel [the eminent musicologist] said that Wagner strove to express artistic truths, not tickle the ear, and therefore his work will stand, while Italian opera, which is founded on sensual enjoyment, must pass away.' Fair enough. Mind you, old Ambrose also remarked that musicians are not commonly distinguished above their fellows by mental capacity. In my experience, I'd say he had a point. However, since meeting and sharing the stage with the remarkable Alfie Boe, my judgement of all things operatic has softened somewhat.

Meanwhile, someone had introduced me to Ry Cooder's eponymous debut album and the initial impact was overwhelming: a fantastic player with a truly original perspective. And my musical direction was awarded further stimulus with the Leon Russell-produced *Getting Ready* by Freddie King. This particular period would prove to be a turning point in my personal development as a guitarist and, with the release of the Allman Brothers Band's *Live at the Fillmore*, my creative disposition was well and truly focused. My confidence was bolstered further after a gig somewhere up north, when a bloke said, 'You're no genius, lad, but you've got talent.' Well, genius does what it must and talent does what it can.

CHAPTER 11

TWO HEADS ARE BETTER THAN NONE

On the week ending 13 November 1971, an article in the news pages of the *Melody Maker* announced:

JUICY LUCY RE-SHUFFLE – FOUR QUIT, GROUP REFORMS. After last week's Coliseum split, there comes news of another British group breaking up. The outfit in question is Juicy Lucy, but this time there is a happier ending – because the group has already re-formed! Vocalist Paul Williams and lead guitar[ist] Mick Moody are the only two remaining members of the original line-up, and they are now joined by drummer Ron Berg and bassist Andy Pyle (both formerly with Blodwyn Pig) and keyboard player Jean Roussel, a former classical pianist who'd subsequently turned to jazz as a vehicle for his inventive approach and style.

Of the previous members of Juicy Lucy who have

left, Californian steel guitarist Glenn Campbell and DeLisle Harper are in the process of forming a new band altogether, sax player Chris Mercer has joined Keef Hartley and drummer Rod Coombes is working with the Roy Young Band.

Said Paul Williams: 'The split was inevitable. We had for some time been arguing about the type of music the band was playing. Juicy Lucy made a name for exciting rock music, and that's what we shall continue to play.'

Juicy Lucy in its re-shaped form has signed a three-year deal with the Deutsche Grammophon Company (Polydor in Britain) for all territories except the United States, Canada and Japan.

Excellent! Paul had managed to rejuvenate the band, I'd stepped into Glenn's shoes and the thirty-five-quid-a-week retainer remained in place. This was a good line-up too; Ron and Andy were an item, as solid as they come, and Jean was a huge talent. In fact, everything about him was huge – physique, hair, clothes, appetite, etc. Being a twenty-eight-inch-waist skinny person, I couldn't figure out how anybody, especially one so young, could be so overweight. Jean wasn't a dope smoker, though one night he asked if he could take a spoonful of somebody's grass and make a cup of tea with it, which he duly did. He spent the remainder of the evening waiting for the effects but nothing happened. That is, nothing until about six hours later, when he awoke sweating from the depths of a psychedelic dream. He stuck to food after that. When he told me that he'd made sweet music with jazz legends Jon Hendricks and Marian Montgomery, I deduced that he must have been paid in carbohydrates. Joking aside, he was one hell of a piano player, with a mellifluous brand of funk that added a touch of class to the band's rock-edged sound. All we needed to do now was to capture that revitalised sound on tape.

Nigel Thomas wasted no time in furthering the band's *modus operandi*, and within weeks we were set up and ready to go at the newly opened Command Studios in London. The Grease Band's drummer, Bruce Rowland, was brought in to produce, and Paul had a bunch of songs co-written with a lyricist called John Edwards that we wasted no time in learning. For covers, I suggested Ry Cooder's version of Alfred Reed's 'How Can a Poor Man Stand Such Times and Live', Taj Mahal's 'Cuckoo' and a rousing version of one of my favourite Chuck Berry songs, 'The Promised Land'. After a few days (and for reasons unknown), we relocated to Olympic Studios in Barnes, south-west London, where we settled into the smaller, more comfortable Studio Two. On the second day, Bruce bounded into the control room: 'Come and have a listen to this!' he enthused. We followed him through to the control room of the larger Studio One, where a band was set up and playing as in a live gig. We listened for a while as they sang and played an original country-rock song with effortless aplomb. At the end of the song, we registered our approval with 'yeh's and nods of the head while producer Glyn Johns reeled back the tape for another take. On the way back to our studio, I turned to Bruce.

'Great little band – who are they?'

'They're a bunch of guys from the States making their first album. They're called the Eagles.'

I found it an education working with Bruce. For a start, he was totally focused on the job in hand, was refreshingly enthusiastic and was instrumental in capturing the kind of guitar sound I'd striven for since my first recordings back in 1968. This was due, in some measure, to the employment of the resident studio amplifier, an original Fender Super model which would have originally housed the standard issue of two ten-inch speakers. However, somewhere down the line and due, no doubt, to over and/or abusive use, one of the speakers had been removed and never replaced. This was a blessing in disguise, as the extra workload directed to the remaining speaker created a warm distortion at a relatively low level. The band was augmented on one or two tracks by organists Mick Weaver and Ian McLagen, the latter formerly of the Small Faces and the soon-to-be Rod Stewart and the Faces. Oddly, backing vocals were provided by the virtuoso guitarist Albert Lee and Chas Hodges, who would eventually settle for Christian-name status as half of the hugely successful cockney duo Chas and Dave.

The assistant engineer (whose name now escapes me) was an extremely nice chap for whom nothing was too much trouble. He did however have one small yet significant flaw – money, or, to be more specific, parting company with it, and had an embarrassing habit of giving sixpence to a tramp then asking for a receipt.

The new line-up played a series of shows (including a short trip to Italy) before taking a Christmas break, then early in the New Year *Sounds*' Ray Telford interviewed Paul and asked him why Juicy Lucy had been unnecessarily 'slanged' in the past. In his reply, he pointed to the fact that the old Juicy Lucy had been getting paranoid about being a musician's band, which in turn created dissension in the band's attitude towards live performances: 'When that sort of thing happens the excitement goes out of it and to play good rock and roll there should be plenty of excitement. Now, though, I've got the band back to where it should be with the excitement.' Here was a man with excitement on his mind.

A couple of paragraphs later, Telford suggested that Glenn Campbell's 'wild and woolly slide playing' was an undoubted attraction in the old band: 'I reckon that Glenn's the best steel player in Britain. I don't know about America but certainly over here there can't be too many people to touch him. But now Glenn's out Mick (guitarist Mick Moody) is playing like he's been let out of a cage and some of the things he's doing come very near to being as good as Glenn's.' That would be due to the excitement then.

After Paul's conclusion that there had been a lot of bad feeling towards Juicy Lucy in the past, and that club gigs were the most satisfying, the reporter rounded off the piece with, 'It looks now as though most of Juicy Lucy's more pressing problems have been solved. The business hassles which have dogged them since their beginning are smoothed out. Maybe now they'll get down to playing music. They can do it.'

We rehearsed in readiness for the forthcoming round of gigs, which took in a short tour of Germany and a string of one-nighters in the UK. Although the welcoming spaces of universities and town halls gladdened our hearts, we'd often find ourselves working up a sweat in invariably gloomy and smoke-enshrouded venues, like Clarence's in Halifax, the Wake Arms in Epping, Cleopatra's in Derby, the 76 Club in Burton on Trent and the Temple in London. The overabundance of black-painted walls in some of these establishments could evoke images of Gustav Mahler at his most despondent. Only the pretty cherry-red finish on my Gibson ES335 guitar seemed to brighten up the grubby stages in some of these places. In defence of such establishments, they *did* exude atmosphere and the overall stage sound was often tight.

Supporting the Grease Band at Hull University was both memorable and inspiring, as I got to witness the wonderful Henry McCullough in full swing. That night, we played in earnest; the following night we played in Grimsby.

The clubs may have provided the opportunity to get closer to the audience, but it was the universities and colleges that paid better – thanks to government grants – and whose hospitality was sometimes extended to incorporate the odd crate of Newcastle Brown Ale. Bloody luxury! Nigel Thomas was, by now, channelling all his energies into the careers of both Joe Cocker and the Grease Band, so the day-to-day tasks were given over to Bernard Pendry, a likeable older man whose experience in the business probably owed more to accounting than dealing with long-haired rock 'n' rollers. However, he seemed genuinely interested in the likes of Juicy Lucy and singer-songwriter Tony Kelly, and, though this was hardly 'change management', he rose to the challenge with newfound enthusiasm. On the floor above us, a young Max Clifford was establishing himself as PR man to the stars and, according to more recent news, other things too. Naturally, Nigel's acts were among his clients. We took delivery of a nice big Mercedes van in which to haul our gear *and* our arses to gigs, plus a brace of enthusiastic roadies in the form of Frankie and Joe, a couple of true 'heads'. Man, these boys liked their dope, and this insouciant bunch would be stoned on a regular basis until further notice!

The band turned up at a college in Warrington to find that no hotel had been booked. Why worry? Have another spliff! Frankie and Joe soon resolved the problem by persuading three girl students to let us all stay at their flat. One or two of the entourage may have gotten more than just a bed for the night, while another one – who shall remain nameless – got up during the night from his drunken slumber and pissed in a wardrobe. We awoke refreshed and suitably decadent, and the kind Lancashire lasses helped us stave off the possible onset of scurvy by cooking us a nutritious breakfast before we left. Having been identified as the person who pissed on the girl's personal items, the nameless one was made to feel about as welcome as an exploding suppository and, therefore, went hungry until we stopped to refuel. When we did stop, the phantom pisser had to settle for a fish-paste sandwich, made and proffered by an ancient woman who looked to be in an advanced state of necrosis.

Just prior to the release of the album, titled *Pieces*, Jean made a wise career move that required no rumination when an offer to join Cat Stevens's band was waved at him. Stevens was, by then, an artist on the verge of huge success, especially in the United States. No doubt the financial arrangement *and* the distinct possibility of even more regular snacks and/ or a proper dressing-room rider played a small part in Jean's decision to leave. He was replaced by rhythm guitarist Dave Tedstone, a rather shy, taciturn individual who cited Kiowa Indian guitarist Jesse Ed Davis as his main influence. After a few gigs, another keyboard player was instated in the form of ex-Vinegar Joe pianist Mike Deacon, then sporting a fine pair of James Onedin-style sideburns. However, his spell with the band was relatively short-lived and he would eventually be replaced by ex-Audience man Nick Judd. Within weeks, Andy Pyle had gone, to be replaced by Belfast-born Chrissy Stewart, the ex-Eire Apparent bassist, whose funky edge was well in keeping with the band's direction. A man with a penchant for a sociable smoke, his down-to-earth and friendly personality made him a firm favourite within the ranks. However, Chrissy had a problem locking into Ron's drumming, which was fundamentally classic British blues-rock. Though Paul disagreed, the majority favoured the cooler, funkier style of Terry Stannard, so it was goodbye Ron, hello Terry. Ruthless but fair. However, after a couple of gigs, Paul bemoaned the fact that he missed Ron's 'clout', so he was reinstated.

Juicy Lucy had been booked to support Joe Cocker on his European tour, which would also help with the promotion of the album. Good old Ray Telford gave *Pieces* a favourable review in *Sounds*, while over at *New Musical Express*, Pamela Holman joined in with yet more positive reactions:

This is the first Juicy Lucy album since American steel guitarist Glenn Campbell left a few months ago. Lucy were re-launched, confident that the new guitarist Mick Moody could fill that gap. Indeed Moody is an exceptional guitarist in his own right, but to replace someone like Glenn Campbell would have been an impossible task. The group realised this, and decided to change their style. So *Pieces* is an album mainly demonstrating that they can produce good music with or without Mr Campbell. Best tracks are on side two. Songs like 'Suicide Pilot', a good rocking number, complete with aeroplane effects at the ending; 'Dead Flowers in the Mirror', which could be described as a drunken lament; and 'How Can a Poor Man Stand Such Times and Live', which has a bluesy feel. If Juicy Lucy continue to put out material of this quality they stand a good chance of a very healthy future.

TWO HEADS ARE BETTER THAN NONE

When Hitler's government authorised the building of the Dietrich-Eckart-Buehne amphitheatre in Berlin to coincide with the 1936 Olympic Games, they could never have visualised for one moment that this monument to opera, classical music and theatrical productions would, less than three decades later, be playing host to a group of long-haired Englishmen performing an over-amplified form of music that had its roots in the blues style of black America. To complete an overall sense of irony, when the Rolling Stones played at the renamed Waldbuehne in September 1965, the crowd responded by trashing the place and causing 400,000 deutsche marks' worth of damage – a hell of a lot of money by today's standards.

I'm pleased to recount that when Juicy Lucy performed there in 1972, there was no such anarchic behaviour, and, in the company of Atomic Rooster, Can, If, Beggars Opera and Hawkwind, we were given an enthusiastic welcome. Coincidentally, our best-received song that day was a cover of the Stones' 'You Can't Always Get What You Want', during which Paul climbed up among the PA speakers to whip up the crowd. Hawkwind featured a pre-Motörhead Lemmy and a dancer called Stacia who wore little more than paint. The German band Can were certainly an odd kettle of fish. They improvised on a theme for the whole length of their set, the bass player wore fingerless gloves and the only verbal communication was provided by a Japanese guy who sat cross-legged on the floor and rattled off elementary German phrases in his native accent. Barking bloody mad!

Afterwards, we took up our usual positions in somebody's room at the hotel, a fraternity of musos and roadies reacting with eagerness as proffered joints of Arabian-Asian origin promised a cool conclusion to the day's events.

A LITTLE BIT OF LINCOLNSHIRE LOGIC.

The Boston Gliderdrome was, as the name suggests, a cavernous place, which was created to cater to the tastes of aeronautics enthusiasts. When Juicy Lucy played there in 1972, it was a regular stop-off point on the one-nighter circuit. One of the venue's more peculiar features was that of a small, middle-aged man who, standing in front of the stage decked out in full evening dress, proceeded to conduct the visiting bands with an imaginary baton! Along one side of the huge dancefloor was a bar, which I attempted to enter for a pre-gig drink.

'Yer can't come in 'ere wearin' that,' commanded the stroppy bouncer in reference to my black 'Indian Joe' hat.

'Why?' I asked, somewhat surprised.

''Cause if I let you in with that on, they'll all come in wearin' 'em.'

I'd been a fan of Joe Cocker since playing support to him on various occasions a few years previously, so it was with great anticipation that I boarded the Manchester-bound tour coach at the Cumberland Hotel near Marble Arch. Cocker certainly had a great band: Chris Stainton on keyboards, Jim Keltner and Alan White on drums, Alan Spenner on bass, Neil Hubbard on guitar, Rick Alphonso, Fred Scerbo and Milton Sloane alias the Westport Brass, Felix Falcon on assorted percussion and Gloria Jones, Viola Wills and Beverly Gardner on backing vocals. One serious band! As we headed up the M1 motorway, I surmised by the amounts of joints being passed around that this was not going to be a tour for the faint-hearted. It would be a great pleasure to be able to stand at the side of the stage and observe such talented artists, even if some of them were, shall we say, slightly over the limit. Mind you, there were very few in this particular entourage that wouldn't be out of it at some time during the next three weeks.

Backstage after the show, from inside the somewhat limited confines of a window-sided phone booth, Joe showed off his skills in multi-tasking by attempting to speak on the telephone *and* snort a generous amount of coke directly from a small bag.

We flew to France for shows in Paris and Lyon before making the short hop to Brussels. Most of us were happy to share a joint and have the odd drink, but there were a few who lived a more 'buy and try it' existence. After the show in Amsterdam, Joe's road manager – a jovial Welshman called Plum – invited some of us up to Joe's suite at the Hotel Akura for a nightcap (or whatever the equivalent is in marijuana). An hour or so later, we arrived at the suite in question and made ourselves comfortable. I enquired as to Joe's whereabouts, which prompted Plum to nod in the direction of the bedroom. Through the half-open door, I could see the singer and a couple more of his band prostrate on the king-size bed. I don't know what they were on, but it certainly wasn't sociable hemp. Plum suggested a nice pot of tea, made a headcount – eight in total – and called room service to place the order. I can only assume that the Dutch staff had a problem with Plum's accent, or else they were smoking a more potent crop than we were, because the ensuing delivery was inaccurate to the extreme. Instead of one waiter delivering a trolley laden with tea for eight, we were treated to the remarkable sight of eight waiters delivering eight trolleys of the same, thus making a grand total of tea for sixty-four people and a possible world record for a room-service beverage order.

To the inert souls in the bedroom (or perhaps the Astral Plain), tea was of little consequence.

The soundchecks sometimes gave us the chance to jam with guys from Joe's band, especially Alan, Neil and Alan White, which was a great experience and a genuine thrill. The backline was exclusively Acoustic – an American brand of amplification introduced to us by Leon Russell – and my personal onstage instrumentation was the aforementioned Gibson ES335, a Vox solid-body for slide and an old Neapolitan-style mandolin on which I used to perform a wee Irish jig at the end of 'Diamonds Rolling Down Those Golden Stairs'. It was after one of these soundchecks that a majority-rule vote heralded the return of Terry Stannard, who caught the first available plane and was back on stage for the next show. Ron Berg was naturally disappointed and no doubt hurt, but he took it on the chin and even asked if he could hang out for a few more days, which he did. Gigs in Germany, Italy and France with days off in Genoa and Nice rounded off an enjoyable tour, though we were disappointed not to be given the support spot on the three London dates at the Rainbow Theatre. Managerial skulduggery and another band's attractive record-company support had, no doubt, put the mockers on that. Mind you, we were there a week later supporting Slade, so there was some kind of artistic justice after all.

For the second year running, Juicy Lucy was booked to play at the Turku festival in Finland, and the Chrysalis agency had chartered a plane to fly its artistes there. The journey from Gatwick was undertaken at night, and also on board were Chicken Shack, Wild Turkey, Tir Na Nog, assorted roadies, girlfriends and tour managers. After an uneventful flight, we disembarked at a small airport, picked up our luggage and proceeded through Finnish customs with the confident air of innocent travellers. However, Frankie and Joe had been given a cursory pull by a couple of the local customs officers. Their focus of attention seemed to be a somewhat innocuous tool box, which they opened for inspection. Now, unknown to the rest of us, the two lads had planned a surprise for all and sundry in the form of a reasonably-sized nugget of Lebanese Red (a popular brand of hash), which they'd secreted inside the battery compartment of a hand torch. After a quick eye-scan of the contents, one of the custom officers reached inside and picked up . . . yes, the torch! By this point, I can only imagine that the two roadies were struggling with the bleak prospect of having to spend the next three years in the company of deranged Vikings and gay Russian wrestlers, some of whom would be lying naked in provocative poses in the sauna of a high-security jail. The officer pressed the 'ON' switch and, of course, nothing happened. The Vikings and wrestlers had now been joined by a judge who had nothing but contempt for long-haired rock 'n' rollers, plus the leader of an anti-British organisation.

'Hmm,' grunted the customs man before tossing the inactive torch back into the box and waving them through. Exit two very, very lucky lads. Frankie spoke for them both: 'Fuckin' 'ell, head, that was close!'

Of course, the next day they were two very, very *popular* lads, and we weren't the only band on the bill to enjoy such a welcome toke.

CHAPTER 12

FUNKY SHITKICKERS

We returned to the familiar circuit of one-nighters, which included the Hind's Head in Chadwell Heath, Big Brother in Greenford, Alhambra Rock in Birmingham, Kew Boat House, the Belfry in Sutton Coalfield and the Leas Cliff Hall in Folkstone, a venue which, as far as I'm aware, is still in existence. On the afternoon of the last, I did a session for the 1960s pop singer John Leyton, whose biggest hit had been 'Johnny, Remember Me'. He'd since established himself as a film star, featuring in *The Great Escape* and *Von Ryan's Express*, and had returned home to relaunch his singing career (an unfortunate move that proved to be fruitless). The session, at Morgan Studios in north-west London, was enjoyable; he was extremely nice and, seeing that I was in a hurry to get to the gig in Folkstone, even helped me carry my gear to the van! I wonder if Johnny remembers me. Before I forget – and to illustrate the generosity of the government's grants towards the arts in those days – how about this for a bill: John Cleese, Terry Jones and Michael Palin from Monty Python's Flying Circus, the Hollies, Juicy Lucy and Andy Roberts. It happened at Bradford University and we shared a dressing room with the Python lads – unbelievable by today's standards but par for the course then!

That year, I achieved two small yet significant landmarks in my budding career – headlining at the Marquee Club and playing at the legendary Cavern in Liverpool. According to one William Shakespeare, 'Things won are done; joy's soul lies in the doing.' Well said, my son! I'd played the Marquee several times with Tramline but always in a supportive role, so 4 September 1972 was a big day for me. It turned out to be a steaming gig. The original Cavern was, of course, the launch pad for so much great talent – not least the Beatles – so it was a great privilege to stand where so many had stood before, even though it was a bit of a tip. Sadly, it closed the following year.

Not long after, Paul Williams announced that he was leaving Juicy Lucy forthwith to front drummer Jon Hiseman's new band, Tempest. So it was decision time: carry on with a replacement or call it a day. It didn't take long for the rest of us to make that decision, and, with our ever-enthusiastic road crew and Bernard Pendry behind us, we resolved to continue.

A topical distraction from our minor yet admirable state of optimism was the big to-do in the newspapers regarding Marlon Brando's new film. I have to say that erotic films had little impact on us at the time. Here is my recollection:

A RETROSPECTIVE ABRIDGED FILM REVIEW –
LAST TANGO IN PARIS
Barking-mad permissive French bird has irresponsible
sexual encounters with fat-arsed American pervert then
shoots him.

Our first choice as Paul's replacement was Frankie Miller, a no-nonsense Glaswegian with a gritty and deeply soulful voice. Frankie agreed to do a couple of gigs with us, and before we'd reached the end of the first song at rehearsals we knew we had our man – the job was his! He suggested a meeting with his manager Doug D'Arcy, and I went along as the band's representative. Doug explained that Frankie was on the threshold of a solo career and that it would not be beneficial to him to join Juicy Lucy. We were obviously disappointed, but resolved to soldier on and continue with the search for a new singer. It would be a number of years before I eventually got to work with the inimitable Mr Miller.

Meanwhile, Paul Williams had got wind that the band was to continue with a replacement, and was somewhat miffed by our actions. As far as he was concerned, he was no longer the singer, therefore Juicy Lucy should disband. This was a bit rich considering he'd dropped us all in the shit and gone straight on to a secure, better-paid position.

Bobby Harrison was another singer who helped us out on a gig, and though his admiration for our musicianship and musical direction was genuine enough, the consensus among the band was that he was not the right choice to front Juicy Lucy.

It all came to a head during a singer-less gig in Hornchurch, when our roadies Frankie and Joe came onstage to help render a twenty-minute version of 'Jumping Jack Flash'. Although their hearts were in the right place, their voices weren't. Their vocalising was not dissimilar to a couple of inmates from a mental institution doing an impersonation of Arthur Mullard and Yoko Ono. Not surprisingly, a number of people in the audience asked for their money back, and the knock-on effect on the band's morale was so severe that some of us lost the will to carry on. The end was nigh, and nigh on a few days later, Juicy Lucy ceased to exist.

Parting may be such sweet sorrow to balcony-bound lovers, but to rock bands it's a bloody downer, especially if you've worked hard to achieve a certain level of proficiency. Losing Paul and being denied Frankie in the same week was a lot to bear, but before I had time to wallow in embittered thoughts of what might have been, an opportunity arose courtesy of the aforementioned Mr Harrison.

It's a well-known fact that 'A Whiter Shade of Pale' by Procol Harum has become one of the most recognisable songs in the history of popular music, but what's not so well known is that Bobby Harrison played drums on the original version. This particular version was allegedly a demo, and Bobby was replaced for the actual recording by Bill Eyden, a session drummer who received a flat fee of fifteen guineas. Ironically, Bobby took the matter to court and was awarded a settlement (the amount was undisclosed, but was alleged to be rather more than Mr Eyden's somewhat paltry payment). You win some, you lose some. I can only assume that Bobby applied the same degree of unerring attention to his personal rights as he paid to his personal appearance, which was almost Teutonic in its attention to detail. Being ten years older than me, and with conscription still in existence, he'd been summoned by the authorities to register for National Service with the army.

'I was in the Suez, you know.'

'What, with all those rats and shit?'

There was always a possibility that this 'spit and polish' regime had indirectly influenced such fastidious behaviour with, perhaps, just a hint of vanity too. Bobby had made the transition from the man at the back to the man at the front almost overnight, and, as someone who had never been shy in coming forward, had landed himself a management and recording deal along the way. And on that short journey from the drum stool to the microphone, he'd somehow developed a singing style that was a curious blend of Steve Marriott and Mario Lanza.

The initial recordings for Bobby's solo project took place at Morgan Studios and featured the former Mick Abrahams Band sans Mick: Ritchie Dharma, a Eurasian drummer from Yorkshire, Walt Monahan, a bass player from Northern Ireland, and a Geordie keyboard player called Bob Sargeant. Shortly after I'd arrived at the studio, I was unloading my equipment when I was accosted by the local wide-eyed loony.

'The flies! The flies! They'll get us in the end! There are over a hundred thousand different types and, in their limited life-span of twenty three days, they can lay up to six hundred eggs. What are you going to do?'

'Stock up on fly paper,' I replied.

He mumbled something inaudible and lurched off into his own private insect hell.

A couple of days later, I was ensconced in a large American car en route to the Granary club in Bristol, sharing spliffs with the recently formed Supertramp. A totally unknown commodity and a few years away from stardom, they were loose enough musically to invite me on stage to play a few songs with them. As people were wont to say: 'Nice one, man.'

Although Bobby's partnership with Bob Sargeant was the catalyst that inspired the original ideas, former Procol Harum organist Mathew Fisher was brought in to take the production to the next stage. Trident and Olympic studios were also hired, and other participants included Ian Paice, whose inspired funk-rock drumming added a touch of class to the proceedings, respected session stalwarts Herbie Flowers and Clem Cattini, trumpeter Alan Bown, Chrissy Stewart and Black Sabbath's Tony Iommi. Tony had problems with the rented amplifier (a huge Fender Showman, which looked rather cumbersome next to my tiny Selmer studio model), but returned later to Morgan with his own gear to let rip with a mammoth solo on 'King of the Night'. Before the start of the sessions, I'd got together with Bobby to write the seductively funky 'Long Gone', and, once in the studio, he made a return to the drum stool to join Chrissy, myself and Mathew in laying it down. It turned out to be Bobby's favourite track and led to the inevitable decision to form a band, with an emphasis on down-home funk and bluesy riffs.

There were a number of auditions, including one with the aforementioned Alan Bown and another with a bass player who was so out of his depth that at one point his face took on the expression of someone who'd just been nominated to act as a knife-thrower's assistant. The chosen few turned out to be my friend and ex-Tramline bandmate Terry Popple on drums, ex-Crazy World of Arthur Brown, Terry Reid and Paladin keyboard player Pete Solley, and ex-Ginger Baker's Airforce and Skip Bifferty bass player Colin Gibson. We all had similar tastes in music, a penchant for a joint or two, a sociable attitude towards alcohol and a collective sense of humour, though Colin's tended to veer towards the slightly more bizarre. Bobby's ebullient character coupled with Pete's realistic outlook contrasted nicely with the more laid-back and 'let's see what happens' attitude of the north-east three. Management and recording contracts were duly signed and producer Vic Smith was enlisted to help capture the sound of Snafu. Yes, Snafu – a G.I. acronym for 'situation normal all fucked up', although to parents, prim ladies and men of the cloth, it was translated as 'all fouled up'. Colin had heard the expression on a track titled 'Big-Eyed Beans from Venus' from Captain Beefheart's *Clear Spot* album, and liked the sound of it. Soon after, when the word was mentioned during an episode of Bilko, it prompted him to check out the exact meaning, which he then related to us with mischievous glee!

The Manor Studio, along with one hundred acres of prime Oxfordshire countryside, was purchased by a certain Richard Branson and became the first residential studio in the UK. Soon after it had opened its doors, the established and somewhat eccentric bass player Steve York gathered together a bunch of his favourite players and took over this prestigious location to co-produce an album. Sharing the production (and also engineering) was Vic Smith, who kindly invited me to spend a day in the studio and take part in the proceedings. What do you get if you put a host of hip, stoned groovers in a room together for a few days? Well, with performers such as Graham Bond, Mike Patto, Tim Hinkley, Boz Burrell, Ollie Halsall, Ian Wallace, Elkie Brookes and Lol Coxhill, there was no danger whatsoever of any sort of rational behaviour – this was creative madness at its best! The outcome was an organised jam of jazzy blues songs with rather unconventional titles such as

'Hey God', 'Male Chauvinist Pig Song', 'Black Note Meets the White Note' and 'Women's Lib Song'. The wacky baccy was in abundance and the odd line was chopped out for those with a couple of quid in their pocket. Needless to say, nobody got paid for their efforts and I doubt if anybody bothered to ask.

Many years later, writers Hugh Barker and Yuval Taylor made an interesting analogy when they suggested that if rock was born in the 1950s, the 1970s was when it was in its late teens and early twenties, the period when experimentation and creativity are often at their peak.

It's a great pity that the event wasn't filmed, as I'm certain that the end result would have encapsulated the spirit of the 'rock 'n' roll crazies' in its most quintessential form.

When the album was released a few months later under the title *Manor Live*, the front cover displayed a pregnant giraffe strolling around the grounds while the impressive building looked on, somewhat nonplussed, in the background. Also on the front cover was a list of featured artists under the heading Camelo Pardalis, which I assumed was Latin for 'a cast of characters' or something similar. Many years later, I double-checked via Google as to the exact literal translation. It means 'giraffe'.

After a short period of writing and rehearsing, and armed with a bunch of newly written songs, we joined up with Vic Smith and settled in at the Manor. I can only describe the facilities as first class. They included a state-of-the-art studio, which was housed in the erstwhile barn, large, comfortable bedrooms and an in-house chef who cooked hearty breakfasts in the huge kitchen and later treated us to fabulous dinners in the relaxing atmosphere of the dining room. The lounge area boasted one of those big old fireplaces that always appear sad and incomplete without a log fire burning within, a sound system and a long wooden table just high enough to be able to roll a spliff from comfy armchair level. There was at least one Irish wolfhound, possibly two, though it may have been the same one that just wandered around a lot. Apart from the chef, the staff – who were mostly female – lived in, and were extremely hip to what was going on.

There was a young, scruffy-looking guy called Mike staying at the Manor, who was using up any available studio time – mostly in the mornings when we were stacking the zeds – as part of a project sponsored by Richard Branson. One morning, he asked Pete to add a few bars of fiddle to a piece of his music, and paid him the princely sum of £2 (cash). A few months later, Mike Oldfield's album was released and went on to become a massive worldwide success under the title *Tubular Bells*.

Although Snafu's musical direction veered towards funky rock, three of the songs revealed a curious leaning towards country and bluegrass. This probably resulted from Pete's masterly use of the fiddle and my own burgeoning interest in roots music, which drew from the likes of Ry Cooder, Country Gazette, and Clarence White and the Kentucky Colonels. Through the riffy, wah-wah and keyboard-drenched 'Long Gone' and 'Said He the Judge' to the soul-centred zeal of 'Goodbye USA', 'Drowning in the Sea of Love' and 'That's the Song', these tracks stood out in particular. 'Monday Morning' coupled a mandolin and fiddle-led hoedown with Bobby's lamentation of days gone by, the realisation of the rat-race and the dreaded Monday-morning start. However, optimism was finally restored when the song broke into a lively square dance, which marched with renewed vigour towards the obligatory fade-out. The laid-back 'Country Nest' rejoiced in moving to the country (the lyrics suggested Virginia, rather than Dorset), and not only did I perform on guitar, lap slide and mandolin, I also managed to squeeze in a banjo as well! An underlying funky feel in the bass and drums and some clever vocal inflections added to the overall quirkiness, while Vic excelled in the production department. Completing the trio was another shitkicker, 'Funky Friend', which featured Pete's Doug Kershaw-influenced fiddle and Bobby's light-hearted slant on the home from home. The song concluded with one mighty knees-up where the tempo sped up to a rate of movement which could only be described as frantic, and may have left the listener with the distinct impression that we'd just lunched on amphetamine baguettes. My memories of the session would, however, point to the usual 'custom cigarettes', although there was always the possibility that something of Peruvian origin may have materialised courtesy of staff or hangers-on.

Towards the end of our stay at the Manor, we were visited by artist Roger Dean, who'd been commissioned to design our album sleeve and who was in need of a photograph to adorn the back cover. Roger, whose star was on the rise, had already gained a considerable reputation by creating exotic artwork, which included watercolours, for bands such as Yes, Osibisa, Uriah Heep and Gentle Giant. After a quick reconnoitre, he decided on a dilapidated building in the grounds of the house and we took up our positions, all hair and dopey smiles. After a couple of dozen shots, and having exhausted all possibilities regarding the limited poses offered by the stoned collective before him, Roger decided on an alternative backcloth and suggested the perimeter fence of an adjoining meadow. As we took up our positions by the fence, Colin suddenly let out a yelp of excitement: 'Look – over there!' In the field just a couple of hundred yards behind us, a couple were going at it hammer and tongs. Fantastic! We immediately suggested to Roger that he angle his camera so that he captured not only Snafu but Snafu *and* the alfresco shaggers. Sadly, Roger's sense of humour was not in keeping with our own (or possibly anybody's) and he was having none of it (unlike the couple in the background). What a possible coup – what a wasted opportunity.

At dinner that evening, Vic Smith – whose moustache outdid both mine and Bobby's – expressed everyone's feelings when he announced that the Manor was the funkiest studio he'd ever worked in.

Pete Solley had written a song with one of the guys from Sha Na Na – a gospel-tinged composition entitled 'That's the Song' – and, to get the desired effect on the choruses, we decided to book an American gospel choir from a nearby airbase. The next day, a coach arrived and about thirty people disembarked and stretched their legs in the fine summer sunshine. There wasn't enough available space in the studio, so Vic decided to record them outside on the lawn. As they took up their positions amid the various overhead microphones, their leader/conductor – a big black guy in his forties – wandered into the control room to take instructions. I'd just rolled a nice fat joint made from some fine black hash and, without thinking, I offered it to him. Member of the United States Air Force or not, he accepted it and took a few blasts. Raising his eyebrows, he handed it back to me and glided back to the waiting throng. Surprisingly for a gospel choir, there were two or three white people in evidence. One of them had close-cropped hair, a shirt and tie and shapeless baggy trousers. The men dressed in a similar fashion. The session was a success and the Manor staff enjoyed the spectacle. Later, when we scrutinised the recording, we could hear that a few people were singing slightly flat. We assumed it was the white rednecks, who are generally not 'born with it', and decided to turn them down in the mix. After closer scrutiny, we were pleasantly surprised to discover that it wasn't them after all.

Around the time that the album was being mixed, the band showcased its talents in the Upstairs Room at Ronnie Scott's Club in London and, soon after, headed for Holland. This short tour included a three-day stint at Boddy's Music Inn in Amsterdam and a date at the city's infamous Milky Way. The former was managed by Mr and Mrs Boddy, a middle-aged, somewhat unlikely couple, to say the least. Ma Boddy was a larger-than-life, rather maternal Dutch lady who loved to party and look after 'her boys', while Pa Boddy, a large, bearded man from the American mid-west, was so laid-back he was almost horizontal. They ran a hotel a few blocks from the club and the visiting bands stayed there, residing amid a slightly bohemian atmosphere, distracted only by their two teenage daughters. Holland in the 1970s boasted the most liberal attitude in Europe, and the Boddys tolerated most things, apart from any predatory actions or lascivious thoughts towards their girls. Any movement in that direction would be immediately counteracted by the looming presence of their ubiquitous father. Still, a decent boiled egg could be guaranteed at 'musician-time' breakfast, *vis-à-vis* very late morning.

At the Milky Way, dope and hash cakes could be bought legally from a little table in the foyer, like some sort of surreal Women's Institute for hippies. The audience reaction to our set

frau-beater and a Valium five. The next morning, we were confronted by the downcast faces of Mick and Joe.

'Oo, we din manige to get the back dawr on the van fixed and sum one's nicked the ARP Odyssey synthesiser.'

Poor Pete. It was his new toy – new and uninsured. He made a mental note to file their names under D for Dumb Fuckers.

The band members and their respective ladies hit it off on a sociable level too. Laid-back nights at various pubs and clubs or cosy stoned nights round the record player were the order of the day. Around this time, I took my first and last acid trip – it turned out to be a deeply unpleasant experience in which I had absolutely no control over the proceedings. Once the effects had worn off, I vowed never to dabble with that stuff again.

Back in the real world, our management / record company / agent machine kick-started their Snafu campaign with the impending release of our eponymous debut album. First, a tour with Dutch rockers Golden Earring in November, followed by a string of college and university dates in the UK. In retrospect, I'm not sure if supporting Golden Earring was a good thing or not. Leather-clad and with the emphasis on a rock 'act', they were bound to attract the kind of audience that was not necessarily into Snafu's somewhat casual approach. The 'Earrings' were extremely professional and, although they were not the world's greatest players, they knew how to put on a good show. Their drummer, Cesar, a larger-than-life character with the general physiognomy of a deranged Roman god, would for no apparent reason suddenly jump up onto his stool and launch himself with undisguised gusto over his drum kit, to land, like a champion Russian gymnast, at the front of the stage. It was a considerable stunt and one you were unlikely to encounter at a J.J. Cale concert. Offstage, and bereft of rock-star shape-throwing and outrageous physical feats, they were an extremely nice bunch of guys.

London's Marquee Club was as legendary as they come and, soon after our gig there on 27 November, the following letter appeared in the *Melody Maker* Mailbag under the heading 'I've Been Everywhere':

> Saw Deep Purple at the Rainbow, saw the Who at Charlton, saw Bad Company at the Rainbow, saw Grand Funk and Jack Bruce at Hyde Park, saw Alice Cooper's Wembley gig, and saw Rod Stewart / Faces at the Oval. I also saw Snafu at the Marquee and they gave all of the bands mentioned a good kick up the arse. Thank God for Snafu – Mick, Sittingbourne, Kent.

Being on the receiving end of that kind of plaudit *and* being praised in the same sentence as God could have had serious repercussions regarding one's ego. Only time would tell.

Back on the treadmill of one-nighters, Snafu found itself at the Lafayette Club, Wolverhampton, proffering a small yet distinguished guest list of Ozzy Osbourne plus two to the doorman. Black Sabbath were stable-mates at Worldwide Artists, and Ozzy fancied a night out in the company of his then-wife and her friend. After the show, we were invited back to chez Osbourne, a funky house in a rural area, where we sat in the kitchen, accepted drinks and skinned up. As the drink and smokes started to take effect, Ozzy's attention was drawn to a basket of fresh eggs that was sitting in the middle of the large table. He made a remark about the plain and simple décor that had been chosen to adorn the walls, then immediately sought to rectify this by lobbing the eggs at them. This set the dog to barking and the wife to shouting, so we made our excuses, said our goodbyes and went back to the hotel bar.

We saw out 1973 in the usual moderate to advanced state of hedonism before embracing the New Year. We were also considered worthy of an appearance on *The Old Grey Whistle Test*, where we mimed to 'Long Gone' and 'Goodbye USA'. Five days later, on 18 January, we started out on the European leg of the Doobie Brothers tour – an exciting prospect as they were really starting to make waves. Furthermore, there were changes to the crew: Mick the van-crasher and failed door-replacer had been replaced by Larry Burgess – a true 'head' – and another new face, the seemingly more ambitious Keith Sherman, who would act as both tour manager and sound engineer. It was a combination that would in the long run prove that, as an attribute, sincerity is more attractive than personal ambition.

CHAPTER 13

SITUATION NORMAL

As we hit the road, the reviews for the album started to appear in the music press.

Pete Erskine from *Sounds* wrote:

In the midst of a wedge of seemingly vacuum formed funk albums very much in the wake of the Average White Band, Snafu's first album emerges as the genuine article. It has depth, conviction and integrity. The playing is convincing and totally uncontrived and the vocals are strong without mimicking your archetype production-line soul singer stance; not a single 'y'all' makes its grisly appearance anywhere. The band are Bobby Harrison, percussion and vocals, Mick Moody, guitar and mandolin, Colin Gibson, bass, Pete Solley, Keyboards and Terry Popple, drums. Between them they effortlessly knock off a selection of Crusaders-fashioned material –

like the opener 'Long Gone' whose central riff recalls the Average White Band's 'The Juggler'. Gamble and Huff's 'Drowning in the Sea of Love' and the crisp 'Said He the Judge' – and a few precision-tuned electric/acoustic country things like 'Country Nest' and 'Funky Friend' very much in the vein of Area Code 615. Let's hope there are more albums like this in the coming year (y'all).

Meanwhile, over at the *Melody Maker*, Jeff Ward seemed to be impressed:

A couple of months ago now, this album arrived on my desk under the anonymity of an advance white-label. There was nothing but the odd name to go by: Snafu – US army ironic slang for 'Situation normal, all f..... up.' And it transpired that the group comprised ex-members of Procol Harum, Juicy Lucy, Ginger Baker's Airforce, Paladin and Terry Reid's band. But that was a shock because the group sounded so American in the vein of Steve Miller or maybe Iron Butterfly. It just couldn't be a British band or at least not wholly British with a rhythm section like that but incredibly good it was. It was also damn good. The music had down-home funk and personality. It even got better still on subsequent hearings. First track 'Long Gone' lopes like a prowling wolf, it's lean and hungry and there's immediate atmosphere and inventive guitar – that's former Juicy Lucy man Micky Moody. Drums by newcomer Terry Popple are played slack and sleepy heavy, on the bass drum and snare, but delicate, almost finicky on cymbals. And he has that rare ability among British rock drummers to really swing.

Hear how he whips up the excitement to fever pitch in 'That's the Song' locked into a rock solid backbeat with the bass guitar; the number's co-written by keyboards man Pete Solley and Jocko Marcelliano of Sha Na Na. Bobby Harrison's vital earthy vocals are gasped out into the song fade as the beat motors. Great stuff, it jangles the nerve ends. It's not an album without interesting contrasts either, though the group maintain their basic feel throughout. 'Monday Morning' for example begins with a bluegrass fiddle that later turns into a splendid hurdy-gurdy instrumental section with mandolin after the manner of a traditional reel; 'Funky Friend' is a frantic shitkickin' hoedown; and there's also the Philly hit 'Drowning in the Sea of Love', a Gamble-Huff composition which was recorded not so long ago by Joe Simon. One also should mention Solley's extremely tasteful and melodic synthesiser work, especially in 'Goodbye USA' where Moog is partnered by guitar. Snafu are about to support the Doobie Brothers on a European tour taking their sound 'back' to the States for their own tour in March, where Americans strangely enough could well mistake them for compatriots. The band seem to have aimed deliberately at absorbing the *moeurs* of US rock but their particular combination of funky musicians makes it a natural unforced achievement.

They didn't all wax lyrical, as Ken Hyder opined:

Undoubtedly a fine band, but they came over with more impact on the telly recently than on this album, maybe because they only played their best numbers. On the

138

album there are two or three songs which are as tight as you're likely to get from a British band. But most of the tracks are merely competent, needing a bit more inspiration and originality. Still, it's refreshing to hear musicians – especially guitarists – who are not frightened to play the simple thing that's right for the music. It's that lack of ego-tripping that makes 'Goodbye USA' such a pleasurable piece. Let's have more numbers like this one on the next album.

Before linking up with the Doobie Brothers, we pre-recorded a bunch of radio shows for the BBC, which included *Breakthrough* with Mike Sparrow, Pete Drummond's *Rock On*, *Overdrive* with Colin Slade, *The Bob Harris Show* and Malcolm Jay's *Heavy Pressure*. Most of these sessions were recorded at the BBC's own studios, notably Maida Vale and Portland Place in London. Bobby was especially pleased with his new set of congas, and praised them in a manner that could well have been a future influence on the vocal inflections of the major from *Fawlty Towers*: 'I've got new congas from Natal – in Africa!'

Bobby excelled in playing percussion, an attribute that added another dimension, especially onstage. I added another instrument to my guitar arsenal: a burgundy-coloured Gibson SG Custom that was hanging up in Macari's Musical Exchange on Charing Cross Road. The Macari Brothers – Larry and Joe – were a real couple of characters, and Joe's sales pitch was second to none. In response to my enquiry, he informed me that the guitar had once belonged to 'that Paul Cossack from Free.'

The Doobie Brothers held the rare distinction of having

blown Little Feat off the stage during the Warner Brothers package tour at the Rainbow theatre. The 'Feat' were rumoured to have taken their personal grievances onstage that night, but there was no doubt about it: the Doobies were a great band. We watched their show on the first two Dutch gigs and they were very impressive: 'Listen to the Music', 'Long Train Running' and 'China Grove' were, and still are, classics. However, by the time we reached Amsterdam, we realised that Little Feat weren't the only band with internal problems. After our soundcheck, we were aware of raised voices and some kind of delay in the proceedings. When the band did show up for their soundcheck, they were minus their frontman, Tom Johnson. Before long, whisperings regarding alleged narcotics abuse were in the air. Johnson made the show that night but the vibe onstage was subdued.

Ensconced in a hotel room somewhere in Belgium, and challenged by a bed housing a mattress that seemed to be filled with old metal coat-hangers and bracken, I felt the inner stirrings of a silly moment, which resulted in the following:

Django Braithwaite was a Bohemian wing-nut salesman from Whitby who bred lemurs during Lent and crafted false eyebrows from mouse pelts. Bored with his mundane existence, he signed up with the local division of the Territorial Army, where he met and befriended Gordon Hinchcliffe, the local butcher. Gordon, a devout Catholic, was eventually ostracised by the Guild of Master Butchers for creating crucifixes out of prime-pork sausages. Around this time, his self-esteem was so low he broke down and professed his eternal love to a dust mite. Consequently, he became melancholic and took to training cormorants to shit on the heads of junior accountants. Concerned with his friend's declining mental state, Django extended a hand of friendship but was given 'five' in a Chicago accent. Visibly moved by such a misunderstanding, Gordon broke down and confessed to a lifetime's intolerance to lapwing's eggs.

After the European dates, we flew back to England to play the four remaining shows at Southampton Guildhall, London Rainbow, Oxford Polytechnic and Leeds University. The gig at the Rainbow is one that I've always chosen to forget, but it's now time for me to face up to it in print. Whether or not I had some sort of brainstorm, a serious attack of stage fright or some kind of internal personality feud remains unanswered, but I certainly blew it. During the first song, I took it upon myself to fall to my knees and blast out a guitar solo that would have been better suited to an amateur heavy metal audition. After that, I took to strutting around the stage like some sort of manic Max Wall, oblivious to the artistic suicide I was seemingly bent on. Was it self-destruction? Misplaced ego? Who knows, but the cool muso with the Gibson had disappeared up his own arse. After the show, in a very sombre dressing room, Pete took little time in expressing his opinion – and who could blame him?

Later on, I took some comfort in reports that Keith Sherman's out-front sound was utterly abysmal. We returned to the Rainbow soon after as support for War, and I'm pleased to recount that it was a much happier occasion, which gave us a good excuse to hang out until dawn. Later that day, I had enough energy to roll a joint, sit in front of the television and watch a relatively new cop series called *Kojak* featuring Greek spam-head Telly Savalas – great stuff, Theo!

Around about this time, and in the company of Colin Gibson, keyboard player Kenny Craddock and drummer Alan White, I played on a demo session for an old friend from Middlesbrough: Chris Rea. His manager, another old friend from 'the boro', John McCoy, had blagged some free time at Island Studios in Notting Hill for the purpose of acquiring Chris a record deal. We recorded three or four songs, including 'Fool if You Think It's Over', a catchy little tune that would eventually put the talented Mr Rea on the road to stardom. And Hell.

A few days later, I picked up an album entitled *Shangrenade* by American blues-rock-fusion guitarist Harvey Mandel. I'd been aware of his work with John Mayall and Canned Heat and possessed a couple of his previous solo efforts, all of them showing off his prowess on the instrument. However, I wasn't really prepared for what came out of the speakers when I sat down to listen to this one. He seemed to have developed a new approach almost overnight: a style that centred around flurries of notes that cascaded in an increasingly commanding fashion over a tight jazz-funk backing. How the bloody hell was he doing that? We all found out a few years later when Eddie Van Halen introduced Harvey's visionary style to a wider audience. Nowadays, it goes under the descriptive heading of 'finger-tapping', a technique that requires the player to employ both hands on the guitar's fingerboard.

I still regard Harvey Mandel as one of the most tasteful and innovative guitar players of all time.

In the latter part of the 1960s, Patrick Campbell Lyons had been one half of the psychedelic pop outfit Nirvana, best known for their popular underground hit, 'Rainbow Chaser'. We were introduced to each other by Bobby, and, though

Nirvana had bitten the dust, Patrick was forging ahead with a solo career. As a singer, Patrick was no Joe Cocker – or Jarvis Cocker for that matter – but he did have a good ear for a catchy melody and confidence in his ability as a producer. He was also pretty good at brokering recording and publishing deals – usually in the form of one-off singles – where he would employ pseudonyms such as Patrick O'Magic and Rock O'Doodle! Although the vast majority of his album *Me and My Friend* had been recorded by then, he asked me to overdub on one or two tracks, some of which were odd to say the least. During the time I was with Snafu, I did a number of sessions for Patrick and I always enjoyed them, mostly because they were just a bit off the wall!

The BBC radio *In Concert* series was a popular show back then and regarded as a good means of communication to a wide audience, so Snafu found itself booked into the venue, the Paris Theatre in Lower Regent Street, to perform the statutory four or five songs. The small theatre was full to capacity as the support band, an unknown act by the name of Dr Feelgood, took to the stage. We were at once taken aback by the reception that greeted them, and comforted to know that if the support act was so warmly received, the headliners would surely be destined for even bigger things. Dr Feelgood, a basic rhythm and blues band featuring a guitarist who seemed to be suffering from Restless Leg Syndrome, took the place by storm as we sat in our dressing room taking in a confident toke or two. A few minutes before we were due to go on, Larry came bursting into the dressing room.

'The bloody place is nearly empty!'

'Why? Where are all the people?'

'Apparently, all of their fans wrote in for tickets and

organised coaches to bring them here. They've all fucked off back to Canvey Island!'

We hit the stage to meagre applause and a somewhat diminished crowd consisting of a few Snafu fans, a handful of complementary ticket holders, a vagrant who'd sneaked in from the cold, two Japanese tourists who were expecting to see Cat Stevens, and the commissionaire.

Recovery from such an embarrassing ordeal was aided by a fairly busy schedule of one-nighters in the UK, with more visits to Holland and Germany. We travelled to Swansea for a student ball at the Top Rank and found ourselves on the same bill as local heroes Man. Now, we thought we were pretty consistent with the joint rolling, but we were like novices compared to the guys in Man. As we passed their dressing room, the door opened and, peering in, it looked like the opening scene from one of those old black-and-white films about Jack the Ripper. Cue an Orson Wells-type voice: 'London, 1887. From out of the dense smog, a figure began to materialise. As he came closer, I saw the most hideous face, warped beyond recognition by the madness within. . .'

I read it as, 'Swansea, 1974. Through the pungent smoke, hirsute shapes could be made out, proffering large roll-ups. As the murkiness subsided, the abandoned grin of guitarist Deke Leonard could be seen through the Stygian gloom. . .'

It seemed to work for them though; they went on stage and played their arses off. Outside, we came across a lad who'd been thrown out of the gig for being drunk and disorderly and was in no mood to forgive and forget. 'Land of my fathers?' he growled. 'My fathers can fuckin' 'ave it!'

Capital Radio had begun to establish itself as the number-one London radio station, and Sarah Ward hosted a late-night show which featured two or three songs from live bands. Snafu found itself taking part in one of the earlier broadcasts, and we headed up to Euston Road's Capital Tower to take up the challenge. Our equipment was set up in the studio and we were left to our own devices – the usual large roll-ups and cans of beer – until the producer notified us that we had five minutes in which to prepare ourselves. From her pivotal position in the control room, Sarah could speak to us via a talk-back speaker in the studio and Bobby elected to answer her questions on the band's behalf. For some obscure reason, Bobby steered the conversation towards his ability to tap dance.

'It's been a few years though!' he added tantalisingly.

'Well, come on, let's hear some then!' demanded an intrigued Sarah.

That was the cue for our self-assured singer to leap onto a large flight case and treat us all to a touch of the Bruce Forsyths, which must have been somewhat challenging in a pair of stack-heeled boots. After a mercifully short demonstration, I'm pleased to recount that no further forms of vaudeville-style entertainment were administered by Bobby and that the status quo was firmly restored during the first bar of the first song.

Shortly after, we released a single, 'Dixie Queen', and had the rare distinction of hosting a champagne buffet lunch at the Penthouse club. The event was organised by our record company, Phonogram, and there are photographs of a delighted band posing with various Penthouse Pets to prove it! Once we'd recovered from our glamorous lunch date, Pete, Bobby and myself got together to compare musical ideas in readiness for the new album.

Our management had arranged a new producer, Steve

Rowland – a seemingly multi-talented American who'd produced, among others, Dave Dee, Dozy, Beaky, Mick and Tich and the Herd. He'd also starred in such films as *Battle of the Bulge* and *The Thin Red Line*. We met prior to the recording at our management's office and, on first impression, I couldn't decide who spent more time in front of the mirror: him or Bobby. He had creases in his jeans so sharp that, when he sat down, he kept his legs straight to deter any unsightly knee bumps. He would negotiate a chair like Douglas Bader, and I formed an opinion that he particularly avoided climbing ladders. He had a fine head of hair that was well-groomed and suspiciously unnatural, and no doubt he abstained from wearing racing helmets and performing that party trick where you stretch a condom over your head. Piss-taking aside, he would prove to be a consummate professional and an extremely nice man, though not necessarily the right choice to produce the conundrum of talent that was Snafu.

Situation Normal was recorded at Advision, Air and Landsdowne studios and, due to diversity, drugs and dilemmas, turned out to be an even bigger farrago than *Snafu*. Overall, the album suffered not only from a lack of true direction but also from Rowland's production. Sound-wise, it was far too dry and seemed to be aimed at Radio One listeners, rather than the album market. Steve also liked to finish recording at a 'realistic' time, which meant nothing to the rest of us, who'd adopted a more 'bop 'til you drop' mentality. Later on, it transpired that Bobby and Steve had discussed the possibility of a hit single, but to be quite honest there just wasn't one on this album.

One of the band had been given some coke that was so strong he couldn't handle it. Feeling reckless, somewhat irresponsible and merrily assured from an evening at the local pub, I took it off his hands. Back in my flat with one of the road crew, I chopped out two cautious lines. We soon realised that this was no ordinary coke, if it was coke at all. My companion lay back on the bed while I slid to the floor, where I remained in a helpless and somewhat catatonic state. What the fuck was going on? After a while, I decided to go to the bathroom to relieve myself of some of the beer we'd been drinking earlier. My limbs felt numb and movement wasn't easy, but I managed to crawl to the door like an intoxicated Bionic Man in one of those slow-motion sequences. Ten minutes later, I reached the bathroom, where I somehow managed to pee from an angle of twenty-five degrees. I somehow managed to slither my way back to the room, throw the suspicious substance into a wastebasket, and then remain prostrate until the effects started to wear off. Some days later, I was alerted to the existence of angel dust, also known as PCP – a form of animal tranquiliser normally associated with horse surgery.

Before we departed for our U.S. tour, we undertook a few more one-nighters, which included the Dagenham Roundhouse and Hemel Hempstead Civic Hall. There was, apparently, another appearance on *The Old Grey Whistle Test* of which I have no recollection whatsoever.

CHAPTER 14

SITUATION RELATIVELY NORMAL

It wasn't until we were crossing the Fifty-Ninth Street Bridge into Manhattan that I realised just how strong the grass was. The driver of our record company's limo was obviously no stranger to this lark: pick the band up at JFK airport, make them feel at home with a spliff, and then drop them off at the hotel. His particular hand of friendship ('Here's a lil' present for yooze guys!') was warmly received and immediately smoked. A little later, as we crossed the famous steel structure, the darting effect of the bright sunlight flashing hither and thither through the overhead slats was, in our stoned condition, enough to induce an epileptic fit. Thankfully, it was an epilepsy-free band and the spoon-administered freeing of tongues was not a prerequisite. We were still out of it when we arrived at the City Squire hotel on Seventh Avenue, and relieved to disembark in an underground car park away from the seriously distracting clamour of downtown New York.

After an unfeasibly drawn-out and somewhat bewildering check-in, we finally reached our assigned rooms, where we stared at the TV until the effects of the dope began to subside.

Snafu's schedule consisted of fifteen dates as support to Emerson, Lake and Palmer, two shows with the Eagles, two with Jo Jo Gunne, one with Foghat and an appearance in Central Park, New York with Peter Frampton. Although we'd recorded our second album, we were here to promote the first one. The band – together with roadies Joe and Larry – were accompanied by Keith Sherman (now relieved of his position as failed soundman and reinstated as tour manager) and management representative, Malcolm Koss. After an early night in New York, and having regained the majority of our collective sensibilities, we set out for Williamsport in Pennsylvania. On arrival, my first impression was that we'd arrived in Peyton Place, an opinion perhaps influenced by the town's abundance of one-storey ranch houses that helped make up comfortable, middle-class, tree-lined America. However, there was a twinge of disappointment at the hotel check-in, as neither Mia Farrow nor Ryan O'Neal were there to greet us; we had to settle for Wilbur and Dorothy.

The July sun was blasting down and, as we had a couple of hours to spare before the soundcheck, we headed for the pool area, where like true Brits we stripped to the waist, scorned the idea of sun-tan lotion and took up our sun-worshiping positions. After the soundcheck, we met the guys from Jo Jo Gunne, most notably singer and keyboard player Jay Ferguson, formerly of psychedelic prog-rockers Spirit. He asked to meet 'the guy from Juicy Lucy' and offered his congratulations for recording a good cover of his song 'Mr Skin' on the *Get a Whiff a This* album. It was only when we changed into our stage clothes that the true meaning of sunburn became apparent. Onstage it was even worse: ouch! Guitar strap on shoulder – friction – hindrance – back of guitar on stomach – involuntary movements – pain. ('Gee, those English guys with the red faces move around like Captain Beefheart's Magic Band on speed!') Afterwards, we changed back into our day-to-day clothing with the kind of tortured movements normally associated with victims of extreme arthritis. Needless to say, none of us pulled. Back at the motel, we eased our suffering with beer and an acquired bonus of a popular barbiturate known as Tuinol. The idea, of course, was to stay awake for as long as possible – which we did. Irresponsible but great fun at the time!

The next day, we headed for Nazareth, Pennsylvania, to support Foghat, a band whose personnel were dominated by ex-members of the British blues band Savoy Brown. Nearby was the town of Bethlehem, which prompted my brain to lock on and start scanning the horizon for Wise Men City, Stableville and Herod Falls. The next day – and without a star to guide us – we headed for New Haven to take up our support position on the first of our dates with ELP. For the die-hard ELP fan, watching Snafu must have been like attending a seminar by Bill Gates and having to sit through a talk given by a little bloke in a pullover enthusing about valve radios. We had *no* fucking chance. Opening for the Eagles, Jo Jo Gunne, Foghat and Peter Frampton was sensible billing, but ELP? No – the support spot should have been given to ELO, REM, YAT, REO, PMT, BS&T, etc. ELP was more than just a rock band; it was a show tailored for the arena audience – a spectacle which featured the virtuoso performance and ultimate showmanship of Keith Emerson and the far from supportive roles of Greg

Lake and Carl Palmer. Snafu was a good-time club / small-theatre act and never the twain should have met.

Worldwide Artists Management and the Frank Barcelona Agency got it completely wrong. What were they thinking? After the first couple of shows, it became obvious that this was a mismatch made over the transatlantic phone lines, and as our management company handled both Yes and Black Sabbath, a case of misplaced favouritism was a distinct possibility.

After the show in Providence, Rhode Island, where we'd managed to whip the audience into a state of mild interest, we were visited in our dressing room by a nice fellow who'd enjoyed the show. He gifted us with two or three ready-rolled joints that, he assured us, were spiced with 'just the right amount of PCP'. After my previous experience, I was somewhat reluctant and watched with concentrated attention as some of the other guys sampled the goods. These observations turned out to be very encouraging, and pretty soon I was out there with them: very, very nice! We soon returned to the hotel, high as kites and laden with bottles of beer. Switching on the TV in the designated 'party' room, we were treated to a showing of one of those old black-and-white British music films, the highlight being Lonnie Donegan performing 'Jack o' Diamonds'. Colin made some quip comparing Mr Donegan to ELP, which just about finished us off for the night. Needless to say, Lonnie came off best.

The following few days were spent travelling and providing the accompanying music for the seat-searching throng at great arenas in Boston, Washington and Pittsburgh. Following that, we took a few days off from ELP's 'Show That Never Ends' to play a couple of dates with a band who were destined for seemingly never-ending success.

It was obvious to anyone possessing even the most limited amount of musical taste that the self-contained little band I'd seen recording at Olympic studios were exceptionally talented, and it came as no surprise to find that the Eagles had taken off on their flight to stardom. Snafu supported them on consecutive days in the state of Massachusetts: first at a theatre, then on a lovely summer's day at a small outdoor festival, which went under the banner of On the Green. Guitarist Don Felder had been brought in to augment the sound and, with his original Gibson Les Paul and beaten-up old Fender amp, he was the genuine article – a rock guitarist with exceptional taste. The original guitarist, Bernie Leadon, did not seem particularly happy, and spent most of his off-stage moments wandering around barefoot with his 'chick'. He was a country-music purist at heart, and would eventually leave the band to lead a less pressurised existence. Before you ask, yes, there were women around, though not particularly groupies; this was the 1970s, don't forget, and people were living life to the full in an atmosphere of 'We've never had it so good, so let's go for it!' Not all the women we met on the road were slags or habitual group shaggers; a lot of them were just out for a bit of fun, and I'd say that the majority of musicians are just regular people doing an irregular job. For instance, how many people do you know who work in an environment where alcohol is both sold and imbibed in situ, or where music is played – often at a level of high impulse – which could easily influence the emotions of those within?

On one particular day off in New York, we were chaperoned by our record company representative, who, after the usual pleasantries, produced a gram of fine Columbian coke. Suddenly, he became the most popular man in the room. After the ceremonial chopping and snorting, one of the indulged – a guy who was obviously a newcomer to this sort of thing – suddenly launched into one: 'What's supposed to happen now nothing's happening at all I thought this stuff was supposed to give you a buzz nothing's happening does it make you aware of your surroundings it's a waste of money if you ask me it's five minutes now and I don't feel any different to what I did five minutes ago what's your name again hi I'm Andy I'm from Brooklyn originally but I live in Manhattan now are you Australian I had a friend from New Zealand wow look at that chick she's cute I'm thirsty yeh where's the john?'

Once I'd recovered from this salvo of verbal diarrhoea, I reached for a piece of cheese on a cocktail stick.

'You don't wanna eat that, buddy,' said a pixelated man in a satin baseball jacket.

'Why not?' I enquired.

'Because cheese is overrated. It's just milk's leap towards immortality,' he concluded, before bursting out laughing.

Later that night, we visited the famous Village Vanguard jazz club, where I encountered Joe Beck, a guitarist who'd recorded an experimental album with the renowned Flamenco guitarist Sabicas. Wishing to extend my appreciation of his union with the great Spanish master, I cornered him during the break.

'I bought the album that you recorded with Sabicas. It was a very interesting combination,' I remarked enthusiastically. He looked at me as though I'd said, 'Sabicas was great but you played like you only had one arm.'

He muttered something about it being crap and walked off. Needless to say, when he returned to the bandstand, his soloing received no applause from me, the miserable bastard.

Back on the ELP tour, we had a run of shows that included Pittsburgh, Knoxville, Dayton and Hershey. In Savannah, Georgia, we set out on foot from the hotel in search of a McDonalds and unknowingly approached a notorious gang area before a car with some dudes pulled up and beckoned us over. They kindly informed us that if we turned into the next street, there was a good chance we might not come out the other end, then they drove us to a safer neighbourhood.

A week later, in the drink-and-drug-sodden atmosphere of the Roosevelt Stadium, Jersey City, we were halfway through a ballad called 'Every Little Bit Hurts' with Bobby down on one knee, giving his all. The crowd had shown their appreciation by booing throughout our set, chanting 'ELP-ELP-ELP-ELP' and shouting an assortment of vulgar and vile insults at us. This was one ugly throng. Suddenly, a polythene bag landed on the stage right next to Bobby, who, assuming that it was a bag of marijuana from a thoughtful member of the audience, raised it to head height before turning to survey the exotic contents. It was a bag of freshly shat shit. Naturally, he recoiled in horror and instinctively threw it back in the general direction of the audience. Wrong. Almost immediately, we were bombarded with cans and other projectiles. Suddenly, from out of the baying mob, a bottle was thrown. It flew past my head before smashing against Pete's Hammond organ. Bollocks to this. We unplugged our instruments and made a dash for it while Bobby dropped his trousers and mooned the crowd. The ensuing backstage atmosphere was one of shock and humiliation; this had never happened to any of us before, and I deduced that this was the closest we'd ever been to a dystopian society. I promised myself that I would never set foot in Jersey City again.

We made at least two friends in the American press: journalist Bruce Malamut, who compared us favourably alongside the likes of other British exports (namely the Animals, the Yardbirds, the Zombies and Traffic), and photographer Chuck Pulin. Unfortunately, it wasn't enough. A few days later, we flew home to take stock of our American experience. It had not been a successful venture. Soon after, Pete called Bobby to inform him that he was leaving the band. It seemed that he was not altogether happy with Snafu's development and that the Jersey City episode was the final nail in the coffin. This was a blow, because Pete was an extremely talented musician and a good guy to boot. Keith Sherman was the next to go, though not of his own choosing.

Just prior to our return, we were taken to a very nice restaurant in New York by a charming Englishman called Rupert Perry, then head of Artist and Repertoire at Capital Records in L.A. Keith had seated himself next to Rupert, where he spent the rest of the evening giving it large while the rest of us were ignored. It wasn't Rupert's doing; he was just too nice to tell the overly ambitious Mr Sherman to quit while he was ahead. A plot was hatched that involved a large order of creamy gateaux and the equivalent in doggie bags and, as the unfortunate tour manager stepped outside, he was pelted with said cream cakes. He was somewhat shocked and humiliated, while poor Rupert looked on with a slightly embarrassed expression. In retrospect, I think he knew what was coming.

So there we were, in a state of abeyance, without a keyboard player and with a new album to promote. The first item on the wanted list to be addressed was the keyboard vacancy. Pete's replacement was Brian Chatton, a friendly Lancastrian and, as proven in the first rehearsal, a competent keyboard player and writer. Though he lacked his predecessor's funky edge, his melodic idiosyncrasies would add another dimension to Snafu's sound, especially as Pete's violin-led hoedowns would now be a thing of the past. The band rehearsed in readiness for some forthcoming British dates then hit the road to promote the newly released *Situation Normal.*

Soon after, we were informed that our affairs were to be handled by a company called Quarry Productions. Quarry's most valuable assets were Status Quo and Rory Gallagher – two of the hardest-working artists on the circuit – and the company's first move on our behalf was to arrange a support spot on Quo's British tour in December.

The university circuit was always a bit special in as much as you got to share the bill with other up-and-coming bands. At the University of Surrey in Guildford, we shared the bill with Home and, although any recollections of the performances from that particular night have been well and truly erased, I have retained a brain-cell playback pertaining to the backstage social activities. As per usual, the joints were rolled and smoked, and the distinct possibility of a *gratis* crate of Newcastle Brown Ale was adding to that particular brand of laid-back euphoria to which we'd become accustomed.

Suddenly, our attention was drawn to the encompassing presence of a member of the Home entourage, whose grand entrance as a human chicken was as off-the-wall as it was unexpected. Here, indeed, was a kindred spirit for Colin Gibson if ever there was one! And before anyone could say 'Thai stick' or 'Where's me chillum?' Colin had joined him for what I still consider to be modern man's earliest attempt at a synchronised ritual chicken dance. Our tears of mirth rolled side by side with the joints as they clucked and plucked along to their own cosmic-fowl rhythms; believe me, they needed no egging on (groan).

Later, as we were driving out of the main gates, Colin spotted his newfound loony mate still doing the non-compos-mentis chicken in the middle of the road: 'Stop, let me out!' And he was off for another bout of poultry posturing before we eventually headed for home. Best of all, through all of their newfound kinship, neither of them spoke a word to each other.

Prior to the Quo tour, I received a telephone call from an old friend, the newly appointed Deep Purple vocalist, David Coverdale. We'd known each other since the latter part of the 1960s when we were both part of the music scene back in Middlesbrough, and he was now about to undergo a serious culture shock by moving to Malibu. A suite at the Holiday Inn in Swiss Cottage was his final *pied-à-terre*, and, in the company of Terry Popple and a couple of ex-north-east musicians (who'd settled on rock 'n' roll truck driving as a sensible alternative), we proceeded to do the bleeding obvious – get out of it. A good night was had by all, and Polaroid shots of us 'mooning' were in circulation for a while afterwards. The prize-winning shot, incidentally, came courtesy of Terry, whose undercarriage could be clearly seen due to the unmannerly spacing of his legs.

The Quo UK tour actually went well, apart from the final show, which happened to take place at the Granada in Bobby's birthplace, East Ham in London's East End. He was so convinced we'd get an encore that he went out and bought five West Ham football shirts. These, he assured us, would be the icing on the cake as we charged out triumphantly to answer the audience's demands. Unfortunately, the only demanding shouts were 'Quo-o-o-o-o!' and we were left standing in the wings, milling around like work-seeking immigrants.

In an interview with one of the music periodicals, Bobby opened up his heart and spoke about the difficult seven months prior to the band's successful tour with Status Quo. He recounted some of the problems that had surfaced during the ELP tour, and how the band had started to stray away from its original aims that he and yours truly had set out to achieve: 'To combine Micky's guitar and my very riffy, raunchy voice plus a really funky rhythm section. But somewhere in that year on the road, the keyboard player, Pete Solley, who was very country-influenced and a powerful personality, wanted to write, and the outcome was the second album which was me and Mick and Pete writing together.' He then admitted that the album lacked direction and contained a diversity which detracted from the band's strengths. He also disclosed that he wasn't too happy with the country stuff. Him and most journalists, as it turned out. This, in turn, had led to an 'amicable split with Pete'. The interview was rounded off with Bobby in a positive frame of mind: 'Every band goes through times like this but if you can stick together through it, it brings you closer together and the rest of it is easy going. Snafu are at that point at the moment. The rest of our career is going to be easy.'

The rest of our career kicked off on 15 February 1975 at the Lauphiem Sporthalle, Germany, the first date on a mini-tour supporting Status Quo. The 'Quo' were a decent bunch of guys with a great deal of camaraderie and laddish, in-house humour. They also employed a personal road crew – a trio of various shapes and sizes who they named Lock, Stock and

Barrel. Our own personal trio had now been updated due to the departure of the inept Keith Sherman, and we were pleased to welcome John 'Bruno' Wayte – a shy, likeable man from the Midlands who joined Joe as joint custodian of the equipment. Larry was happy – as Larrys are reputed to be – to take over the tour manager's reins, driving us to shows in our rented Peugeot estate and, given the opportunity, presiding over the lights. My overriding memories from these dates are of Bobby trying to make light of sections of the crowd chanting 'Sta-tus-Quo!' by suggesting 'Sna-a-fu!' as an alternative – what a trooper! The other is making the most of a day off in a nice hotel that featured, among its amenities, a sauna. Terry persuaded me that twenty minutes in the steam does one the world of good, so, armed with towels, we gagged and wheezed our way through the airless, ultra-humid enclosure, only to find Bruno sweating profusely and smoking a cigarette. Quality!

We took a train from Hamburg to Berlin, which in those days meant travelling through that sinister piece of land known as East Germany. There was still an atmosphere of the Cold War around, and anybody familiar with Len Deighton's spy novels will appreciate the paranoia that still prevailed. We half-expected to see Michael Caine walk shiftily through the carriage to rendezvous with a fellow agent, who he'd eventually find slumped in a toilet with a bullet hole in his head.

Time for levity! Prior to the tour, Colin had paid a visit to his local joke shop and purchased a selection of hideous stick-on false noses in readiness for any moments of silliness. And when a customs officer appeared in the next carriage to check people's passports, we knew instinctively that one such moment had arrived. Without any thought whatsoever as to the possible consequences of our actions, Colin, Terry and me quickly chose a rubber nasal appendage each and secured them onto our existing facial organs. Cretinous grins were then adopted to complete the picture as the bovine-faced official reached our seats. His initial reaction to such folly was, predictably, one of surprise, followed soon after by restrained annoyance (as would be expected when confronted by three idiots who'd chosen to look like rustic fuckwits from a Pieter Broegel painting). Would he call for the plain-clothed, gun-carrying members of Erich Honecker's fearsome Stasi, who were no doubt secreted among the passengers? Or would he just regard us as unfortunate, infantile by-products of the decadent west and shake his head slowly in disgust?

Mercifully, he chose the latter and we were spared the humiliation of a night as guests of the state security.

At a large hall in Berlin, Status Quo's tour manager, Bob Young, was fine-tuning the band's backstage arrangements. Unlike Herr Honecker, Bob possessed admirable leadership qualities and a charm that was as effortless as his banter. He was the band's official lyricist, and even joined them onstage for the Doors song 'Roadhouse Blues' to play harmonica and incur the relentless wit of Messrs Rossi and Parfitt. Early on in the tour, he found me sitting backstage picking some rural blues on an acoustic guitar and joined in on harmonica. We hit it off immediately and sparked off a friendship that would eventually incorporate musical creativity and extreme silliness – a winning formula in anyone's book. And some of it will appear in this one – just wait and see!

CHAPTER 15

SITUATION FAR FROM NORMAL

In March 1975, Charlie Chaplin was knighted, the North Vietnamese were on their way to capturing Saigon, construction was started on the Trans-Alaska Pipeline System and King Faisal of Saudi Arabia was shot dead by his nephew. The following month, Bill Gates founded Microsoft, and a faction of Red Army terrorists took over the West German embassy. As if we cared. The only kind of headlines that would have triggered off any kind of reaction in our collective mindset would have been: 'ALL EUROPEAN MUSIC VENUES TO CLOSE' or 'ROLLING JOINTS, BOOZING AND GETTING OUT OF IT IN GENERAL TO BECOME CAPITAL OFFENCES.'

On our travels, we would encounter neo-Buddhists extolling the virtues of this mysterious religion while countering their newfound vegetarian diets with huge spliffs and permissive sex lives: 'Fancy coming back to my place for a quick mantra and some partner swapping? If you get the munchies, don't eat the bananas – they're for the shrine.' Sometimes – usually in Oxford Street – you'd be affronted by shaven-headed groups from the Hare Krishna movement wearing eastern leisure suits, chanting something obscure and tapping lamely on cheap percussion instruments. They were harmless but irritating – a leftover from the hippie 1960s and still seeking inner peace from the selfish, self-possessed world outside. One day, I was walking along Wardour Street carrying a guitar when one of them approached me.

'Hey, brother, come and play for us tonight!'

'What are you going to pay me with – rune stones?'

'We shall enlighten your day.'

'I've just remembered, I'm working.'

'Where?'

'Anywhere, man.'

Not listed among those memorable events of March 1975 are the club dates and preparations for the twelve-date British tour Snafu would undertake in May. The support spot was taken by another Quarry signing: four lads from Liverpool known collectively as Nutz. Typical Scousers, they were down to earth and likeable, especially the singer, Dave Lloyd, who divided his time onstage with visits to the bookies.

'Not now, Dave,' pleaded the guitarist, Mick Davenport. 'We're ready to do the soundcheck.'

'I won't be long,' responded Dave with a knowing grin. 'Just extend the intro 'til I get back!'

We visited the Queen Margaret Union in Glasgow, where we played to a lively crowd. Afterwards, one of the students told us about a club where the audience was so hostile they lined up in front of the stage and performed a Hakka before the first song. Thankfully, the audience at the Uni showed no particular inclination towards the game of rugby or, more importantly, premeditated and intimidating war dances. In between gigs, we continued to write songs with the emphasis on funky rock and readied ourselves for the all-important third album. Our management had secured an album deal with Capitol/EMI, with the added bonus that we were to record it at the Manor. In between gigs, I was happy to indulge in a spot of session work, which included joining Colin and Terry on a track for Alan Hull's long-awaited solo album, *Squire*.

I think we'd all learned from our lack of foresight regarding *Situation Normal*, and resolved to put a great deal more effort into the writing and general direction of the new album. Pre-production rehearsals went well, and we headed back to the Manor with a positive attitude, various nuggets of hash and a bottle of Jack Daniels. Renowned keyboard player Tim Hinkley was brought in to add a down-home spirit that just wasn't in Brian's musical genes. To his credit, Brian remained secure in his own talent and unfazed by Tim's more cavalier approach, content to double up keyboard parts with him and work on arrangements for his own songs. Highly rated engineer Bob Potter was given the task of getting the best out of the self-indulgent bunch now rolling up and tippling on the studio floor, though in all honesty he was happy to be in the thick of it with the rest of us. Having worked with the likes of the Grease Band and Joe Cocker, he probably found our excesses quite tame in comparison.

The album was completed at Island Studios in London, the final tracks being 'Hard to Handle' and 'Lock and Key'. Tim was the driving force behind both numbers, and it was no real surprise that he became a permanent replacement for Brian, who seemed happy to concentrate on songwriting and other ventures. Tim would bring a real rock 'n' roll edge to the band and a boundless enthusiasm which could be, to put it mildly, very infectious. He made his band debut at the Dagenham Roundhouse on 2 August 1975, followed a couple of days later by a gig at the Marquee. There would never be another dull moment with Tim around!

A couple of weeks later, we arrived at the Reading Festival and found ourselves in the company of Thin Lizzy, Supertramp, String Driven Thing, Ozark Mountain Devils, Alberto y Los Paranoias, the Kursal Flyers, Zzebra and Alan Stivell. Great names!

A man in patchwork denim with the complexion of putrefied cheese was wandering about, mumbling something about trying to make inner peace. Somebody suggested four tablespoons of Andrews and a large prune. Some of us ended up in a portacabin-cum-dressing room drinking something called Limoncello – a drink with such a high sugar content that, after just one small glass, I could feel the initial stirrings of type two diabetes. Mixed with black hash it proved to be an interesting combination of sugar rush and herbal incapacitation.

Early in September, we completed a BBC radio *In Concert* performance, which, I'm pleased to say, was very successful, with the added bonus of having an audience that didn't fuck off back to Canvey Island before we went on. We also found time to record three songs for the *John Peel Sessions*, before heading back to Germany for a short tour with Status Quo plus a handful of festival-style events. A couple of these were with Thin Lizzy, and the adventurous Mr Hinkley wasted no time in becoming Phil Lynott's partner in crime. After one show, we spent most of the ensuing early hours trying to track them down, moving from club to bar only to be told, 'Ah, ze big guy and ze little guy! No, zey came and zey vent.'

At the Circus Krone in Munich, David Coverdale and his lady, Julia, appeared backstage before our set. We hadn't seen each other since his 'mooning' send-off to the States, and he was now resident in Bavaria. After the show, we went to a cosy little bar where he spoke about his wish to record a solo album – it soon became apparent that all was not well in the Deep Purple camp.

Playing a relatively short support spot meant that we were ready to act like people with mental disorders by 9pm. The ever-present booze, the easily obtainable dope, the occasional Valium and the very occasional Mandrax: all of these distractions could, or would, play a part in our post-gig activities. Mostly, it would see us propping up bars, skinning up joints backstage and in hotel rooms, or simply chatting up women. Seldom did things get out of hand, though we did have our moments. Late one night in a room at the Holiday Inn in Wolfsburg, somebody decided that crumbling a Mandrax instead of hash into a joint would make an interesting change. Well, it certainly took things to another level, inspiring one of the gathering to adopt a *real* rock 'n' roll attitude and sling a coffee pot out of the window. Thankfully, the sedentary effects of the barbiturates prevented any of us from turning into Vandal Berserkers. There were, however, some heated exchanges at the check-out later that morning, when it was discovered that said coffee pot had landed on the roof of the Italian High Commissioner's car, causing considerable damage. Camaraderie prevented those present at the time of the offence from spilling the beans, but the guilty party was already at the top of the list of suspects and would be seriously scrutinised for the rest of the dates.

The new album, entitled *All Funked Up*, was released to tie in with a December tour supporting Nazareth and to promote our single – the revamped version of 'Lock and Key' – we appeared on a brand new TV show called *Supersonic*. Tim fancied himself as a bit of a guitarist and, though he'd played electric piano on the original recording, chose to throw a few shapes as rhythm guitarist for the show. Thankfully, we were only miming, so he could throw as many shapes as he wanted to my original rhythm track. He also decided to go the whole hog and invest in a pair of tight, bright red velvet trousers for the occasion. Unfortunately, the step up to the stage was a little too high and the extra stretch proved too much for the material in question. You could hear the sound of velvet parting company from its seam at the other end of the studio. Tim soldiered on, bare-arsed but proud, to an audience of enthusiastic punters, including one young lady who looked like Bolton's answer to Holly Golightly.

Nazareth were a good bunch of lads and their no-nonsense slant on good old British rock 'n' roll never failed to bring the house down. Their audience seemed to accept Snafu in a way that Quo's often didn't, and I don't recall hearing any shouts of 'Naz-ar-eth' during our set either. Nazareth's tour manager was a likeable guy called Harry, who we immediately christened Harry of Nazareth, thus giving a sense of the biblical to the proceedings.

'Got the stable ready for Christmas, Harry? Ha ha!' I'm sure he'd heard it all before.

Pete Makowski from *Sounds* accompanied us to the

Above: The boys in the white shirts: our classroom band, The Roadrunners, pose for a shot in 1965. Paul Rodgers would later go on to find fame with Free and Bad Company, of course...
(*l-r*) Paul Rodgers, Dave Usher, me, Colin Bradley.

Right: Looking lean and mean in London, sporting a trusty Telecaster. 1967.

Above: Rome, in 1969, with Lucas and The Mike Cotton Sound. An early lesson in soul music. I still love it.

Below: Relaxing with Snafu in 1974. Situation normal… for the time being!

Left: Young and Moody. Taken on an album photoshoot on Parliament Hill.

Right: Nice titfer, all the way from Saville Row.

Below left: A lost weekend in the Channel Islands with Rick Parfitt of Status Quo (second from top). A good time was had by all! c.1980

Right: Legendary DJ Tommy Vance once referred to this line-up as the definitive Whitesnake. (*l-r*) David, Bernie, Neil, Ian, Jon and myself.

©*Virginia Turbett/Getty Images*

Below: A very early Whitesnake performance, featuring Pete Solley on keyboards.

Above: David and myself taking a break between songs during rehearsals at Shepperton Studios.

Below: Marsden and Moody: undercover agents for the blues! *Saints & Sinners* session, Clearwell Castle, 1981.

Above: Developing my Southern Rock vibe for early Whitesnake. 1978.

© *Getty Images/Fin Costello*

Below: The Moody and Marsden guitar duels were always a high point. Exciting, creative, but, most of all, great fun.   © *Getty Images/Fin Costello*

Above: Man in Black with matching Les Paul Custom. © *Haydn Hart*

Below: All smiles and Goldtops. © *Sarah Reeve*

Above: The Micky Moody & Ali Maas *Black and Chrome* photo session 2016. We scrub up well!

© Alwyn R. Coates

Brighton Dome and gave us a very favourable mini-review in his forthcoming article:

> It was a stormer. They have the same musical magic as bands like Kokomo and AWB's – when it works, it works! Moody was particularly inspiring showing his versatility on the ol' axe. 'We were told that you're not allowed to get up or clap your hands,' Harrison told the audience. They got up, clapped their hands, cheered and demanded an encore.

The Naz's are still touring today and I've got just one question for Dan and Pete – if you ever get to read this, who *were* the Banana Sisters?

Snafu confirmed its transition to 1976 by performing on 1 January at the Great British Music Festival, a three-day event which took place in a ginormous hall at Olympia, London. From our basement position on the bill, we could look up and see who had to follow us: Jack the Lad, the Baker Gurvitz Army, John Miles, Barclay James Harvest and Procol Harum. Considering that most people must have been somewhat fragile from the previous night's traditional celebrations, I seem to remember it as a satisfying experience. Of course, being first on, we had the rest of the day to indulge ourselves at a leisurely pace and enjoy the proceedings. Particularly entertaining was the idiot dancing, provided on this occasion by a girl called Mandylion and her partner, who bore a worrying resemblance to one of the Cardassians from Star Trek (though none of us knew that at the time). To top it all, we each got a free poster in the form of a mirror, which was a nice touch.

The *All Funked Up* album is sometimes referred to as the

band's 'great lost album'. Oddly enough, I have no reviews for it at all in my own personal archive, which is food for thought. Did it ever get reviewed, or had I lost interest in people's opinions by then? Personally, I think it's a bloody good album that must have received some sort of attention, so sadly it may have been the latter. Perhaps it was the transatlantic phone calls from David Coverdale – then struggling to get through a Stateside tour with the self-destructing Deep Purple – that had had an effect on my feelings towards Snafu.

We travelled back to the Manor to record another single, 'Are You Sure', a cover of a Staples Singers song, after which we set out once more on that well-trodden path of one-nighters. There is, thankfully, a recording of a live concert from a BBC radio show at the Paris Theatre which captures the band in full flow. Tim had injected a new vigour into the proceedings, which clearly shows through on the recording – the band was rocking.

Also featured in Snafu's line-up by then was a friendly character called Brother James – a Caribbean percussionist with enormous charm who became an unofficial (and mostly unpaid) member of the band. He would just turn up and play, exuding good vibes via a dazzling smile. Unfortunately for me, it just wasn't enough to bolster my enthusiasm. Though I was unaware of its importance at the time, David T. Wolf's comment would ring true: 'Idealism is what precedes experience, cynicism is what follows.'

The only review I have in my possession from this period is a simple two-liner from one of the major music papers. It's regarding 'Are You Sure' and simply states, 'Nice slide guitar embellishes this mellow version of the gospelly Staples Singers song. Rather good.'

SITUATION FAR FROM NORMAL

The Deep Purple tour reached London for two shows at the Empire Pool, Wembley, in mid-March, and it soon became obvious that this particular rock 'n' roll circus was being led by jugglers and Pierrots. A personal invitation from David secured me not only a place in the VIP box but an opportunity to ride in his hired Jaguar – nice! I was picked up at home by his personal assistant, John 'Magnet' Ward, a long-haired individual with a western moustache – a look I myself favoured.

Backstage at the arena, amid an atmosphere somewhat subdued for a rock 'n' roll gig, it appeared that everybody had their own dressing rooms, which is not uncommon at that level. However, in this case, the reasons seemed to be more paranoiac than practical. Magnet ushered me into David's room where, after a hug, we got stuck into the brandy. He briefed me on the state of play – who was talking to who, who was out to lunch, etc. – smoked another Marlboro and then hit the stage.

It was not a good show. The atmosphere on the stage was subdued, eye contact seemed to be minimal and signs of enjoyment were almost non-existent. At some point in the set, Glen Hughes went into Hoagy Carmichael's 'Georgia', and many in the crowd reacted with the kind of apathy that's usually reserved for teenagers at christenings. It was like Prince breaking into 'Dust My Broom'. To add insult to injury, the P.A. system went off completely during one number, reducing the mighty Deep Purple to the status of a band playing without the aid of microphones in their local pub. Thankfully, the problem was solved before the end of the song.

As instructed, I made my way backstage during the encore and spied Magnet waiting in the wings amid a small group of personal assistants. I'd like to suggest a collective word for *that* particular group of personal assistants: a 'lightstep', because these guys must have been treading on bloody eggshells for months. Within seconds of the final chord, we left hurriedly in the direction of the Jaguar and sped off to the hotel of David's choice – in this instance, the metaphorical Le Valium Cinq (incorporating fags and booze).

A few days later, Deep Purple had a *really* disastrous gig at the Liverpool Empire and it was all over bar the shouting. That would be left to various lawyers and would include shouting in bars and other associated puns.

Sitting at the bar in the Speakeasy, listening to the maudlin ramblings of a once-successful bass player whose marquee value had, by then, plummeted to that of mere bivouac status, I was informed of the death of Paul Kossoff. It was a shock to say the least. I'd known him since 1967 when he worked as an assistant at Selmer's music shop in London and, though our paths hadn't crossed for a long while, we were members of the same fraternity – baby-boomer blues guitarists. That particular year, I'd made the move from Middlesbrough to London with the Wildflowers – a group which also included my old school friend Paul Rodgers – in the hope of some sort of recognition. When the band folded (soon after the infamous 'Summer of Love'), the two Pauls would extend their friendship to a permanent musical partnership and Free was born. Whatever brought about Paul's metamorphosis from a pleasant teenager from a seemingly secure, loving family background into a reckless young man dependent on hard drugs is academic: it was still a tragic loss.

CHAPTER 16

FRESH FIELDS, FIRES AND FARTS

976 would prove to be an interesting and fruitful year. David Coverdale was back on the blower with plans for a solo album, and I was invited initially to the Arabella Hotel in Munich where he was holed up, then to the home he shared with Julia in Wartaweil on the shores of Lake Ammersee in Bavaria. It was in this truly beautiful location that we continued with our writing. I would listen to David's ideas, occasionally adding my own interpretations, or suggest chord sequences and melodies towards new songs. In the evenings, we'd sit out on the patio, or else retire to the local *bier stube*, where Herr Coverdale was known affectionately as the Wartaweil cowboy. On our return, we'd either continue with our writing or head down to the basement to play table soccer, taking on the identities of former school football heroes in match-winning penalty shoot-outs. This was a long way from Deep Purple, and David was finally enjoying a stress-

free existence. To round off the day, we'd often indulge in a nightcap consisting of a brandy with a Valium chaser before wobbling up the stairs to bed.

Some mornings I felt as though I'd been bounced upon by Rover – the giant balloon from *The Prisoner* – or fired head first from a trebuchet.

Spring turned into what would eventually become known as 'the long hot summer of '76'. A drought act was passed, along with a hosepipe ban and water rationing, as temperatures soared to 35° centigrade. As people laboured in the unprecedented heat, road surfaces began to melt and bush fires sprang up in Devon. Clad in my lightest clothing, I returned to the Coverdale abode in Wartaweil to continue with the writing, pausing only to imbibe fine German beer. Situated nearby and overshadowed by its formidable monastery was the small town of Andechs, a place where the Benedictine monks had been brewing beer since the fifteenth century. And boy, could they brew beer. Julia drove us out there one sweltering afternoon to sample the wares and, of course, quench our thirsts. I can't recall David's preferred tipple that balmy day but I sank two or three steins of the stuff. Halfway down my second, I began to feel the effects and looked instinctively towards the label on the bottle for some kind of explanation. Although my vision was beginning to falter, I learned that the brew had a strength of 6.9 per cent and contained only the finest spring water, five types of malt, barley and, judging by my deteriorating condition, low-grade surgical spirit. On our return to the house, David retired to his bedroom, somewhat tipsy. 'Arl carry on wida rite'n,' I declared to Julia, who smiled sympathetically before joining the other inebriate upstairs. Determined to make a good start on the lyrics to a new tune, I tottered across the patio and walked rather unsteadily towards the invitingly shady confines of a large tree. I had the title, 'Celebration'; now all I needed were the verses and a chorus.

Two hours later, and refreshed from his snooze, David discovered his co-writer fast asleep under a tree, a note book beside him with just one word scrawled across the top of the heat-curled page: 'Celebration'.

One evening, an old acquaintance of Julia's turned up with her boyfriend, so we retired to the patio to continue our writing session. It was only a matter of minutes before she joined us.

'Julia tells me you make records.'

'That's right.'

'Well, tell me one thing I've always wanted to know. How do you get that little hole in the middle?' We decided to hot-foot it to the *bier stube*.

The next day was blisteringly hot and, by mid-afternoon, *mein hosts* had decided on a little siesta, prompting me to take a short stroll towards the lake. At the bottom of the garden there was a small jetty, which, under different circumstances, would have been handy for tethering a motorboat or, perhaps, diving for plundered loot. However, on this particular day, its sole purpose was to provide a distraction for a thumb-twiddling guitarist. David had forewarned me not to throw cigarette butts into the lake, as it was a health hazard to the swans, so I stubbed out my Marlboro underfoot before returning to the house for inspiration. Forty-five minutes later, the garden was swarming with firemen, most of whom seemed to be in a hurry to reach the jetty. I soon saw why – the bloody thing was on fire. Oops! Of course, the hot weather got the blame and 'passive arsonist' was not added to my CV.

We went into the air-conditioned Kingsway Studios during the first week of August to start work on David's album with the impressive cast of Tim Hinkley on keyboards, DeLisle Harper on bass, a young drummer called Simon Phillips and former Deep Purple bass player Roger Glover in charge of production. Simon, of course, went on to become one of the greats in the world of rock drumming and went on to play with the Who, Priest, Toto – oh, just Google the rest if you don't already know. The great saxophonist, Ron Aspery, who was a mutual friend of both David and myself, added his unique style to a number of tracks, and backing singers Helen Chappelle, Liza Strike and Barry St John helped put the icing on the cake.

I'd first met Ron back in the late 1960s when I was still living in Middlesbrough; he was playing in a local band called Rivers Invitation while I was a member of their chief rival outfit, Tramline. After a stint with the Eric Delaney Band, he returned to the north-east, in particular Redcar, to take on a residency at the Starlight nightclub. It was here that I had the pleasure of jamming with him and two other extremely talented and original musicians – Colin Hodgkinson and Tony Hicks – with whom he'd formed the nucleus of the house band. Although they accompanied the usual array of cabaret artists, they lived for the final hour when the majority of the punters were too busy getting legless to realise what was going on.

Unbeknown to most of them, they were being treated to some highly original arrangements of songs by Robert Johnson, Cannonball Adderley and Leadbelly, as well as band originals, which were influenced by anything from Charlie Parker to Jimi Hendrix. The trio would soon emerge from obscurity and present their unique brand of jazz-fusion under the name of Back Door.

The Kingsway recordings were enjoyable; although the material was diverse and, to Deep Purple fans in particular, somewhat unexpected, I had the feeling that David had got a lot of things off his chest. When Ron had finished his overdub session, he invited me to guest with Back Door at 'an early gig in Reading' on the following weekend and, true to his word, picked me up at the arranged time in his little VW Beetle. We stopped at a couple of pubs en route to fill our bodies with strong Pils beer. It never occurred to me to ask which venue the band was booked into; I just assumed it would be some sort of intimate jazz club. Needless to say, I was rather taken aback when he turned into the backstage area of the Reading Festival.

'Just a little jam then, Ron?' I asked wryly.

'Oh, aye – fill yer boots!' he beamed.

Acting as driver and personal assistant on the sessions at Kingsway was Willy Fyffe, a former member of Deep Purple's crew and grandson of the famous Scottish character actor and comedian Will Fyffe (who was perhaps best known as the writer of that well-known song 'I Belong to Glasgow'). Willy exuded 'good vibes', was very witty and also displayed talents in both music and art; we were destined to see a lot of each other over the next few years, both professionally and socially.

After the Back Door gig (we were positioned between A Band Called O and Sassafras – by 'eck, those were the names!), I was invited to join them a few days later at the BBC studios in Bush House in central London for a pre-recorded World Service broadcast. On arrival, I gazed in awe at a truly remarkable building, which, on its completion in 1923, was declared the most expensive building in the world at a cost of $23 million. As we were setting up our equipment, a true legend of popular music entered the room: Brian Matthew, host of the 1960s pop show *Thank Your Lucky Stars*. I was blown away. As a kid, I'd watched this guy on TV every Saturday night without fail as he introduced a who's who of pop's kings and queens, including the Ronettes, the Supremes, the Beatles and the Rolling Stones. He'd also hosted the influential Saturday-morning show *Saturday Club*, though I like to think *that* particular shindig was pre-recorded: if not, he must have been knackered by 8pm.

'Hi, guys. I'm Brian,' he announced. We nodded knowingly. 'Fancy a drink?' The words 'bull' and 'red rag' sprang to mind. In the bar, he bought us all a pint. 'Usual double brandy, Mr Matthew?' the barman asked. He gained immediate and everlasting respect.

The World Service was – and still is – a highly informative and educational radio format, and Back Door were expected to not only play but also submit to individual interviews. Colin was first up and was asked to pigeonhole his blues influences. Due to some sort of inexplicable verbal peculiarity, he exaggerated certain pronunciations with a controlled chirrup: 'Well, the bluesss ssssingers traveled from Missssissssippi to sssshhhicago and people like Robert Johnssson and Sssson Houssssse were very influenssshhal.' Ron went next and, when asked to describe his technique, especially his amplified saxophone sound, he replied, 'I've got my saxophone and an amplifier and a bug, and I just plug them in. I don't know that much about it really.' Newcomer Adrian Tillbrook explained that his new Arbiter drum kit was an 'Autotune model' and had to be assembled by using a ratchet. Special mention was made of his club in Hartlepool, the Full Circle Club, which specialised in a full circle of music played by a full circle of musicians. He also enthused about an obscure Indian musician named Ranjit Poalie. We were none the wiser. When it came to my turn, I was introduced as a 'special guest of Back Door' and stood opposite the smiling face that was Brian Matthew.

'I believe that, as well as regular guitar, you play steel guitar too. Do you play it horizontally?' he inquired.
'Only if I've been at the brandy,' I replied. His eyes widened. 'No, I play slide or bottleneck-style guitar, usually from a vertical position.'

He grinned appreciatively as the others chortled in the background. After the session, we retired to the subsidised bar and spent a happy hour with a happy bunch.

CHAPTER 17

ONE SPLIFF
TOO MANY

Using his influence, charm and brazen premeditated cajolery, Bob Young managed to persuade the studio-bookings secretary to grant us a bit of free time at Phonogram's recording studio near Marble Arch, which in turn enabled us to record our first co-written song – the jaunty 'Warm Winds'. Good old John Coghlan was happy to provide the drumming, which in this case warranted the use of brushes as opposed to sticks – very un-Quo! The session led to more songwriting assignments and pretty soon we had enough material to make some rough demos. These were created at a small studio in Battersea, and the sessions were engineered by a guy who was very proud of his ex-BBC recording console. In true BBC fashion, the big old volume faders opened away from the operator, rather than towards, and Bob was convinced that specks of rust fluttered down as they were motivated. The studio owner/engineer seemed a little on the bored, perhaps blasé side, which, to me anyway, signified that he was either unhappy in his work or had never quite got over that session he did with Stockhausen.

The next day, we proudly played our minimalist recordings to David Oddie at Quarry, who gave us the thumbs up to go ahead with the project. Together with fixer/producer Stuart Taylor, he secured a deal with Magnet Records, a company known more for its blatantly commercial pop renderings than cool, bluesy sounds. Apparently, they were looking to broaden their horizons and appeal to the kind of people who wouldn't normally opt for the label's big guns, Alvin Stardust and Darts.

First off, we needed a producer, and I had no hesitation in suggesting Roger Glover – a man with fine musical credentials, broad tastes, good ears, a warm personality and who was not averse to the odd spliff. He happily accepted our offer and recommended the small but funky Central Sound studio in Denmark Street, London. Around the same time, I was asked to perform at a showcase gig for Graham Bonnet, late of the Marbles and possessor of the awesome voice that propelled him to prominence in 1968 with 'Only One Woman'. Also in the line-up was a multi-instrumentalist by the name of Graham Preskett, who played almost everything, could write, read and arrange music like most of us write, read and arrange our own names, and was a charming and funny man to boot. We had no hesitation about asking him to join us in the studio. And to complete the small but extremely efficient combo, we brought in drummer Terry Stannard, my old bandmate from Juicy Lucy who'd since played with Kokomo. He was just the man to provide the tight grooves we were looking for. Roger brought his bass and a variety of percussion instruments and, apart from the occasional sojourn to a pub by St Giles Circus, we stayed in, skinned up and locked on.

The studio was at basement level at the back of the property, while at the front was a barber shop, which displayed a sign to warn customers of the low doorframe. It read 'Mind your Head' – a piece of worthy advice judging by some of the coiffured creations we saw leaving the salon.

We went into the studio armed with nine songs: six Young and Moody originals, one by Bob and Francis Rossi (which had previously been recorded by Status Quo), a cover version of Robert Johnson's 'Four Until Late' and Elizabeth Cotten's 'I'm Going Away'. The last was taken from a cassette that Ron and Colin had given me, and was such a heart-rending performance that we just had to do it. Recording the songs was a great pleasure; there was no bullshit, no ego problems and no pressure, and they took just six days to record and three days to mix. In fact, I met up with Roger many years later and he still has very fond memories from the recording of the album. One day, he bounced in with the new J.J. Cale album, *Troubadour*, went straight to the turntable and put it on. By the end of the second bar, his face was beaming; by the end of the third, so was everybody else's. Roger's inspiration helped fuel a feeling of togetherness and creativity throughout the recording, which was almost cottage-industry in its approach.

Bob and I took a twin room at a hotel in Bayswater while we recorded our album. The sessions all went well and there was no shortage of both Lebanese and Moroccan fortified herbs. Once back at the hotel, we'd head for our room, order cans of Guinness and sandwiches, and listen to a cassette of the day's recordings on our tape recorder while eagerly devouring our supper. The obligatory joint was rolled and

winter and saw that good ol' boy Jimmy Carter elected into the White House; taking part in the official celebrations were the Allman Brothers, who rocked their way into the history books. Other milestones included the Band's last gig – which was filmed under the direction of Martin Scorsese as *The Last Waltz* – and the release of *Hotel California* by the Eagles. By 'eck, those lads had come a long way since those sessions at Olympic Studios. And the Sex Pistols blighted live TV with obscenities during an interview with Bill Grundy. Mind you, the smug Grundy seemed to possess the sort of nauseating personality that would make anybody want to swear.

To warm my heart (and the rest of my body), I would sometimes retire to a cosy pub and, taking the broadest view of George Bernard Shaw's belief that music is the brandy of the damned, order myself a large Courvoisier. Soon after, I was accosted by the pub bore, a man with a fondness for the sound of his own voice who liked nothing better than to drone on and on about his drunken escapades (and I always thought that alcoholics were anonymous). He was also an idiot. When he first became a dad, he went down to the pub to celebrate his newfound status as a palindrome. Yes, it was time to head off home, switch on the TV and watch *When the Boat Comes In*. ('You shall have a bloater, when the boat comes in.')

A few days before Christmas, I decided to hit the town and hang loose. The day started off innocently enough with a hike around the annual Christmas parties that the established record companies hosted to celebrate their musical and corporate achievements. I'd probably indulged in my fondness for brandy at half a dozen establishments before falling out of a cab outside the offices of A&M Records on London's New Kings Road. Once inside, I instinctively fell in with some familiar faces: a friendly though dubious bunch of musicians, roadies and hangers-on. Taking what I considered to be a sensible stance, I ordered a pint of lager with the optimistic view that it would somehow dilute the effects of the cognac. Under the circumstances, it was a commendable effort. However, my inability to say no to a proffered joint was to be my undoing. I was no stranger to a spliff, but on top of all that hard liquor?

It only took one toke to render my legs incapable of sustaining their supportive role, which in turn caused the rest of my body to stagger momentarily like a newborn baby deer. I collapsed in a heap on the floor and, within seconds, was dragged unceremoniously to an office behind a makeshift bar and laid to rest. Or so I thought.

Enter one Mitch Mitchell, erstwhile drummer with the Jimi Hendrix Experience – a man with a passionate fervour for the maniacal.

'Come on, Moody. On your feet, man,' he enthused, and, by roughly encouraging my body to rise to an angle of approximately forty-two degrees, administered the simple nauseate to persuade the contents of my stomach to display itself across the immediate area. Unfortunately, one passer-by – a well-known chanteuse – sustained a direct hit on her funky stilettos and was not impressed.

'For fuck's sake' would have been unfamiliar parlance to her many fans but was quite appropriate in this case.

CHAPTER 18

CANED IN CANNES

In January 1977, and in the company of Bob Young, David Oddie, Alan Crux and Colin Johnson from Quarry Productions, I found myself on a plane to Nice. On the journey to France, large Bloody Mary in hand, I finally accepted the fact that nearly everything I liked was either illegal, permissive or a health hazard. A little voice inside my head said, 'So what, you're only twenty-six. Enjoy life – indulge!' Another little voice retorted, 'Hey, my name's Conscience, and if you keep listening to him you'll end up in big trouble.' I thought, 'What's with the little voices - am I mental?' Somewhere in the background, an impromptu burst of laughter from my travelling companions helped restore my compos mentis and reassure me that there *is* a difference between rational thinking and schizophrenia. Well, self-analysis is much cheaper than trekking all the way to Harley Street and paying somebody a fortune to be told something that you already know. We touched down amid the welcoming warmer climes of the Côte d'Azur with seasoned attitudes and preparative livers, casual visitors to a country of which I had serious doubts. How can you trust a country that produces over two hundred kinds of cheese?

Once through the *Gitanes*-scented customs, Johnson and Crux took a cab and headed for their hotel, while Oddie, Young and Moody headed to the harbour for a two-day residence on board a yacht belonging to Rod Stewart's manager and head of Riva Records, Billy Gaff. We were in Cannes for the world's biggest annual music fair, Midem, where we would meet up with the men from Magnet and, in turn, sign a deal for a Stateside release with United Artists. We boarded the vessel, which was moored close to a small square, and were shown to our quarters – a two-berth cabin with no ship's cat to swing around. Still, Young and Moody's blossoming friendship regarded 'sleeping' as an afterthought: 'collapsing' seemed to be more in keeping with our joint mentality.

And off we went – in for a centime, in for a franc.

We dined at a restaurant in the company of various acquaintances, including publisher Terry Oates and his wife Mandy, then headed off to a huge bar in some hotel or other. The place was heaving with publishers, accountants, record executives, hangers-on and artists such as us, all making a concerted effort to get completely blitzed. Not the worst situation to find oneself in!

I was only halfway down my first drink when I became aware of somebody trying to catch my eye. I turned to face the object of my distraction and found myself looking into the smiling face of . . . Ian Hunter from Mott the Hoople? No, I didn't know Ian Hunter and this guy was somehow different.

He beckoned me to join him, which, out of a sense of curiosity, I did.

'Mr Moody, good to see you, my friend. Have some champagne!' He spoke in a German accent, though I was still none the wiser.

'Hello, er, how are you?' I responded with the rictus grin of a confused man.

He motioned towards a large man standing by his side: 'This is Zigi.' Zigi was none of the aforementioned movers and shakers. I'd come across enough heavies – or shall we say minders – in my time to recognise that look of emotional detachment. He broke off his gimlet gaze to nod his head slightly in my direction, like Grendel keeping one eye open for Beowulf.

'So what brings you here?' asked my mysterious German friend. I explained my purpose for the visit while racking my brain for a clue to his identity. Why I didn't just ask him outright who he was I'll never know – let's put it down to embarrassment and shyness. 'Come with me,' he said, and led me towards the toilets. There are only two reasons for a man to lead another man into a toilet area: to take part in some devious sexual activity or to chop out a line. Thankfully, he chose to do the latter. It would be another thirty minutes before his identity was revealed.

After our second visit to the gents, the mystery man was replenishing the champagne glasses when the penny finally dropped.

'Ya, I miss the Zoom Club but I needed to move on, get another club,' stated our mystery man.

Any sense of anxiety I had about being in the company of a total stranger suddenly fell away and I gawped at him like the surprised subject on *This Is Your Life*. Was this really the same Cooky Dahl who used to look like a model from a Pringle golf-wear catalogue? I was now in the company of a man whose recent transformation from Vince Hill to Ian Hunter was staggering to say the least.

'When was the last time you played at the Zoom?' he enquired.

'Oh, let me think, Cooky. Yes, Cooky, with Snafu back in 1974, I think, Cooky.'

Our noses twitched in unison. I continued to get loaded free of charge and, when Bob and David announced that they were leaving, I brushed them away with a slurred, 'See you back there soon.' Two hours later, I staggered into the early dawn and hailed a passing cab.

'Where to?' asked the cabbie, a doleful man whose looks were redolent of the cemetery.

'The cream-coloured boat, you know, Billy Gaff's,' was all I could muster. He stared at me then gesticulated with his arm, sweeping it in a semi-circular motion across the harbour where a neatly moored armada of several hundred yachts awaited my selection.

'You have a large choice, monsieur,' he answered dryly. My glazed eyes followed his sweep. 'Yes,' I thought. 'A bloody large choice.'

By now, my body was entering the first stages of self-induced toxicity, the cab driver was in no apparent mood for sympathy and I had no fucking idea where I was going. It was looking like the beach for me when, from somewhere in my subconscious, an image of a small clock tower appeared. I made a gesture with my hand that might or might not have suggested the probability of height, before offering my impersonation of a public clock: 'Tic-toc-tic-toc – Boing! Boing! Boing!' My cabbie – a man who looked like he'd been buffeted by life's travails – took on the expression of a man who'd suddenly found himself in the company of an intoxicated lunatic within the close confines of his own car. 'Clock tower, clock tower!' I shouted excitedly. His eyes widened then softened as his instinct for survival recognised my cod-vaudeville attempts to point him in the right direction. 'Ah, ze clock tower – *oui, voilà!*'

The following evening, after an afternoon in the recovery position – i.e. horizontal – we met up with Roger Glover and headed for the sumptuous clifftop villa that Magnet Records had rented for the duration. Once inside, we were greeted by representatives from the record company, who showed us to the bar. Oh, well, if we must. From there we headed for the terrace to enjoy the panoramic view of Cannes. From such a vantage point, one could observe the events that would unfold as the evening wore on: prospective diners looking forward to some fine French fare, businessmen with their attaché cases, drinkers swaying from one bar to another and inebriated fools searching for their boats. Soon after, we were introduced to Artie Mogul, the president of United Artists Records – a big fish in that morally polluted ocean known as the music business. After the usual pleasantries and small talk, we signed the contract that would secure Bob and me a release in the USA – a potentially big step forward for brand Young and Moody.

Also at the gathering was another new Magnet signing: Chris Rea, an old friend from Middlesbrough who I hadn't seen since his demo session at Island Studios two or three years before. And the 'Isn't it a small world?' section was completed by his manager, John McCoy, who I'd worked with in Tramline back in the late 1960s – all in all, a splendid gathering! Naturally, the partying didn't stop there and, later that night, we headed once more for the bars of Cannes, where the absence of Cooky Dahl meant that I had to rely on others to supplement the extortionate prices that were being charged for drinks.

The next morning, as the Mediterranean sun blasted down through our unopened porthole and into the airless pit where we lay, the recumbent mess that was Bob Young looked across from his bunk and uttered the immortal line, 'Would you happen to have a teaspoon so I can prise the tongue off the roof of my mouth?'

CHAPTER 19

STUDIO FEVER

David Coverdale's first solo outing – entitled *White Snake* after a song we'd written together in Wartaweil – was released in some territories in February but, due to issues with the powers that be, its British release was delayed until April. David decided to soldier on and it was back to the somewhat chillier shores of Lake Ammersee to assist with the follow-up. The writing and pre-production went so well that a call was made and a studio was booked. Within weeks, we were settling into studio two at London's Air Studios, which was situated atop an imposing building, which in turn looked down commandingly over Oxford Circus. Top o' the world, Ma! Tim Hinkley was back in the keyboards chair, but the rhythm section this time was a far cry from the reserved DeLisle Harper and boy wonder Simon Phillips. Behind the kit this time was a true veteran of British rock, the former Sounds Incorporated, Jeff Beck and May Blitz drummer, Tony Newman. And on bass, one of my favourite players, Alan Spenner.

On the first day, we were set up and ready to record by 1pm but there was a slight hitch: producer Roger Glover was attending the celebratory playback of the album he'd just produced for Judas Priest. We waited patiently, eschewing the bottle of brandy that was perched invitingly by the control desk. Even the notorious Mr Newman, a man with a, shall we say, large than life personality (that preceded him in all directions), was noticeably subdued. A little after 7pm, the studio door burst open and a red-nosed Roger, obviously the worse for drink, stumbled in. ''Ello, lads. More champagne – put it on my tab, ha, ha, ha!'

Tony Newman's eyes widened before taking on a demonic gleam. Then, with a sardonic grin, he announced, 'Oh, it's one of those albums, is it? Pass the brandy!'

The incident set a precedent for the rest of the sessions and, although Roger sought to restore his credibility, it was rock 'n' roll city all the way! Not that Roger minded: he enjoyed a good time as much as the next man and the music didn't suffer as a result of this. However, with Tony at the helm, Hinkley and Spenner bringing up the rear, and me and Coverdale offering as much encouragement as we could muster, studio two would be no place for the squeamish. We slipped into a natural routine: run through and record the songs in a sensible, professional manner sometime between noon and 10pm with the aid of spliffs, coffee and an early-evening imbiber and/or toot; start to feel the effects of studio lag; and then decide to call it a day and finish off whatever stimulant we'd been drawn to. It was at this point that Tony would come into his own, which, in retrospect, was like being entertained by Al Murray's creation, the Pub Landlord, only fifty times more excessive. His own particular 'mind and matter' test stipulated that if you couldn't walk in a straight line and say 'bunny rabbit' unimpeded, you should go home. If you could, have one for the road and head off round the corner to the Speakeasy Club and continue indulging until unable to carry on.

Alan didn't always make it to the 'Speak'. He seemed to have an additional clause in his agenda that probably involved the use of downers, and some nights we'd have to call for a cab to take him home.

After one particular session, we were readying ourselves for the short walk to the Speakeasy when the tape operator popped his head round the studio door and asked us to come to the reception area. The sight that greeted us was not a pretty one. Poor Alan Spenner was lying spread-eagled on his back with an embarrassing stain around the crotch of his jeans. Further investigation showed that he was comatose and had indeed pissed himself. We tried to kick-start him but he was having none of it. 'Go-sleep, go-sleep,' is the most that we got from him and, bearing in mind that most of those present were not exactly in a state to qualify for a medical licence, we took the executive decision to help him into the studio and bed him down for the night. Earlier that day, Roger had taken delivery of an Oberheim polyphonic synthesiser, and the large cardboard box that had housed it was of a size comparable to Alan's dimensions. We padded it out as best we could with cushions and, with a collective effort, managed to get him inside, taking care to lay him on his side in case he might vomit.

We returned at noon the following day and he was still in

it! We finally managed to rouse him with the help of strong black coffee, and guided him to the gents to freshen up before continuing with the recording.

Alan was a lovely guy who never had a bad word to say about anyone. I went to see the reformed Kokomo at the beginning of the 1990s and Alan greeted me with that huge grin of his, but during the performance he seemed uneasy and distant. It was shortly after that I heard of his passing from a heart attack. What a bloody waste. Rest easy, Alan. You've been sadly missed.

In April, as the *Young & Moody* album was about to be unleashed on an unsuspecting public, David flew in from Germany to do the rounds of press interviews and found himself in the paradoxical position of promoting an album while putting the finishing touches to the follow-up. Writing in *Sounds*, Geoff Barton started off by making a comparison with other solo releases from within the Deep Purple camp before airing his own views:

And now, along comes David Coverdale's *White Snake*, an album perhaps destined for less trumpet blowing and dancing-in-the-streets than is usually the case with a solo effort of this type.

Why? Several reasons, I suppose. First off, the release of an LP by a one-time Purple member is hardly a novelty any more – although *White Snake* was recorded way back in mid-1976 it's taken until now to find its way on to British record racks and a whole lot of water has passed under the bridge between times. Second, David Coverdale was not a member of the classic Deep Purple line up and as such is still tagged with the label 'Ian Gillan replacement'. Dumb, I know, but when it suits them, fans can have disturbingly long memories. Third, Coverdale has no plans to tour the country to promote this album, at least not for the immediate future. Fourth . . . oh, to hell with it. You get the message – there's a chance that *White Snake* may not receive the attention it deserves. Which would be oh so wrong.

'I don't wanna scream no more,' Coverdale said shortly after Deep Purple had smoked on the water for the last time – and shortly afterwards, he dashed into the studios and recorded *White Snake*, releasing his frustrations on nine highly varied tracks. Nine tracks where he can strut his stuff minus inhibitions and – lo and behold – actually *sing*.

No 'Wooaayeahyeahs' here, just an intelligent, pleasing selection of songs, good-time rock 'n' rollers such as 'Lady' running hand-in-hand with the afro rhythmic 'Celebration' and the balladic 'Peace Lovin' Man'.

Highspots come in the forms of 'Blindman' a lurching, loping, Free-like number and 'Goldie's Place', mean and sleazy, the red lights glaring bright.

Lyrically and musically excellent – Coverdale's band includes Mick Moody on guitar and powerhouse drummer Simon Phillips – this album comes as a pleasant surprise, and reveals facets of the vocalist's talent that were never really allowed to surface with Purple.

There are duff moments, of course – 'Hole in the Sky', *not* the Black Sabbath tune, is rather tedious and deadly ponderous at times, for example – but for the most part *White Snake* bares its fangs and bites down.

The Air recordings were finalised at the end of April, beginning of May at Musicland studios in the suburbs of Munich – an established favourite within the Deep Purple camp. On my return to the UK, I headed for the Manor studios to take part in the recording of Graham Bonnett's first solo album. I considered myself lucky to get in on this one as the producer, Pip Williams, was an excellent guitarist in his own right. The fact that David Oddie was Graham's manager and mentor may have swayed things my way, methinks. Noted session man Dave Markee was handling the bass duties (make a note of that session man) and we got on like a house on fire – a joint smoker-in-crime with a likeable nature. I also got to play with ex-King Crimson drummer Mike Giles – a true English eccentric – and keyboard virtuoso Tony Hymas, a man with the kind of wry humour that always does it for me.

Graham was a sweetie: down to earth and modest with a daft sense of humour, which also did it for me. Another enjoyable experience, and, as Muddy Waters was wont to say, 'Things was clickin', man!' This statement brings to mind the positive outlook of partially-sighted Norman Johnson, a white, middle-class blues singer from Lemon County, California, whose major miss, 'Squeeze My Orange 'til the Juice Runs Down My Blender' failed to deter him from a life of tranquillity and well-being. When his health deteriorated, he sank into a taciturn demeanour, which his wife later described as 'like a Trappist monk with laryngitis'.

As the *Young & Moody* album hit the reviewers' desks in advance of its official release, I headed off to Chipping Norton Studios to play on Gerry Rafferty's first solo recording. It was at this point that my lifestyle, coupled with inner conflicts relating to my personal life, finally caught up with me. After months of constant work and reckless living, the quiet, laid-back, rural atmosphere of Oxfordshire brought me down to earth with a large bump. The first thing I noticed (apart from the peaceful surroundings) was a difficulty in tuning up correctly – something I'd never had a problem with before – and an inability to concentrate on the matters at hand. Together with a stomach ache and a case of the shakes, the growing paranoia that was now starting to take hold was further exacerbated by the presence of such esteemed company – the prodigious talents of former Joe Cocker, keyboard player Tommy Ayres, highly rated drummer Henry Spinetti and bassist Gary Taylor, who'd been a member of the Herd and Fox. At the end of the first day, I confessed to producer Hugh Murphy that I was unable to continue. Both he and Gerry were gracious in their concern for my health, though this didn't compensate for my own disappointment at missing out on a very musical experience. More disappointingly, I never got to play on a future classic, 'Baker Street'.

The *Melody Maker* singles reviewer, Caroline Coon, brought a certain amount of cheer with her headline review of Young and Moody's newly released single, 'Chicago Blue'. Under the heading 'The sidemen who came in from the cold', she showered us with the kind of praise we all like to hear:

It's great when hardworking sidemen come in from the cold. I've not had the pleasure of meeting the Moody half of this duo, but one of the pleasant bonuses of going to a Status Quo concert is the sight and sound of Bob Young. He has written songs for the band, looked after their personal business for years, played harmonica and generally added to the earthy, unpretentious level-headedness of their persona.

Now we find that Bob's singing is as good as everything else about him. Mick's guitar is indeed remarkable. Combined, they've created a very English Country Music sound – casual, expansive and sensitive, but rock hard.

The song, with a beautiful arrangement, is a slow burner which becomes more appealing with every spin. I especially like the line 'how beautiful you are, especially when the lights are off. . .' Now is that a compliment or not? The outstanding single of the week.

A hit.

Naturally, there was a certain amount of jubilation from all concerned, though in reality it was just one person's point of view. However, Magnet Records sent out flyers to its retail outlets that proclaimed, 'A new album by Young and Moody destined to set your cash tills ringing!' It also revealed that the campaign was backed by ads in *Melody Maker*, *Sounds*, *NME* and *Record Mirror*, as well as extensive radio advertising, and advised any interested parties to 'STOCK UP NOW WITH YOUNG AND MOODY.' The adverts in question revealed that, 'Something made Bob Young, the other member of Status Quo and co-writer of many of their hits, and Mick Moody of Juicy Lucy and Snafu, one of the most sought-after session men in the world, get together with Roger Glover of Deep Purple. That something is "Young and Moody".' Next to a picture of the album cover is a quote from Roger, which reads, 'The happiest album I have ever been involved with.'

From the stories I'd heard about ego clashes in the Deep Purple camp, it must have been the equivalent of escaping the sexual advances of Hillary Clinton in favour of a 'come to my hotel room' invite from Michelle Pfeiffer.

Such was Roger's enthusiasm for *Young & Moody* that he arranged for our first cover version – a reworking of 'Close Your Eyes' – on his next production, an album for ex-Playboy bunny, Barbie Benton. Apparently, Barbie had appeared in an episode of *McCloud* and had wowed them in Sweden, prompting Playboy Records to turn our bunny girl into a country singer. She brought her own steel-guitar player to the sessions, where an all-star band of Simon Phillips, Tony Hymas and Graham Preskett provided the main ingredients while no doubt wondering what the hell they were doing in such an environment, apart from earning money. I was kindly invited to supply the guitar parts for a couple of tracks, including the above-mentioned, which, when you've co-written the original song *and* guitar part is, er, relatively easy. Barbie was a cute li'l thang from the button-nosed School of Mostly Physical Attributes, USA, who had a distracting habit of bending down and touching her toes during the session. Although this particular manoeuvre suitably enhanced her pert *derrière*, it cut no ice with Tony, to whom artistic endeavour meant much more than having a nice arse. His grimaces of distaste were a picture of absolute disgust, prompting the rest of us to bite our lips in order to avoid a fit of the giggles.

The *Young & Moody* album was receiving favourable reviews in the music press and even the country-music writers had taken a shine to us. Pete Smith at *Country Music Roundup* started his article with, 'I was beginning to think I'd never hear it! A British country/rock outfit beating the yanks at their own game.' His review continued in the same vein and he named it his album of the month. Although it was nice to gain praise from 'Britain's Number One Country Music Paper', the fear of ending up onstage at some 'chaps an' spurs' event sponsored by a home-improvement centre in Nuneaton was never far from my thoughts. Throughout this maelstrom of activity, Bob and I spent a lot of our free time together, writing, being silly (great fun!), drinking and getting stoned. Magnet Records was already making enquiries about the next record and we wasted no time in preparing it. Roger was eagerly anticipating the event and made some inroads regarding slightly bigger studios. Mind you, most studios were slightly bigger than Central Recorders, if not a lot bigger.

Magnet took out more ads in the music press in the form of praiseworthy quotes from the aforementioned reviews, including a rather nice personal commendation from Mr Coverdale. We also undertook a short tour of radio stations to help promote the album, with stopovers at places like Blackburn and Sheffield. Being a non-driver, it was left to Bob to point the car in the right direction. After one particularly heavy night on the booze, Bob had to pull over onto the hard shoulder of the M6 motorway for five minutes while he tried to regroup his brain cells into an order that discouraged waves of nausea, dizzy spells and projectile vomiting. Author Philip Norman coined the title *The Road Goes On Forever*, but Young and Moody added an appropriate subtitle: 'But Sometimes You've Gotta Stop Before You Smash into the Back of a Lorry.'

In a markedly fitter state, the tried and tested team of Young, Moody, Glover, Preskett and Stannard went back into the studio with the addition of Dave Markee on bass. This time we found ourselves at the renowned Sound Techniques studio in Chelsea, where, back in the 1960s, such names as the

Yardbirds, the Who, Pink Floyd, Elton John and Jethro Tull had laid down tracks. From the early 1970s, it had earned itself a worldwide reputation for capturing the sounds of British folk and folk-rock artists such as Fairport Convention, Nick Drake and Sandy Denny among others. We'd been writing on and off since the last album and had eleven complete songs to throw at the other guys. As per usual, the wacky baccy was never far from hand and the vibe in the studio was certainly conducive to making sweet music and having an enjoyable time. And we did. We even brought in the marvellous Henry Spinetti and his drums to beef up two or three of the tracks.

Sadly for Elvis Presley, nothing would be happening for him. I was visiting a lady friend in Munich when I heard the news of his untimely death. Another bloody waste.

Unfortunately, the men at Magnet Records were not impressed with the result of our recording sessions, claiming it was 'far too eclectic for Magnet Records'. Naturally, we were all disappointed but, personally, I was far from distraught; there was so much going on at the time, you just moved on. In 1970s speak, it was all part of life's rich tapestry, or, as they'd say today, the zeitgeist.

Hindsight is a marvellous thing but foresight is a gift bestowed upon the smarter souls among us . . . though, sadly, not in this case. Years later, some of the tracks were released on a Young and Moody compilation, so it wasn't a totally wasted exercise.

CHAPTER 20

HEROES AND DYLANS

We arrived at Ian and Jacky Paice's beautiful house near Henley in a semi-inebriated state, which was pretty much par for the course at the time. David had been invited to a party the Paices were hosting and, for some long-forgotten reason, I found myself heading up the M4 in a car driven by Willy Fyffe, in the company of Mud's drummer, Dave Mount. An odd combination, you might say, but Willy had been working with Mud and found that he and Dave had things in common – namely having a few bevvies and a good laugh. We'd assembled at the Sun Inn in Barnes for 'liveners' before heading to a Chinese restaurant, where, from a table situated next to George Best and his companion, we enjoyed a sake-soaked meal. Once we'd crossed the threshold at chez Paice, we gratefully accepted the offers of large vodkas and tonic, and mingled with the throng. We'd been carrying that throng around for days and felt it was high time it was mingled. A couple of hours later, Dave Mount had cornered both Ian and Bad Company's drummer, Simon Kirk, and was trying to convince them that they should get together the next day and record a version of the 1960s instrumental hit 'Wipeout'.

'Just imagine the three of us bashing away together while someone like Jeff Beck plays guitar. Da da da da da da da da, da da da da da da da da, bum, bum, bum bum boooom! It'll be fantastic!' The expressions on the faces of Messrs Paice and Kirk suggested otherwise.

Meanwhile, I'd been waffling on to Jon Lord, though I think the only decipherable word he caught was 'brandy' because ten minutes later, while I was trying to focus on the billiard balls, he appeared at my side with a bottle.

'I've just been down to the cellar and brought this up especially for you,' he announced proudly. I closed one eye and, with much squinting and moving of the head, managed to decipher that it was some form of glass receptacle.

'Great,' I replied, before taking the bottle from Jon's hand. Removing the stopper, I took a generous swig before plonking it down on the billiard table. After the initial shock, Jon grabbed the ONE HUNDRED-YEAR-OLD BOTTLE OF NAPOLEON COGNAC and quickly removed it from the immediate vicinity.

When it became *really* apparent that his vehicular companions were beyond help, Willy bundled us into the back of the car and set off for home. We got as far as Barnes in south-west London before he was pulled over by the police.

'Now then, can you tell me where you've been this evening?' asked the larger of the two officers.

'Oh, we've been to a party and just I'm dropping these

two off home,' replied Willy, gesturing to the back seat. The copper craned his head slightly to get a better view.

'There doesn't seem to be anyone in the back seat,' he responded suspiciously.

'Well, there was ten minutes ago because I heard somebody moaning the opening sequence to "Wipeout",' confirmed Willy.

The copper opened the back door to discover the comatose forms of Mount and Moody sprawled on the floor between the seats like the unfortunate victims of a sarin gas attack.

'Perhaps you'd better get them home as soon as possible,' he concluded.

Tim Hinkley's 'Heroes' was a who's who of hip musicians, some of them household names, who hung out and made music with the irrepressible keyboard player. His aim was to present a brotherhood of performers who shared a common ground in rhythm and blues and a natural enthusiasm for having a good time. From its inception in 1976 through to the end of 1977, Hinkley's Heroes would see the likes of Eric Burdon, Roger Chapman and Mike Patto in the vocal spot, with Polly Palmer, Boz Burrell, Tim Bogart, John Halsey and Mitch Mitchell hovering in the flanks. A whole wash of guitarists were queuing up to take part and it was not uncommon for three of them to be onstage at the same time. Among the throng of string-benders were Jim Cregan, Henry McCullough, Mick Ralphs, Brian Robertson, Charlie Whitney, Bernie Holland and Bobby Tench. Throughout all the indulgences, madness and general chaos, those involved possessed a camaraderie that would remain unbroken through thick and thin, drink or drug.

Tim invited me to join in the festivities – replacing Henry

McCullough for a number of shows – in a line-up that featured former Jimi Hendrix drummer Mitch Mitchell, former Patto drummer John Halsey, ex-Jeff Beck singer and guitarist Bobby Tench, madcap fusion guitarist Bernie Holland and legendary bassist Tim Bogart. Singer/guitarist Isaac Guillory provided not only the support spot but the splitter van in which he was happy to drive us to and from gigs. And adding a sprinkling of extremely good vibes was roadie Larry Burgess, late of the now defunct Snafu, who smiled all through rehearsals with the dreamy physiognomy of the habitually stoned. Having come straight from the airport after a trip to Munich, I was only too happy to share my duty-free bottle of Rémy Martin with all and sundry. It was soon drained of its contents, which provided not only a healthy glow to the faces of the imbibers but a warm sense of inspiration.

The shows were centred on the university circuit, with a show at the infamous Golden Lion in Fulham, West London, thrown in for good measure. Apart from the obvious musical and social high spots, my most vivid recollections from the shows are a risqué a cappella version of 'Swing Low Sweet Chariot', complete with expressive gestures, and Mitch Mitchell's tap-dancing interlude. Fabulous stuff! On another occasion, Tim introduced Isaac as 'Tonight's special guest – Bob Dylan!' The new messiah for the night shuffled on to tumultuous applause as we launched into a pre-arranged Dylan-cum-Band version of 'The Weight'. The crowd loved it and shouted for more. Afterwards, we got loaded until we crashed out and I woke up with a sore head and another treasured memory.

Sitting in the backstage dressing room of a provincial university prior to a Hinkley's Heroes gig, various band members and crew mulled over the quality of the hash. Fact: for a nice sociable smoke, there was Lebanese red (Red Leb), Lebanese gold (Leb Gold) and Moroccan (Rocky). For a slightly stronger buzz, you could enjoy black from Pakistan (very pliable) and that no-nonsense stuff from Afghanistan. And let's not forget the notorious Nepalese temple ball. From personal experience, I acknowledged that a few too many brow-furrowing hits on the last could render one horizontally conspicuous for longer than originally planned. And then there was that oil that you could spread on to the Rizla paper before adding the tobacco. . . Just then, we were distracted from our ponderings by a cadaver-like man who was noticeably too old to be a student. Dressed in a coarse jute shirt, cut-off Oshkosh dungarees and inflatable plastic moon boots, he entered the room and was moving with some difficulty towards an available chair. He gazed bleary-eyed around the room with red-veined and virtually closed eyes, and started to babble incoherently about his current physical state and the advantages of medieval trepanning – a pathological attention-seeker if ever I saw one. I quickly came to the conclusion that he must have dwelled somewhere between the distant past and the local cuckoo's nest, then handed him a joint in the hope that he would soon return there. It seemed to do the trick.

After the first hit, he muttered 'Tempus fugit, baby!' then, with an ashen face and legs that seem to be taking their instructions from an alternative source, staggered out of the room.

Amid this madness, I received a call from former Juicy Lucy manager Nigel Thomas asking me to come along for a play with Boxer, a band put together by the incomparable singer Mike Patto. I'd known Mike since my days with Zoot Money back in 1970 and had great respect for him as a no-bullshit frontman who sang from the heart and always in the company of good players. He'd formed Boxer a year or two before and had felt that the original line-up was maybe a tad too self-indulgent, hence a proposed change of personnel. Looking back at this particular period, I suddenly found myself in the enviable position of being 'flavour of the month' in the popularity stakes. Modern parlance denotes this as 'up to the minute and desirable', and, if that's true, I don't think I've been there since! It was an impressive turnout: former Vanilla Fudge and Beck, Bogart and Appice bassist Tim Bogart; Chris Stainton from Joe Cocker and the Grease Band on keyboards; J.J. Cale's drummer Jimmy Karstein; and, of course, Mike on vocals. I recall that we had an inspired jam session, which was hardly surprising given the talent in that room, spurred on by the presence of an impressed Richard Branson, who stood alongside Nigel wearing a huge grin and raving about the band's potential. He signed Boxer to his Virgin label the very next day, though I later declined the offer.

To alleviate his boredom between tours and recording – or as a possible means of escape from the nauseating strains of 'Save Your Kisses for Me' (a ditty which seemed to emanate from any functioning radio at the time) – Status Quo's drummer, John Coghlan, decided to put together a band featuring some of his musician mates. The emphasis was on fun and, with the incomparable Jackie Lynton on vocals and humorous interludes, there would be no shortage of that! John asked me to fill the lead guitar spot alongside singer-guitarist John Fiddler (late of Medicine Head), Pretty Things keyboard player Gordon Edwards, newly elected Quo member Andy Bown on bass, keyboards and guitar, and Bob Young on harmonica, backing vocals and general good vibes.

We played to a packed house at the Marquee, where, in the middle of the set, John brought out his one-time drum tutor, Lloyd Ryan (who was resplendent in full evening dress), for a pupil/teacher head-on drum feature. Though somewhat out of context, it proved to be entertaining and John got to show his teacher what he could do. I'm sure he was impressed.

'Two silver stars, lad, and get your bloody hair cut!'

After our disappointingly short stint prior to Juicy Lucy's demise, it felt good to be working with Frankie Miller again. A truly great singer, he'd built up a solid following in the UK with bands that had, over a relatively short period, included Henry McCullough, Chrissy Stewart, keyboard player Mick Weaver and guitarist Ray Minhinnett. I was invited to join his band, and was privileged to be part of the impressive group of musicians which made up the latest incarnation of Full House: Procol Harum drummer B.J. Wilson; former Ace singer, keyboard player and composer of 'How Long', Paul Carrack; Chrissy Stewart on bass; and a brass section consisting of my old Juicy Lucy bandmate Chris Mercer on tenor sax and Martin Drover on trumpet. An interesting itinerary informed us that we would perform a handful of shows – including the Reading Festival – in England, and then fly to the United States for four or five shows in the Detroit area. This rather unusually short visit to the state of Michigan may well have been the result of the mutual admiration that existed between Frankie and local lad Bob Seger, who, having achieved success with 'The Fire Down Below', had acknowledged Frankie's 'Ain't Got No Money' as a major influence on the song. He would later record a version of the latter in a show of gratitude, leaving Frankie to reciprocate by performing a medley of the two songs in his live show.

Prior to Frankie's Anglo-American tour, I took a French lady I'd befriended out to dinner and, in good old 1970s style, ended up back at her place in her rather nice boudoir. Things were going rather well when, just as we'd progressed to that point of absolute submission, she let out a harrowing cry and burst into tears.

'Bloody hell, what's wrong with you?' I asked, somewhat surprised.

'I'm so unhappy with my life. I've got some Valiums in the bathroom cabinet and I'm going to take them all!' she replied with as much despair as she could muster.

'No, you won't. I'm going to flush them down the toilet – right now!' I concluded.

I leaped from the bed and, although somewhat hindered by my state of, by now, semi-arousal, managed to get to the bathroom, rummage around the cabinet and find the potentially life-threatening medication. However sensitive I was to her over-emotional outburst, I quickly concluded that this was more of a *cri de coeur* than a threat of impending death and, moreover, that the Valium would be put to much better use in the hands of a sensible abuser than an over-emotional Gaul. So on the way back to the bedroom, I slipped them into my coat pocket and got back into bed where, after a short period of reconciliation, we carried on where we'd left off.

'Who did you fly here with?'

'Apart from the band, I don't know. The rest were complete strangers to me.'

The Stateside mini-tour got off to an inauspicious start due to the over-economical stance taken by Frankie's management regarding the travel arrangements – notably those offered by Laker Airways. A few weeks beforehand, Freddie Laker had introduced his long-haul, low-cost, no-frills 'Skytrain' service between London Gatwick and John F. Kennedy, New York. The company's initial offer was on a 'first come, first served' basis, which, while being beneficial to bakers and milkmen, was not necessarily the ideal scenario for musicians and insomniacs. And so, true to form, we found ourselves at the wrong end of the queue and consequently missed out on places for the flight. D'oh! The following day found us all at Heathrow boarding a scheduled, fully priced flight to Detroit, where we were picked up by the promoter and driven to the downtown branch of the Holiday Inn. Once we'd checked in, we headed for the bar, where we found ourselves in the company of various members of the Grateful Dead, though it could have been Hot Tuna, or the Phil Lesh Band, or the Bob Weir Group or . . . oh, who knows? They were good company, whoever they were.

The following day, we set out for our first show at a nice old theatre in the suburb of Royal Oak, on a bill that also featured fellow Brits Crawler. Originally Back Street Crawler until the untimely death of Paul Kossoff, the band now featured ex-If guitarist Geoff Whitehorn. Rumour had it that former Rolling Stone Mick Taylor had been offered the job originally but declined, citing that he didn't want to replace another guitarist who'd died. Peter Green was next, but he also refused the position as he was 'not ready to return to the stage'. Or anywhere else for quite a while, as it turned out. Geoff had no such disposition regarding the deceased or the demented, and seized the opportunity to establish himself firmly on the rock scene. He did cut a dash, adorned with a black Les Paul Custom guitar and a pair of trousers that seemed to have taken their inspiration from the kind worn by cinema commissionaires. Nice stripes, man! Backstage, the on-site catering was second to none and B.J. in particular was extremely pleased to find that a nice black hash from Pakistan was available on request.

Afterwards, we headed back to the cosy confines of the Holiday Inn bar, where Frankie decided that he fancied a 'carry-oot'. He was informed that a fried chicken and burger place was a half-mile walk away, which struck him as a practical way of both eating and exercising. However, downtown Detroit in 1977 was not a safe place to wander around at night. Like many American cities, the affluent had moved to the suburbs, leaving the once grand centres as ghettos and no-go areas. Undeterred, Frankie and one or two of the others set out on foot with the kind of bravado that the rest of us balked at, returning thirty minutes later with the self-satisfied grins of the brave and well-fed. The following afternoon, I was sitting in a hotel room talking to Paul Carrack when there were two or three distant cracks not dissimilar, one would imagine, to gunshots.

'Those two or three distant cracks were not dissimilar to gunshots,' remarked Paul.

'One would imagine so,' I responded.

We scanned the surrounding landscape (now mostly parking lots) from the window, but were unable to discern any form of heightened activity, so we returned to our conversation before readying ourselves for that night's show.

The following day, I was perusing the local newspaper when my attention was drawn to a small headline: 'WOMAN SHOOTS SON DEAD OVER CADILLAC KEYS.' The location given was two blocks from the hotel at the exact time we heard the shots. I would be giving the chicken burger a miss that night too.

We drove the sixty miles from Detroit to Toledo, Ohio for a concert supporting local Michigan heroes Brownsville Station, best known for their hit 'Smokin' in the Boys' Room'. What a strange-looking bunch they were: one appeared to be wearing ballet tights, Ronald McDonald's shoes and Buddy Holly's glasses, while another one's genetic make-up seemed to have bequeathed him the unfortunate combination of Max Wall's head and Ronnie Corbett's body. I waited with bated breath for his version of Max's song, 'The Boy with the Impeccable Feet', but it never materialised. The poor guy was somewhat vertically challenged and was, allegedly, very superstitious. Consequently, he always avoided walking under a black cat. Meanwhile, the drummer had settled for an animal-skin adornment in the style favoured by Tarzan, offset by a fetching dog collar. They weren't a bad band though, in the 'kick-ass' style of rock, and treated the audience to a performance of their latest single, 'Martian Rock'. Yes, these lads were definitely on a planet of their own, Mars or otherwise.

Browsing the many-channelled TV, I came to the conclusion that American sport was shit. What's so clever and entertaining about basketball when the average height of the players is seven and a half feet and the baskets are only marginally higher? They should try using midgets – it would be far more interesting. Baseball? We call it rounders, and it's a children's game. And American football is a convoluted imitation of our noble game of rugby, where real men don't wear crash helmets and body armour. Pah!

On our final day in Detroit, I came face to face with the salient features of a true legend – Colonel Saunders, the alleged creator of the world-famous Kentucky Fried Chicken, who was checking out of the Holiday Inn at the same time as us. He looked as immaculate as he did in the famous logo – all silver hair and white clothes – and put even Bobby Harrison to shame in the 'picture of perfection' stakes.

Just what *did* he think of the Brits and the Grateful Dead-heads?

Back home in England, there was a phone call from David Coverdale, who was eager to get a new band up and running and planned to hold auditions as soon as I'd wound up with Frankie. I met up with David in London's West End and, after a meal and an alcoholic top-up at the Ship public house, we headed the few yards down Wardour Street to a private drinking club called La Chasse. Entrance was gained by throwing a coin up at the first-floor window and waiting for your presence to be detected; this could sometimes mean three or four well aimed shots before the face of a raving Irish barman called Frank appeared at the window, acknowledged the entrant as a suitable candidate for alcoholic oblivion, and then sent someone down to open the door.

The place was about the size of an average semi-detached house's through-lounge, and was always filled with cigarette smoke. Closing times could vary and were usually heralded by Frank's commanding call of 'Everybody out!' The only requirement needed to undertake this particular manoeuvre was the ability to walk down the stairs, open the door and pass through it. Given the rampant rate of indulgence, it was no surprise to find that not everybody was successful, especially if you'd settled in at the small bar with the likes of Crawler's Rabbit Bundrick and Terry Slesser-Wilson, Frankie Miller and roadies of notoriety such as Jack McGill, Baz Ward and a guy called Mike, who always drank from a glass boot.

HEROES AND DYLANS

I would sometimes run into former Family and Streetwalkers guitarist and songwriter Charlie Whitney on my nocturnal carousals, and always enjoyed his personal greeting of 'What's your racket?!' What a character – when it came to drinking, there were no grey areas with this man. He seemed to abide by a 'feast or famine' rule, whereby his choice for the evening was either one small Martini or lots of anything. One night at La Chasse, he was helping out behind the bar and, on my entrance, immediately suggested I try one of his own concoctions, the curiously named Hopalong Cassidy. Having agreed to sample his wares, one could only look on open-mouthed as he proceeded to travel from left to right along the optics, stopping at regular intervals to disperse a generous amount from the chosen bottle. Having already made an enthusiastic start to the proceedings at the Ship, it required only one Hopalong Cassidy to render me nine-tenths unconscious, with just enough life force in my unsuspecting body to allow me to slither down the stairs, crawl out of the door and collapse in the gutter. After thirty minutes – and with some help from a passing Samaritan – I'd recovered sufficiently to hail a cab, and a kindly – albeit wary – driver drove me home.

The following morning, nursing a hangover of apocalyptic proportions, I decided that, in future, I'd be better off taking my chances with Japanese fugu fish.

Somehow, amid this sometimes bohemian existence, I still managed to listen to some great music. The Crusaders with Larry Carlton on guitar always did it for me; in fact, anything that featured Carlton – notably Steely Dan's *Royal Scam* – was as good as it got as far as I was concerned. Little Feat, with Lowell George still in charge, were as cool as the proverbial cucumber, *Wired* by Jeff Beck was still on the turntable and the rejuvenated Doobie Brothers with Michael McDonald and Jeff 'Skunk' Baxter were an exciting prospect. I liked the gutsy, funky stuff spearheaded by Sly Stone, Larry Graham, and the Meters, and the roots music coming from Ry Cooder and Taj Mahal. And let's not forget the jazz-fusion of *Heavy Weather* by Weather Report, featuring the outrageous bass playing of Jaco Pastorius. Then there was rock, bluegrass, crossover bluegrass, Cajun, blues, progressive folk and . . . hell, loads more! Honestly, we were spoiled for choice.

Frankie Miller's Full House started its nineteen-date British tour on 10 November 1977 at Coventry's Lanchester Polytechnic, supported by Meal Ticket, a band who'd opened for Bob Seger and the Silver Bullet Band a short while before. What an incestuous little business! What next – Brownsville Station opening for Meal Ticket? Bob Seger's Full House? On 1 December, Frankie and Full House played a London date at the Rainbow in Finsbury Park, and after the show I was pleased to see Bernie Marsden with David. I'd known Bernie since the early 1970s and, during the intervening years, we'd crossed paths at various motorway service stations en route to and from gigs. He'd been part of the Deep Purple off-shoot, Paice Ashton Lord, whose attempts at super-stardom had floundered. The three of us retired to the Speakeasy, where we had a bonding session of such positivity that the idea of a twin-guitar line-up for David's new band became more than just an idea – it became a reality.

Within days, auditions were being planned and a piece of rock history was about to bear fruit.

Putting a hard rock band together in 1977 was more a

labour of love than an everyday occurrence. Although the punk phenomenon had already entered into its passé stage, the popularity of bands like the Jam, the Clash, the Stranglers, the Boomtown Rats, Talking Heads, Television and Elvis Costello had been instrumental in introducing 'new wave' to an eager public. Thankfully, new rock acts like Foreigner had helped create a 'new rock wave' of classic-vocal/guitar-led outfits, and evergreens such as Z.Z. Top, the Allman Brothers, Joe Walsh and Led Zeppelin proved to be an inspiration in such transitional times.

Despite all this transition, I managed to work on some new songs with Bob Young and played on a few session dates, which included the debut album from the aptly named Chanter Sisters. And for a spot of 'quality time', there was always the TV. *Roots* was a fictional twelve-part series about the history of a black American family, and centred around a character with the unforgettable name of Kunta Kinte. I would eventually refer to him as Kunty Kinty and this suspect moniker would be put to best effect when delivered in a Birmingham accent. Throughout such levity, I was sensible enough to stick to the five-a-day diet. Pints, that is.

Early December in the old industrial part of Islington, north London, was far from an attractive proposition, but E-Zee Hire rehearsal studios was one of *the* places for professional rock bands to get their act together. David, Bernie and I were about to take the first musical steps towards David's rock 'n' roll vision in the company of Chrissy Stewart and drummer John Shearer. Chrissy was my first choice for the bass spot, though there was little chance of him leaving Frankie Miller's funky set-up to join what would essentially turn out to be a hard rock band. Shearer had been recommended to David as an extrovert technician who had, reputedly, 'the biggest drum kit in the world'. Well, I must say, when Mr Shearer removed his drums from their cases, it looked like a miniaturised version of a large oil refinery squatting self-assuredly on the dilapidated carpet of studio two. Once this village of percussion had been erected, we had a play, and, though time has put the kibosh on any particular memories, Shearer obviously failed to impress as, the next day, another drummer was in evidence. There's obviously some truth in the old adage: 'It's not the size of the boat, it's the motion of the ocean.'

Chrissy and Paul Carrack played together at some point and Tim Hinkley also dropped in to have a blow. We had fun and some great music ensued, but it was obvious that David's musical direction was at odds with that favoured by those particular guys. After the session, Paul took us to see some friends of his who lived nearby to smoke a few sociable spliffs. The hosts owned a German shepherd dog by the name of Satan, which prompted David to remark (in his own inimitable fashion), 'Have you taken him out for some exorcise?'

We persevered in the company of drummer (and Cozy Powell lookalike) Dave Potts, having endured the rudimentary and vastly inexperienced bass-playing efforts of some chancer who'd obviously blagged his way in with the intention of cutting a musical swathe through lesser mortals. Far too eager to impress, he failed miserably. And he looked so out of shape he must have felt like Proteus after a fortnight in Benidorm. We were awaiting the appearance of another bassist when we received a phone call to say that he was unable to make it. Rather than cutting short the allotted time given to Dave Potts, Bernie suggested bringing in a bass-player friend of his who lived nearby to help out and, fifteen minutes later, a studious-looking chap called Neil Murray entered the equation. Having trodden the boards with the likes of National Health, Cozy Powell's Hammer and John Hiseman's Coliseum, Neil was no stranger to holding his own in the company of the kind of people who took no prisoners. And not only did he rise to the occasion, he impressed everyone to such a degree that he was asked back to accompany ex-Chapman-Whitney Streetwalkers drummer Dave Dowle soon after.

A day or two later, we had our rhythm section and we adjourned for Christmas and New Year secure in the knowledge that, once a suitable keyboard player was found, we would have our band.

Due to David's prior commitments regarding press interviews and a tour of radio stations to promote his new solo album, which had been entitled *Northwinds*, our quest for the right keyboard player was delayed. However, a series of live dates was being lined up in the form of low-key venues, which David referred to as the Back to the Roots tour and would serve to promote both David's album and the new band. It was mid-February before we resumed rehearsals, this time a couple of hundred yards down Market Road at the Dickensian-sounding Halligan and Heape. This presented us with a larger room and the friendly face of manager Jack McCulloch, the elder brother of former Thunderclap Newman and Wings guitarist, Jimmy. A handful of keyboard players stand out in my memory, most notably ex-Sensational Alex Harvey Band's Hugh McKenna, Montana Red, Tony Ashton and Brian Johnston. McKenna was a seasoned pro and an obvious contender, but it was difficult to gauge his appeal as he spent most of the time soloing on a small synthesiser. Montana Red turned up in a small van with Montana Red emblazoned on its sides, which led some of us to believe it may have had other connotations.

'The name might have been on it when he bought it,' remarked Bernie. 'It could have been worse – Eric Jones the Plumber would have been a terrible stage name.'

'Montana Red's not his real name,' I countered. 'It's Montana Smith!'

He was wearing a flat cap similar to the one worn by Harold Steptoe, which evoked, in certain individuals, the need to utter Harold's well-known catchphrase, 'You dirty old man!' whenever possible.

Tony Ashton was an old bandmate of Bernie's from back in the Paice Ashton Lord days, and both David and I had enjoyed nights on the town with him. I think he only popped in for a blow, as hard rock 'n' roll was never really Tony's thing. In the end, the keyboard spot went to an amiable Scotsman called Brian Johnston – an experienced player who'd worked with Dave Dowle in Streetwalkers.

Such turns of events put me in mind of a quote from Mahatma Crapington's book *The Scourge of the Loft Conversion: Height Rage and the Compulsion to Displace Roof Tiles*: 'Let not the least lose, for the water pressure of life will enlighten the fingers of destiny.'

CHAPTER 21

THE SNAKE'S FIRST BITE

Prior to rehearsals for the Back to the Roots tour, we'd assemble at the White Horse pub in Market Road, an establishment managed by a local character called Joe Hitchcock, a former champion darts player. After a few visits, we learned that, during the 1950s and 1960s, he'd earned a reputation as a formidable showman, hosting exhibition matches in which he employed novel appendages like coins and bottle-tops. Such items would be placed on a volunteer's ear or nose and then noisily removed by one swift throw of Joe's dart! Another original trick of his was to place a cigarette in the participant's mouth, step back to the oche, then, with the deadly accuracy of an Amazonian warrior, pitch a six-inch nail at said cigarette. There is no evidence of him ever causing any injury, and his consistency within the dart-throwing fraternity would eventually earn him plaudits such as 'The Demon of the Dartboard' and 'Treble Twenty Wizard'. In short, he was the first ever darts superstar, revered by thousands, a legend in his own time. By the time our paths crossed, he was already an old man, shuffling with some difficulty around his pub in old carpet slippers.

'Hey, Lally, Davey and the boys are in! Nice bit of York ham for your lunch, lads?' Crawler had been rehearsing at E-Zee Hire one week, which prompted Joe to keep us in the loop: 'We 'ad them Crawlers in the other day. They like their beer . . . and my York ham!'

David Coverdale's Whitesnake made its debut at Lincoln Technical College on 3 March 1978 to an almost capacity audience of about two hundred people. Right from the start, there was a great camaraderie within the band and no ulterior motive other than to go out and enjoy ourselves – which we did. Quintessential rock 'n' roll! We heard later that the place would have been besieged, but a lot people thought that it was a hoax: a recent member of Deep Purple would never consider performing at such a venue. Well, compared to a Purple show, this was more like a humility fest – just the lads getting out there and doing it. We did it again the following night at the Leas Cliff Hall in Folkestone, and the following night at the fabled Lafayette Club in Wolverhampton, where another ex-Purple man, Ian Paice, was conspicuous by his presence. David had jokingly referred to Paice Ashton Lord as Plaice, Haddock and Cod, so I found it difficult to keep a straight face after the gig when we chatted to Ian. Images of fish swimming to and fro around a giant drum kit kept appearing before my eyes, so I legged it back to the dressing room for a beer.

A few days later, we headed to the north-eastern seaside resort of Scarborough to entertain the patrons of the Penthouse Club. We checked into a hotel close to the promenade and, prior to the gig, were joined in the bar by Geoff Barton from *Sounds* and Robbie Dennis and Berni Kilmartin from our record company, EMI. Robbie informed us that he was holding the EMI expense account, whereupon the bull and the red rag were reunited. The orders came firing in from all directions like an amphetamine-enhanced cattle auction:

'Large brandy and coke.'

'Large brandy.'

'Pint of best.'

'Pint of Pils.'

'Large vodka and tonic.'

'Half of shandy.'

The place suddenly fell silent as we looked round to see which despicable member of our entourage had committed such a heinous crime. A half of shandy? Our stares fell like one huge unblinking eye upon a little old man who'd somehow become entwined in our party at the bar and who now looked about him with a certain amount of apprehension in his rheumy eyes. Once the misunderstanding had registered, we continued where we'd left off.

'Pint of Guinness with a Jameson's top. And a half of shandy for our mate.'

'Whiskey and dry.'

'Gin and tonic.'

We hit the stage an hour or so later with a particular kind of confidence that comes from professional experience and rather large amounts of hastily drunk alcohol.

Towards the end of the set, I caught sight of our tour manager, Ossie Hoppe, leaning on the bar chatting to a young lady with long dark hair. From where I was standing – or possibly swaying – she looked rather nice and, when the last chord of the night had been put to bed with the obligatory drum crash, I put down my guitar, leaped from the low stage and positioned myself between her and a startled Ossie.

I looked her straight in the eye. 'You're nice – are you a gypsy?'

She smiled, and then shook her head slightly. 'Not that I know of. Are you?'

There must have been the thought of Belgian-born gypsy guitarist Django Reinhardt flashing quickly through my mind because I answered, 'Yes, from Belgium. My name's Tom.' I heard Ossie snort before he walked off in the direction of the band room to inform the others that I'd assumed a new identity.

'You sound like a northerner,' she replied, giving me a quizzical look.

'I'm from northern Belgium,' was the best I could offer. 'Would you like to come back to the hotel and drink some red wine, like us gypsies do?'

'Good idea,' she said with a smile, and off we went. Back at the hotel, we encountered the night porter.

'Red wine for us gypsies, please,' I requested.

'We've only got bottled Guinness at this time of the night,' he countered lugubriously.

'All right, that'll do. Four bottles,' I said. 'And a packet of *Gitanes*.'

He shot me a look that spoke volumes. Volumes on the behaviour of drunken tossers. We took possession of our bottled Guinness and headed to my room, leaving everyone else to savour the night porter's stout supply, though I recall that dressing-room brandy was doing the rounds too.

The following morning – or more likely lunchtime – we gathered in the foyer for our short drive to Harrogate, with some of us looking rather the worse for wear. My little Rose Lee had departed earlier with the confused air of an honourable Romany to take her place back in the real world. Willy Fyffe gave me a knowing smile and raised his eyebrows.

'Successful night then?' he teased.

'Oh, marvellous. Three times!' I answered, with the unconvincing braggadocio of the truly hungover. Such a questionable statement was a cue for David to let loose with one of his expressive laughs before declaring, 'Belgian Tom's Hat Trick!' while another voice intoned, 'Yeah, three strokes, more like!'

The young lady in question turned up at a gig in Doncaster a couple of weeks later, where, after a pretty convincing show of affection, she proceeded to canoodle with some bloke during the show. Wrong. It didn't take too long for me to get a post-show message to her via Ossie – knob off, you trollop. Ten minutes later, Ossie appeared in the dressing room to inform me that Loopy Lou was locked in a ladies' toilet threatening to slash her wrists with a nail file. Great – there's nothing like finishing off a good night by trying to persuade a nutter with Munchausen Syndrome not to do anything rash. Much to the relief of the bouncer, we managed to persuade her to come out, and I did the gentlemanly thing: took her to the hotel bar and plied her with drink until she passed out. Mission accomplished, I helped her to my room, put her to bed and slept on the floor. The amendment to my little black book was instantaneous.

In the minibus to Harrogate, I sat back and waited for my brain cells to recover and listened to the surrounding banter.

David and Bernie: both intelligent guys with a natural sense of humour; Willy: always up for a laugh but with genuine loyalty and sincerity; Dave: a bundle of energy with slightly more youth on his side than the rest of us; Neil: quiet and sensible with a great head for detail; and Brian: the amiable Scotsman who liked a sociable drink or ten. I made a quick synopsis: great singer, excellent musicians, decent chaps one and all. Evocatively, my thoughts stretched back to my erstwhile school mates grafting away in the steelworks, factories and offices back in Middlesbrough, and I concluded that life was pretty good! We bypassed a Yorkshire town which had been tarnished by the sins of its forefathers, ruthless individuals who'd sanctioned the building of blocks of flats in the brutalist style of the early 1960s: characterless, charmless and utterly desperate, testaments to the greed cultivated by shameless architects, crooked councillors and heartless builders. Put your foot down, Willy, and take us away from this blight on the landscape.

When we arrived at PJs club in Harrogate, we found the road crew sitting in the truck outside the venue.

'Fucking stage is too small. Can't get the PA system on it,' growled a disgruntled roadie.

'Well, at least you don't have to carry the gear in,' stated a voice from our bus. I mentally reviewed the final line in my synopsis of the band: great singer, excellent musicians, decent chaps one and all . . . and with a refreshingly positive and optimistic outlook.

Most of the venues on the Back to the Roots Tour were small but we averaged audiences of around three hundred and fifty. However, we drew 1,500 people to our London show at the Music Machine, which broke the previous attendance record. In the audience (or at the bar) were Thin Lizzy's Brian Robertson, bass player Jimmy Bain and Bernie and Neil's former bandmate Don Airey. Cozy Powell showed up at Basingstoke Tech and, after a show in Doncaster, we found ourselves in the same hotel as Brian Clough and his Nottingham Forest team. We played the Coatham Bowl, Redcar, to a sell-out crowd of 850. The following day, the *Evening Gazette* started off their news piece with, 'When Saltburn rock singer Dave Coverdale returned to his old stomping ground, the Coatham Bowl was bursting at the seams.' And one fan reported that 'hundreds of people stood at the front. Other people had to stand on chairs to get a glimpse of the band.' By the end of the tour, we'd had four more shows cancelled: three due to problems David was having with his voice and another due to an undersized stage. We'd also dumped Brian Johnston, whose playing lacked the dynamic range that was required, plus some of his after-gig alcohol-induced verbal ramblings were irksome and sometimes too tedious to take.

Geoff Barton travelled to Scarborough to review the gig:

The first thing you notice as the band squeezes on to the small stage at Scarborough Penthouse is that David Coverdale still *projects*. Much, much larger than life, like he's making his comeback in a 100,000 capacity astrodome rather than a sweaty, sleazy little club (where long hair, denims and flares still hold sway) in a town on the Yorkshire coast. Consequently, his stage personality is overwhelming, his charisma is immense . . . and you get the feeling that you're witnessing the beginning of something just a little bit special.

David Coverdale's Whitesnake are still a young,

inexperienced outfit, but the potential is there, everywhere you look. Mick Moody and Bernie Marsden convince totally in their roles as twin guitarists; Neil Murray, away from the complex confines of Coliseum 11 and National Health ('At last I'm playing with my heart, not my head') is a joy to watch on bass, his spread-fingered hand speeding up and down the neck like a scuttling spider; Dave Dowell [sic] impresses on drums; and keyboardist Brian Johnston plays a Jon Lord role with style and panache, even though he's hardly been in the band long enough to catch his breath.

And Coverdale . . . well, I'd almost forgotten what a dynamic singer and performer he is. Unlike his *Northwinds* album (reviewed elsewhere in the paper), tonight we were treated to a whole host of up-tempo numbers. Purple songs 'Lady Luck' (introduced solemnly as 'A song that Tommy and me wrote'), 'Mistreated' and 'Lady Double Dealer' amongst them. Indeed, the version of 'Mistreated' (and here's where I incur the wrath of thousands of readers) was far superior to Richie Blackmore's Rainbow rendition. *Believe* me.

Other tunes included 'Only My Soul' and 'Breakdown' (both off the new LP), Bobby Bland's 'Ain't No Love in the Heart of the City', an off-the-cuff blues-breaking boogie instrumental entitled 'Breathalyser', an improvisation for the second encore that included snatches of 'Rock Me Baby' and 'You Shook Me'. . .

It was a short set (at the moment, Whitesnake don't know many songs), rough and ragged at times (due both to malfunctioning monitors and lack of rehearsal) . . . but even if they'd only played *one* song the inherent greatness of David Coverdale's new outfit couldn't possibly have gone by unnoticed.

Go see 'em and you'll just have to agree. No doubt about it.

On 7 April we went into good old Central Sound to cut a four-track EP as a kind of taste of things to come. A couple of days before, I'd treated myself to a 1953 Gibson Les Paul 'Gold Top' model, in its original state, for £600; within a couple of weeks, in an effort to improve the sound, I'd had the pick-ups removed, rerouted and replaced with modern 'Humbuckers'. While this *did* improve the sound, it would eventually reduce its value when sold as a vintage instrument. When I came to sell it in 2009, its condition was far from pristine as well, but I still made a handsome profit. Its new owner, Richie Sambora from Bon Jovi, was, I believe, very happy with his new acquisition.

Now bereft of a keyboard player, I suggested my former Snafu colleague Pete Solley as a suitable replacement for the recording and, given Pete's faultless musicianship, was hardly surprised that he did a good job. David and Bernie had written the perfect opening song for the stage act, 'Come On', and, together with David's rockingly risqué 'Bloody Mary', we also cut another band original, the slide-fuelled 'Steal Away'. This was a natural progression from the Snafu track 'Lock and Key' and featured Dave Dowle's syn-drum interlude, an effect that added almost a touch of disco to the proceedings, though we preferred to think of it as a touch of fusion. The record was completed by a song that David had originally played to me in Bavaria during the preparations for *Northwinds*, the plaintive blues that Bobby Bland had put on the map – 'Ain't No Love in the Heart of the City'. By way of injecting a bit of originality into the tune, I borrowed John Lennon's simple but memorable riff from 'Come Together' and tailored it to suit the song.

It was good to be back at Central Sound, and Willy soon commandeered one corner of the control room to set up a mini-green-room-style table of brandy, beer and a few soft drinks. Sociable-strength hash was in evidence, usually by way of yours truly, and the camaraderie seemed to grow stronger as the tracks took shape. The icing on the cake was the inclusion of legendary producer/engineer Martin Birch, a man with strong character and an impish sense of humour. Perfect!

It's no secret that back then a lot of people were taking Valium to help them relax and, eventually, sleep. Rock musicians were prime candidates considering the lifestyle they lived, and at least three of us in the band were partial to popping the odd one or two. At the time, there was a doctor in Harley Street who'd earned himself a reputation as a man who understood the needs and musts of the habitual night owls. Sitting in his waiting room could be a bit like being in the Speakeasy minus the bar and music. I remember leaving his surgery one particular afternoon with a prescription for one hundred blue Valium (10mg strength – i.e. the strongest available) plus a repeat script for another hundred. And I only went there to have my ears syringed! Having made my way to the nearest dispensing chemist, I wasted no time in processing my script, and a few minutes later I was treating myself to an 'early-doors' tranquiliser.

By the time I got off the tube at Fulham Broadway, it felt as though I was encased in cotton wool, 100 per cent carefree and ready for almost anything (as long it could be done from a seated or sprawled position).

You had to treat these and other 'downers' with respect though, especially if coupled with alcohol, or you could find yourself in trouble. Once you'd gone over the limit, the effects could range from irrational behaviour to death, depending on the amount pro rata of pills and booze consumed. I once observed someone who was out of his head on brandy and Valium attempting to gain entrance to his flat; it was like watching a frostbite victim trying to open a deck chair with a spoon. Thankfully, the unlucky ones were few and far between as most indulgers chose the one-or-the-other method, thus giving the mythical sandman a good opportunity to sprinkle the sand of sleep into the eyes of the needy.

The band rehearsed for a couple of days to give Pete Solley a chance to learn the set. Although he wasn't a contracted member of the band, Pete had agreed to add keyboards to the new album and join us for the forthcoming gigs. On 25 April 1978 we played to 700 people at the modern Reading Hexagon, from where John Mahoney of *Record Mirror* gave us a praiseworthy review. David's relationship with Ritchie Blackmore was, allegedly, far from rosy, so it was rather ironic that, having lauded the quality of my slide guitar solo, he rounded off the paragraph with, 'I thought he resembled and played like Ritchie Blackmore in every way possible.' His reaction to our performance was extremely positive. Even minor ailments couldn't stop us: 'Coverdale, despite having a cold, was the focal point on stage with his dynamic antics, friendliness towards the audience and, of course, his gift of ceaseless vocal energy that gave every song guts and sheer power.' Dave Dowle came in for compliments too: 'I cannot ever recall seeing a drummer work up such a sweat on one number than Dave Dowle did on this one ['Come On']; he was brilliant.'

The following day, things were a little less taxing and we recorded a couple of songs for Capital Radio in London, after which we went our separate ways, domiciled to go home and practice (well, play along with some of our favourite records), go down the pub, possibly conduct a clandestine affair, create some new song routines then, er, go back to the pub and repeat at will. A week later, we hit the soundstage at the renowned Shepperton Film Studios to mime our way through all four songs from the *Snakebite* EP. The resulting film (cable TV didn't exist then) was to be used as a showcase for the band's talents, and was scheduled to hit the screens of the cinema circuit in its capacity as a promotional supplement to the main feature.

We rocked 800 people at the St Albans City Hall (where Bad Company's Mick Ralphs and Simon Kirk were in attendance), then drove afterwards to the Post House hotel in Leicester – where we managed to persuade the barman to stay open half the night – before heading off to the north-east the following day at the Ashington Regal. In the crowd that night was a local singer called Brian Johnson, who'd had a taste of success with a band called Geordie and was still waiting for his big break. As it turned out, he didn't have to wait too long.

Our promotional film, entitled *Snakebite*, was set to accompany a film called *Bilitis*, and band, crew and management were invited to the premiere at the ABC in Shaftesbury Avenue. It was to take place at midnight, and we were invited to a pre-viewing soirée at the Belgravia abode of the band's manager, John Coletta, where we were joined by Don Airey and a relative of one of the assembled – a shifty-looking individual who was later seen helping himself to the contents of the silver cutlery draw.

We wasted no time imbibing most of our host's alcohol supply then headed off to the cinema in a convoy of high-spirited expectancy. We watched our performance with both delight and amusement; Neil appeared on the screen miming along to Bernie's backing vocals, which impelled Don to laugh out loud and remark, 'Neil, you've sold out!' At one point, it exaggerated the dimensions of my expensive fedora. This prompted David to yell out, 'He looks like a Belgian nun!' There was much guffawing, and guitar tech Steve Payne's laugh was particularly manic. The main feature was a pretentious French romantic affair, all soft focus and white lace, which was described as 'the coming of age of a boarding-school teenager on the verge of a full erotic awakening'. No it wasn't, it was soft porn! A poncey art film that we refused to take seriously. Pretty soon our shouts of 'Cor, look at the jugs on that!' and 'Go on, my son. She's gagging for it!' had reduced the respected confines of the former Saville Theatre to a flea-pit in Toxteth. Behind us, the director and representatives from the film company were tut-tutting into their cravats.

We had an album to make and, to prepare ourselves more fully for the impending recording sessions, David, Bernie and myself agreed to spend some time together to pool our musical ideas. By way of the local jungle telegraph, the band's management directed us to their local newsagent, which had a basement room for hire, and once inside we found ourselves negotiating the rickety stairs. It was an austere setting, which provided us with not only a brace of chairs but also an overwhelming smell of cat urine. As Bernie set off in search of another chair and a can of air freshener, David christened our *place de l'inspiration* Cat Piss Studios. It's with credit to our enthusiasm and fortitude that, within days, we had rough

CHAPTER 22

OH, LORD! THE TROUBLE WE'RE IN!

Enthusiastic social drinking was by now an almost daily occurrence, and, if I wasn't in the company of the band, I'd usually end up in a pub with Willy or one of the many willing participants in the grand game of Getting Gradually Pissed. We always drank more than was good for us but were hardly in the Ernest Hemingway league, though, in all fairness, he probably didn't skin up a spliff or two for a nightcap. Interestingly, when Hemingway reflected on his hard-drinking days, he said that he wished he'd gone through the good times stone cold sober so he could have remembered everything. Then, on further reflection, he added that, if he had, the times probably wouldn't have been worth remembering. Personally – and from what I've read about the man – I think these remarks were either self-deprecating or else he was looking for an excuse to cushion his behaviour. Or maybe booze provided him with just the right amount of Dutch courage necessary to take part in the First World War as well as the Spanish Civil War, tussle with potentially life-threatening giant fish, take part in African safaris and write a book that earned him the Nobel Prize in Literature. Whatever his excuse, I'm glad he enjoyed a good drink because he bloody deserved it!

For a long time, my maxim was: 'Never trust a man who doesn't drink.' Later on, having been made aware of the misery and distress that's sometimes associated with the stuff, I settled on a slightly mellower outlook on life: 'You can always get the measure of a man by the shoes he wears.'

When we appeared on *Top of the Pops* to promote our single, 'Bloody Mary', we were already ensconced in Central Sound laying down tracks for our debut album. The *Snakebite* EP had been released and the initial press coverage appeared in the 3 June edition of the trade rag *Music Week*, which devoted a whole page to it, with one half displaying an EMI-placed advert announcing, 'Snakebite's gonna leave its mark in the charts.' The remainder was devoted to a David Coverdale-Geoff Barton interview in which Barton's praise was almost too good to be true. The following week, his employers at *Sounds* featured another record-company-sponsored ad that declared in big bold lettering, 'THERE'S NO SERUM FOR COVERDALE'S SNAKEBITE.' Emerging from the soundproofed confines of our windowless environment, we performed at the Alkmaar Festival in Holland and took part in a BBC Paris Theatre radio recording. This was followed a few days later by an appearance at London's Lyceum where, like the Music Machine, we drew an estimated fifteen hundred people. A week later, we travelled to Birmingham's ATV television studios to record a version of 'Lie Down' for a new rock show called *Revolver*.

Returning to London in our hired coach, we were only a few miles north of the infamous Blue Boar service station when we were flagged down by a representative of our management. It appeared that there had been a technical problem regarding my recorded guitar sound, which in turn had reduced its tonal qualities to that of an elementary banjo player. I returned forthwith to register my annoyance before righting the wrongs of the ridiculed.

From within the limited pile of crumpled cuttings that serves as my press archive, I have retrieved a small review (of unknown origin) for the *Snakebite* EP which proves that not everybody in the music press was enamoured by our creative output: 'Another four-tracker, this time from ex-Deep Purple man Coverdale. Absolutely run-of-the-mill fodder with grimacing guitar breaks. Mix Free, Purple and the Stones and then white-wash. Functional music. Picture cover: white vinyl.' Hopefully, he didn't throw his *gratis* copy away in disgust as they're worth money nowadays.

From out of the blue, there came something of a very positive note (cue heraldic trumpet holding a confident semibreve). Jon Lord was joining David Coverdale's Whitesnake! David had spoken at length to him regarding the chances of a permanent position behind the keyboard, whereby Jon had enthused about the band's rhythm-and-blues roots, the premeditated lack of Deep Purple influences and the down-to-earth attitude within the fold. Bingo! And though our time working with Pete Solley was sadly cut short, let's face it: players of Jon's pedigree are as rare as rocking-horse shit. To celebrate his joining, Whitesnake dropped the 'David Coverdale's' prefix and the Lord spoketh: 'Excellent – I'm looking forward to this!'

Jon spent five days at Central Sound replacing Pete's

overdubs with his own, then joined the band for a three-day rehearsal to familiarise himself with the band prior to joining in with the rest of us mime artists to perform 'Bloody Mary' on ZDF TV in Germany.

During a brief hiatus prior to the onset of Whitesnake's first major tour, we went our separate ways and, apart from telephone contact, saw little of each other. However, we did gather at photographer Fin Costello's studio for a session that produced the back cover shot for the forthcoming album. Alternative poses for publicity purposes were also undertaken, including standing up, sitting down and, after a prompt from Fin, standing at a sideways angle. The session culminated with a pose that featured one sitting down, three standing and two standing at a sideways angle. Those two great virtues – mischief and silliness – were never far from hand, thus providing the recipients with images of men apparently happy in their work.

We also filled out questionnaires for press handouts, which resulted in the kind of things I used to mull over in magazines when I was a young pop fan. Nothing had changed: 'Name, Date of Birth, Town of Birth, Favourite Food, Favourite Film,' etc. Bernie provided the best reply: question – 'Biggest Fear in Life'; answer – 'Joining Yes'. Being a non-driver, the best I could muster for 'Favourite Car' was 'Jon Lord's'. Jon had a lovely Rolls-Royce Phantom in which he would coast to rehearsals with his keyboard technician Stuart Wickes. Rumour had it that he once donned a chauffeur's cap and drove Stuart – comfortably ensconced in the back seat reading the *Daily Telegraph* – to a Deep Purple rehearsal. Sometimes Stuart would take the wheel himself, though, personally, I would have thought twice about letting a roadie ride my bicycle.

Trouble was released to coincide with the tour, and the ubiquitous Mr Barton was first off the mark in the typewriter stakes, citing that the most dominant musical style on the album was jazz-rock. Yes, 'Nighthawk' and the incessant 'Free Flight' had struck a chord – or should I say riff – with him and, in his view, this 'particularly metallicised version [of Whitesnake] was undeniably due to the efforts of bassist Neil Murray'. He had a point. Neil and Bernie were well into that particular musical genre at the time, though two tracks out of ten hardly qualified Whitesnake's overall musical style to be deemed 'jazz-rock'. Then the predictable Deep Purple comparisons:

> Other than this jazz stuff, we have the usual macho lyrics and David Coverdale bellowing them out over raucous DP retreads (although Whitesnake will never be able to recreate raw Purple power, they do their 'damndest' on such rabble-rousing tracks as 'Don't Mess With Me' – and their 'damndest' is quite often enough).

'Trouble' and 'Love to Keep You Warm' are described as 'shoulders-back, lip-pouting, Free-style strutters' and 'Lie Down' as 'an unpretentious, but rousing singalong', whereas 'Day Tripper' is a 'slow and loping, [an] altogether rather neat rendition'. And good ol' 'Belgian Tom's Hat Trick' was 'available on album at last'. His lasting impression was one of optimism that the next album would find its direction, and, with the inclusion of Jon Lord and another track like 'Ain't No Love in the Heart of the City', 'we could be in for a real treat'.

Meanwhile, oblivious to the opinions of the press and the peripheral yet necessary input provided by management and agencies, we knuckled down to the real thing and rehearsed, in readiness to support that famous cliché: 'Who does not love wine, women and song, remains a fool his whole life long.' And though we were pretty *au fait* with most of the song part and were particular devotees of alcohol, the remainder was equal to, if not more important than, any lyric, chord sequence or bottle of brandy. Irrespective of their standing (or other positions, come to that), and be they wives, girlfriends or casual acquaintances, it was the women who provided us with our life-blood and inspiration. And judging by the audiences on the 'Roots' tour, this band attracted a healthy proportion of girls. The chicks came to rock and the intense bearded men stayed away in droves – what a result! Two days before our first major tour, we performed live to the camera men, floor managers and Annie Nightingale at the BBC's Wood Lane soundstage that was *The Old Grey Whistle Test*. This was not the most stimulating of settings, but the camaraderie shone through and 'Trouble' and 'Lie Down' hit the spot.

A couple of days later – on 26 October 1978 to be precise – we celebrated our rapid ascent from clubs to concert halls by performing the initial show of our first major tour at the City Hall, Newcastle.

That mixed air of excitement and tension peculiar to any first night hovered around the backstage area as people prepared themselves for the big moment. Roadies and technicians had busied themselves with last-minute checks and preparations as we readied ourselves to leave the hotel, accompanied by local lad and *Sounds* scribe Phil Sutcliffe, our guest critic for the evening. A couple of weeks later, Sutcliffe's observations would be published under the title of 'Viper Trails', where, after a brief resume about Deep Purple's demise, Whitesnake's beginnings and the welcome inclusion of Jon Lord, he slipped comfortably into 'fly on the wall' mode: 'Seven o'clock and Coverdale is wracked with nerves (as he never was in the last days of Deep Purple). He wanted to be alone, paced his room, came down to the bar after all: "Why do I always die a thousand deaths before I go on?" No answers.'

The unspoken and obvious answer was to have a drink with the rest of us, which he did. This band exuded a strong camaraderie, which was based on mutual respect and equality, though Sutcliffe may have been somewhat off the mark when he stated that the members of Whitesnake were 'all on strictly equal shares'. If he was referring to the financial side of things (which I presume he was), this was never as cut and dried as he may have perceived, and, as far as I was aware, Bernie, Neil, Duck and yours truly were, allegedly, on 'strictly equal shares' in the form of a weekly retainer, though. . . Oh, hang on a minute, the image of a faceless individual has just appeared in my mind's eye wearing a large hat bearing the titles 'Editor, Publisher and Legal Representative', and has formed a mouth bubble that reads, 'Move on, lad, move on!' So I'll hand you back to the capable quill of Mr Sutcliffe, whose written record of that night recalls many happy memories:

We all piled into the coach for the half-mile drive to the Newcastle City Hall and reassembled in the spacious dressing room area. Moody took his black hat out of his elegant white box (a quality titfer this – £28 worth), withdrew to a side room with Marsden and began to boogie. Pretty soon Lord emerged and said: 'It's like a bar in South Carolina through there.' Neil Murray sat practicing while reading the Melody Maker. Coverdale was pacing again as Magnum finished their set: 'I'd like to have gone out there and clocked them but I can't because of the crowd thing. I have to be foetal, a new birth every time. Like that?'

Our wordsmith in evidence was more than kind in his review but singled out two songs that 'elevated hot and sweaty entertainment to the magic of minor miracle.' Under David's guidance and powerful vocal delivery, these two beauties would soon evolve into *tours de force* in our live performances. Now, on with the show:

'Ain't No Love in the Heart of the City' (by Bobby Bland sidemen called Price and Walsh): A low moan of pleasure from the crowd at the taut, subdued guitar intro, a blue moan from Coverdale and then the song starts to swing low, heavy and gentle, always circling back to that hypnotic title line; Moody plays a beautiful solo all pain and strength, stoic; I suddenly realise just how young this audience is, mid-teens mostly, and I'm wondering whether such lived-in emotion can really mean much to them – when they tell me; Coverdale senses something as he, Moody and Marsden finish the unaccompanied middle chorus and he tells the band to stop . . . the crowd's voice rises as one to take the song while Coverdale stands at the edge of the stage, both imploring and appreciating; it's a moment of total sharing, spine-shivering, hair-on-end, tear ducts prickling, every comic trick your body can play on you in response to deep feelings; Coverdale stands stunned, wiping his cheeks with the back of his hand.

'Mistreated': the most astonishing line I've ever heard is Coverdale gathering into that bellow of 'I've been mistreated' that sort of passion that enabled Blind Boy Samson to pull down the Philistine temple; the song is magnificent and raw, an insight like an old master's painting of a butcher's shop, life as red meat; at the end Coverdale throws his head back and howls like a wolf and we roar at him; 'You like the blues? Of course you f***ing do – all northerners like the blues and don't we know it!'

Backstage after the show, emotions ran high. One of the road crew kissed Jon Lord, who called out to everybody that it was the best he'd felt in three years, since Ritchie Blackmore left Deep Purple. David was visibly moved by the whole thing and even stated that performing sometimes transcended sex. Jon was not convinced. 'You old tart!' he said with a laugh then, to all in earshot, declared, 'Years of planning couldn't have improved tonight. It was absolutely right, absolutely correct. I even kissed Micky Moody – I must be mad!'

Meanwhile, Bernie was caught up in an interview for a fanzine, where he said, 'This is *me*, the first time I've played the way I really am. Whitesnake is a loud band.'

Caught up in the momentum of the evening, we headed for a night club, where we indulged in a libation of justified proportions. And the last word from Phil Sutcliffe:

Later at a night club:

Lord (on his knees): David, will you marry me?

Coverdale: Well . . . we'll talk about it tomorrow on the road.

Oh, the humour, the humour! Willy Fyffe was a natural comedian, full stop, and Bernie wasn't far behind in that respect. David was blessed with a quick and clever wit, Jon cultured and urbane with a streak of silliness and Neil, though shy and reserved, could deliver a well-aimed one-liner when he was able to get a word in. In fact, David once said that being in a rock band was the only job where you could act like naughty schoolboys and get away with it! Sitting on the coach wearing a clown's mask with a cigarette up each nostril and waving at unsuspecting motorists gave credence to that particular sentiment. Another prank centred around that seemingly now-defunct practice which encouraged hotel guests to place their shoes outside their rooms on retiring for the night, secure in the knowledge that the night porter would remove them during their slumbers, polish them to a regimental finish and return them to their original position. Or so they thought.

While the night porter was attending to the drink-and-sandwich orders, one inebriated guitarist (of north-country stock) would be mixing and mismatching said footwear in an act of unsolicited mischief that would often bypass mere door-to-door redistribution and extend to placement on various other floors. The highest scores on the 'giggleometer' were usually attributed to extreme swaps – e.g. a direct exchange of size-ten Doc Martens for size-three stilettos. Such schoolboy *schadenfreude* would, in most cases, lead to an aggregated ball of early-morning confusion as guests scoured the corridors in search of their missing property, after first bollocking the unknowing desk clerk for employing a cretin to perform such a straightforward task. Whether this, in turn, led to confrontations and/or late professional appointments could only be surmised, as the perpetrator would be tucked up in a warm bed, oblivious to any such encounters. Tee hee, Plug, go and tell Smiffy!

Sometimes the silliness would take on a more spirited stance, though any rumbustious behaviour would always stop short of actual bodily harm or vandalism; TV sets were much more useful in their rooms than lying in a shattered state on the pavement below. I wasn't alone in this pursuit of irregular conduct or, as some would say, the 'rock 'n' roll crazies', a condition reputedly caused by overexposure to wild music and its effects on the mind! Bernie had his own grasp on madness which, in contrast to my instinctive practical-joker/piss-taker/acting-the-goat style, had a creative touch and a boundless energy attached to it. A good laugh was never far away! The two of us seemed to meld effortlessly into a developing double act that carried itself off stage and into the ensuing social setting, which would usually turn out to be the hotel bar (and corridors, in my case), night club or disco. Working with another lead guitarist requires equal measures of musical understanding, mutual respect and, in an improvised section, an almost telepathic gift of knowing what comes next.

The Marsden/Moody combination would continue to blossom for some time to come.

The audiences were consistent in their enthusiasm as only rock audiences can be, although the sight of so much hair, denim and leather every night could motivate my imagination to set forth some unusual alternatives: a hologram of the Tolpuddle Martyrs rushing the stage prior to their passage to a penal colony, for instance; or Our Lady of Fatima making a brief visitation to a group of peasant children close to the PA speakers. The real die-hard fans would sometimes wait at the stage door to bid us a final farewell:

'David, come back and see us again soon.'

'Don't worry, we won't forget you!'

'Great playing, Bernie. What year is your Gibson Les Paul?'

'Cheers, it's a 1959.'

'Micky, I loved the slide solo. Where do you get the hats from?'

'Harrods, twenty-eight quid!'

'Neil, did the Corinthians ever reply to Saint Paul's letters?'

'I believe so. When he was stationed in Esphesus, it's likely that he was in regular contact with his converts. I particularly liked his second letter, which referred to a previous effort that was largely misunderstood: "I wrote to you in an epistle not to company with fornicators."'

'Jon, great to see you back on stage. We love you.'

'Bless you.'

'Goodnight, Duck.'

'Goodnight.'

One night, after a show in the provinces, the band and crew were gathered in the bar of a down-to-earth hotel where the slightly harassed night porter was trying valiantly to cope with the demand for alcohol and food. Somebody suggested that we quicken the proceedings by raiding the kitchen and making our own sandwiches. Good idea! So we mounted a commando-style raid through the darkened and empty lounge, reached the partly lit kitchen area and prepared for the ensuing challenge. Our raider-in-chief slipped his hand through the door and switched on the overhead strip lighting. Suddenly, we were aware of a sizzling sound and rose up from our crouching position to find Bernie frying an egg! We collapsed in fits of laughter and somebody fell into an ice-cream freezer that Bernie had left open. Sadly, the night porter was alerted to our tomfoolery and closed the kitchen, though not the bar, thankfully. Sometime later, I retired to my room with my girlfriend at the time. I noticed that she had packed a pair of edible knickers in her case. Though somewhat inebriated, I grabbed them and managed to consume most of the gusset and part of the rump. By way of reciprocation, I proffered my worn-only-once Marks & Spencer briefs, but she gave me a quizzical look. Sadly, the paper underwear was insufficient sustenance and I was hungry again by 4am.

It wasn't all jolly japes and giant piss-ups; some had, shall we say, a more focused eye for the girls than others, but I'm not going to go into any of that. It was the 1970s, for God's sake.

It was a great feeling to be part of a twin-guitar-led band, especially as one of my all-time favourite bands was the Allman Brothers Band. 'Belgian Tom's Hat Trick' in particular gave Bernie and me a chance to duel to our hearts' content. And with guitars in mind, George Harrison turned up with Ian Paice at the New Theatre in Oxford, and afterwards the former Beatle was not slow in giving us his opinion.

'Noisy bastards! But I liked the slide solo,' he uttered with that unmistakable scouse drawl. Well, coming from a famous slide guitarist and an ex-Beatle, it was a compliment to be treasured.

The tour climaxed at the Hammersmith Odeon, where the show was recorded for posterity and, as we would soon learn, a Japanese release. Geoff Barton was in attendance and very much enjoyed the, er, first half of the show. In *Sounds* he wrote:

SNAKES AND LADDERS

After 'Mistreated', everything got self-indulgent with gratuitous solo spots and the evening lost its spark. Coverdale spent a lot of time off stage and when he came back he started shouting instead of singing . . . But what the hell. The first part was magical, for which we should be thankful. But if only Whitesnake could have managed to maintain that level of excitement *all the way through* . . . Ah well, with Jon Lord now with the band and with the ghost of Deep Purple gradually laid to rest (although some bozos still insisted on calling out for 'Child in Time' – Deep Purple are dead, won't they ever learn?) the future cannot hold anything but riches for Whitesnake.

Newcastle, Edinburgh, Glasgow, Brighton, Birmingham, Bournemouth, Hanley, Manchester, Ipswich, Portsmouth, Cardiff, Bristol, Oxford, Bath, Redcar, Liverpool, Leicester and London – in fact, all 31,650 of you – we had a great time!

CHAPTER 23

LIVE IN THE HEART OF EUROPE

Baden-Baden is a beautiful spa town in Germany's prosperous state of Baden-Wurttenburg: in short, a Teutonic Bath filled with lots of rich wrinklies. Hardly the setting for the fun-loving Whitesnakes, you might think – and rightly so. However, the marketing department at our record company EMI Electrola thought that an appearance on the *Pop 79* show would do us no harm at all. And the prospect of a two-night stay – bar and restaurant tab courtesy of EMI – was as enticing as they come, especially as we only had to mime our way through one song. Also on the show were Boney M and an incredibly straight-looking middle-aged man who must have had some kind of *in* with the show's director. He reminded me of the kind of entertainer you'd find at a second-rate night club in Yorkshire performing a song-and-dance act. Yet here he was on a bill with a big disco act and bunch of raving rockers; an ageing singer who made

Vince Hill look like Captain Beefheart, carrying a briefcase which bore one of those GB stickers you see on British cars driving abroad. He took no time in pointing out that those were his initials, so I can only assume that he was a George Barnes or a Geoff Black, though it could have been Gary Brown, or even Gerald Blenkinsop. Genuinely Boring would definitely have fitted the bill but, unless somebody has access to the TV company's archives, I guess we'll never know. Then again, anyone desperate or bored enough to want to scour the archives of some long-forgotten pop show in order to discover the identity of a non-entity in a Marks & Spencer golf sweater and grey slacks must be as daft as I am for dredging it up.

GB sang one of those awful, pseudo feel-good songs complete with a chorus that suggested we should 'Get it together, don't mind the weather, peace to the world, yeah, peace to the world,' a refrain that produced sniggers and lip-biting from the next act on – i.e. us.

Bobby from Boney M seemed like a bit of a lad – an observation that was soon confirmed when we he was spotted perched up in the lighting rig smoking a joint! After our bit, Bobby danced his way onto the stage, danced his way through the song, then danced off towards the dressing rooms. After the show, we wined and dined, then wined some more (courtesy of EMI), then headed for a club (probably the only one in that particular town), dragging along with us that somewhat reluctant custodian of the credit card, EMI Man. Not long after we'd secured a table with a dancefloor view, Bobby from Boney M sashayed past, threw us a wave, leaped into the air with a half-revolving twist and landed at the bar, where he ordered a drink and chatted to anybody within earshot. After a swift imbiber, he hoofed it back to the dancefloor, where he stayed for most of the evening.

Ten days later, we were back in a snow-covered Germany for a series of dates supporting those jovial jocks Nazareth, whose line-up had recently been augmented by former Sensational Alex Harvey Band guitarist Zal Cleminson. It was good to see the lads again: the last time, for me anyway, had been supporting them with Snafu. And recognising Zal was hardly a no-brainer as, like most people, I'd only seen him wearing a mad puppet outfit and white-face Pierrot make up. It was only through his appearance onstage in his civvies that we finally managed to get a look at the man behind the mask. This was a good package, and there seemed to be a fair amount of mutual respect between both acts. There was some good drinking done after the shows, where local clubs often played host to the boys in the bands and where moral compasses twitched alarmingly in all sorts of directions. By the end of the night, some of them had gone west and remained there.

Towards the end of the tour, we found ourselves in a TV studio on the outskirts of Munich, where we were required to mime our way through 'Lie Down (I Think I Love You)'. After a performance by a German band fronted by a singing gargoyle, the producer of the show, *Plattenküche* (which translated means 'Record Kitchen', as the studio was set out like a kitchen), beckoned us over to set up our stage positions next to a large dining table. He then requested that Jon play a schmaltzy piano intro over the presenter's introduction. I can only assume that this quirky bit of showmanship was meant to lend a slightly 'cooky' aspect to the proceedings. To be quite honest, it was shite, but that was their prerogative and, if the show helped to establish the band, mission accomplished.

As they say in Lancashire, 'It were a laugh!' And the laughs continued later at the Sugar Shack, Munich's best rock disco, where some of us took to the dancefloor in an uninhibited display of boogieing and improvised mating dances (some of which proved to be successful).

Back home, both David and Jon figured in the *Sounds* readers' poll, and Whitesnake performed at a successful sell-out concert at the Hammersmith Odeon in aid of the Gunner Nillson Charity Foundation. A week later, we became aware of the existence of one Mick Wall, whose arrogant, musically bigoted meanderings would, over the following years, crop up when you least expected them and pollute the air with an unwelcome presence, like dog shit on your shoe. Employed by *Sounds*, his 'review' of the Hammersmith show hovered somewhere between anarchy and deep-rooted nastiness: the kind of unpleasant views aired by one whose life has been soured by frustration, inadequacy and envy. The headline – 'A LOAD OF OLD COBRAS' – gave some indication of what to expect. Before he'd even started on the band, his spittle-infused bile was directed at the 'fat boys grinning hysterically, fantasy guitar heroes strung out on the frantic intensity of imaginary, fantastic guitar riffs . . . I swear we were sitting in some destitute pre-war amphitheatre peopled by desperate gonzo lemmings prepared to leap from the balcony come the climax to Micky Moody's first excruciatingly dramatic guitar solo.'

Ooh, what a charmer. After swiftly dissing the band's recording abilities and their immediate future, he turned his attention once more to his favourite guitarist: 'Moody will never play in a group of musicians as distinguished for their recordings as Procol Harum.'

Eh? Just what was he on?

Ad nauseum: 'And neither will Coverdale or Lord ever again re-live the mad, sometime glorious experience of multi-decibel rock that Deep Purple came to stand for.' Onto the scrap heap with them, then! Other ridiculous statements included, 'Coverdale is *not* a good singer. He's a powerful warbler, really a very average front man, and an unimaginative and abysmal songwriter.'

Further on, his ungoverned pen, bent and twisted with anger, cited a song, 'Losing You', a title which bore no resemblance to anything Whitesnake had recorded, as something 'with ridiculous vocal histrionics that held the audience transfixed', then admitted that the band were expert craftsmen who knew what worked best to move and excite an audience. Fair enough . . . oh, just a moment, the paragraph is still in motion . . . '"Belgian Tom's Hat Trick" must be a boring number to play . . . it's transformed, incredibly, into one of the major highlights of the set.' Next, it was Jon's turn for the chopping block: 'Jon Lord's Gothic keyboard somersaults [solo spot] are performed adequately, without the benefits of depth, real imagination or feeling. But, Goddamn, the kids lap it up.' His piece ends with him having to witness the sight of Whitesnake's triumphant finale, which, according to him, had the fat boys, the middle-class fawning axe heroes (ah, a leftie of course – surprise, surprise) and the lemmings vanishing by their hundreds.

In a nutshell, we were at the mercy of a man who had no idea what it felt like to be one part of a happy medium. Or a happy anything, come to that.

In their next edition, *Sounds* published the following letters:

[Dear Sir,]

I hope this is one of several letters you will receive about Mick Wall's 'review' of Whitesnake, for quite honestly I was shocked and outraged at the moronic, unfair and downright untrue comments contained in it. In short it was mindless garbage. It should never have been printed in the first place because Wall only saw half the gig. How can you write a balanced review if you haven't seen the whole concert? I'd like to give you a proper account of the proceedings.

I've no idea what Wall was talking about when he was giving us all this shit about Coverdale's voice lacking 'depth' and 'quality of phrasing'. What about 'Mistreated' and the enchanting 'Ain't No Love in the Heart of the City'; there was certainly no lack of conviction and sincerity in these songs. Micky Moody delighted us with some of his masterful slide playing to which both Coverdale and Bernie Marsden had a good freak out.

What's all this crap about 'Trouble' and 'Take Me With You' closing the set? Actually Michael dear boy, 'Trouble' was played towards the beginning and 'TMWY' was the second of three, not two, encores. If more proof is needed to show what a prat Mick Wall is, and how superb Whitesnake are, what about this: Jesus, a most discerning concert goer, was there and was merrily freaking out in the aisles, OK?

Oh, by the way, I just ignored silly, immature comments like 'Coverdale is not a good singer' and that he's a 'very average front-man' and 'an unimaginative and abysmal songwriter.' I think most intelligent people will realise how wrong all those statements are. Si, Stevenage.

PS Oh yes, what's this song called 'Losing You'? I have never heard it.

[Dear Sir,]

I would like to say what a prat Mick Wall is. His report on Whitesnake's concert of 3 March is the worst I've read in years. Not only did he call David Coverdale's singing average (it is brilliant), he also said he is a pretty bad songwriter. In my opinion *Northwinds* is one of the best albums ever released.

Furthermore he did not even know which order the songs came in and he even credited a song which has never been written. Has anybody heard of 'Losing You'? The only thing he got right was that the group will go places.

Martin Kennedy and Sarah Dickens, Stevenage, Herts.

We left Mick Wall to contemplate his egalitarian views on the *misère de vivre*.

Having experienced the often respectful, occasionally self-possessed and sometimes contentious opinions from ambitious young journalists (and Mick Wall), it was an honour to meet and spend some time in the company of one of the true gentlemen of the music press: *Melody Maker*'s editor-in-chief, Ray Coleman. Although Ray was of older stock – and, in our company, seemingly like a kindly uncle – he was a genuine lover of music with a natural regard for the positives in people. Joining the band for a one-off in Paris, he interviewed David and Jon for a *Melody Maker* piece headed 'WHITESNAKE: ON THE LADDER'. The reunification of Lord and Coverdale was an obvious topic.

DC: 'All I could offer Lordy, when he came back, was good music and the chance to get back to the roots after all that Hollywood-with-long-hair trip. . .' And the sourness of the alleged acrimonious relationship between Messrs Coverdale and Blackmore was touched upon.

DC: 'I think he's become the Frank Sinatra of rock 'n' roll. I think he believes his own press releases . . . he's an amazing staggering musician . . . his biggest problem is his attitude.'

In Ray's own words, 'If Coverdale is the heart of Whitesnake, Jon Lord is the lungs.'

JL: '. . .that slippery, fateful trip downwards, feeling sorry for myself, complemented by the fact that I had no money problems so didn't need to work . . . I had to go back on the road . . . I just had to get back and play small halls again.'

Although the attendance was somewhat slight for the spacious indoor Olympia Stadium, Ray enjoyed the gig and was very complimentary when the edition in question appeared in the newsagents a week or two later. After the show, in the snug confines of the hotel bar, the Moody-Marsden fraternity impressed him with their knowledge of beat groups of the 1960s – complete line-ups and instruments played!

CHAPTER 24

NOBODY EXPECTS THE SPANISH TOUR

The mid-afternoon temperature of 14° centigrade came as a bit of a shock as we disembarked at Valencia airport resplendent in our new quilted, fur-collared and personally inscribed tour jackets. In the arrivals hall, we were met by the promoter – a somewhat uncertain individual with a non-existent command of the English language. His interpreter – a doubtful man with the breath of an unemptied Korean-restaurant dustbin – led us to a parking space containing a small collection of Seat cars, which left us wondering if this was our chosen mode of transport or some sort of automobile club display alerting people to the dangers of non-roadworthy death traps.

So there we were, heading for our hotel in a micro-fleet of senior-citizen limos, with a night off to acclimatise ourselves before our opening show in Valencia. One of the other Seats overtook us and we could hear the operatic strains from an occupant in the back seat: 'Valencia, stick your head between your legs and whistle up your Barcelona!' Ha, ha! This was going to be fun and we'd be at the hotel in a few minutes.

Thirty minutes later, we were still riding in convoy on the sunlit motorway.

'Where's this bloody hotel then?' somebody intoned.

'Maybe they closed for a siesta and we have to drive around until they wake up and reopen it,' I responded.

The chortles that ensued were not in evidence twenty-five minutes later when, fidgeting with Arctic-strength tour jackets, we found our patience being severely tested. The driver of our car – an individual with some knowledge of our mother tongue – finally admitted that the town of Valencia was hosting some sort of business convention and that all the decent hotels were booked, hence our relocation to another town. Or possibly another *province*. We arrived at our hotel two hours later, picked up our room keys, and the beer drinkers among us went straight to the bar for a very large San Miguel.

The following afternoon, we assembled in the hotel foyer for the two-hour bloody journey back to Valencia, only to be informed by tour manager Ossie Hoppe that our truck had been delayed and that the concert had been rescheduled for the next day. There was a short period of disappointment and passive moaning before Ossie suggested that we utilise our energies into a game of football, under the pretence that a healthy kickabout would do us the world of good. Well, it would certainly keep the Tequila Sunrises and Marlboro Reds at bay for a while. Soon, the massed white legs of rock 'n' rollers were blinding the eyes of hotel staff and transient donkeys, and great footballing names like Coverdale, Marsden, Moody and Fyffe, together with the ace German centre-forward Hoppe, were pitched against other assorted madcaps and hangers-on. These included part-Spanish journalist Robert Mills who, having steadied his long dark hair with a headband, inspired me to christen him Tonto, a nickname which, unbeknown to him, would stand the test of time. It would eventually earn him a place in the Whitesnake Hall of Fun, Wind-ups and Piss-takes alongside a distinguished cast of promoters, agents, crew and musicians. The game was good fun, though short-lived for those among us whose regular excursions into late nights of indulgence proved to be a distinct disadvantage.

Later on in the bar, Dave Dowle informed us that there was going to be a big street party the following day: 'They're having one of those siestas!'

We emerged once more for a Groundhog Day gathering that promised yet another longer-than-imagined journey to the mythical Valencia. The band members plus Ossie, Willy, Robert Mills, the promoter and two hangers-on once again shared the joys of the Seat (pronounced Say-at) with the ratio of three passengers to a car. With the promoter behind the wheel and Willy in the front seat (pronounced *asiento*), I leaned back as far as one could in a Seat seat barely big enough to accommodate one person, one unused tour jacket and a hat box containing a Harrods fedora, to contemplate the landscape.

A few minutes later, the car began to judder before slowing down and, amid a string of Iberian curses from the direction of the driving seat, we drifted gently to the side of the road where our predisposed promoter proceeded to slowly and purposefully head butt the steering wheel. After a few seconds of contemplation, we came to two immediate conclusions: a) we were last in the convoy, at least a mile behind the others; and b) mobile phones were not yet an option. The main priority was to get me to the gig and, with no means of communication, that meant only one thing – hitching a lift.

Those old, world-weary cynicisms that we'd all uttered at one time or another suddenly came into perspective as we stood at the side of the dusty motorway, our thumbs indicating the direction of a place I suddenly felt destined never to visit: 'I'm only in it for the glamour'; 'Oh, the fame, the money, the luxury of it all!' After ten minutes, our gesticulations – and, in the promoter's case, probably prayers – were answered when our chariot of deliverance first indicated, then pulled into the roadside. Chariot? No, something slightly bigger – a car transporter with a consignment of shiny new Seats chained up together like some futuristic Black Maria for badly behaved automatons.

'We're in!' yelled Willy excitedly.

'Waita una momento,' countered the increasingly pessimistic promoter. I could feel another nickname coming on – Chief Black Cloud, in honour of the particular nimbus that seemed to hover permanently above his head. After a brief consultation with the driver, he returned to deliver the solemn news.

'The *hombre camionero*, 'e say only two people,' was delivered with such doleful assertion that it sounded like one of us was about to be read the last rites.

Bad news for Willy – the driver didn't speak English and, under the circumstances, it made sense for old Black Cloud to stay with yours truly, just in case I ended up at some Seat retail outlet in Alicante. Obviously, Willy was not impressed, but, bolstered by a promise from the promoter that the 'Ah Ah' (or whatever the rescue service was called) would be informed as soon as we reached the venue, and with a fresh packet of Marlboro Reds and an admirable acceptance of professional resignation, he settled back in the Seat seat and awaited his destiny.

As the late afternoon sunshine began to fade, I climbed up into the cab clutching my gig bag, hat box and tour jacket, nodded my hellos to the kindly driver and settled down for the final episode of that long, eventful journey to Valencia.

'*Inglés*?' enquired our host on wheels.

'Yes, er, *si*,' I replied.

'Ah, Bobby Charlton!' he responded.

'Alfredo Di Stefano!' I countered, with memories of the great European Cup final of 1960 when Real Madrid thrashed Eintracht Frankfurt 7-3 still etched in my brain. 'Three goals against Eintracht.'

'Ah, *magnifico*, *magnifico*!' he shot back, his memory clearly evoked by snatches of my recollections from that sublime day for Spanish football. The promoter looked on, non-plussed.

There's only so much that an Englishman with almost no command of the Spanish language can say to a Spaniard with a similar non-grasp of English and, with the pessimistic promoter chewing his nails in the corner of the cab, the conversation soon evaporated along with the final strains of daylight.

We motored along at a steady rate until a few miles outside of Valencia when, for no apparent reason, we ground to a halt. From then on, we crawled along at a snail's pace, which gave Pessimistic Pedro (another nickname born out of tedium) the chance to gnaw his jagged nails down to the quick.

It was starting to get uncomfortably close to show time when the source of the go-slow was made known – a set of traffic lights at the end of the motorway! I was almost sure that, if

Franco had still been in power, the idiot who was responsible for this feat of unsurpassed incompetence would have been shot. Fifteen minutes later, we rumbled past the red, amber and green face of stupidity like a liberated tortoise and, after a brief stop at a pay phone to give Chief Black Cloud a chance to inform the others of our impending arrival, headed straight for the theatre. Soon, the car transporter was negotiating a gossamer-thin course between parked cars before coming to a noisy, air-braked stop outside the venue. Waiting on the pavement was a welcoming party of various band members and road crew, who were only too willing to display their hilarity at the sight of one very frustrated guitarist who would not necessarily see the funny side of things until one large cognac had passed his lips.

A few minutes later, the brandy started to do the trick and I pulled on my Spanish boots and joined the lads onstage for a well-received performance, while somewhere on a darkened motorway Willy was opening his second packet of cigarettes.

The following day, we took to the stage in a town close to San Sebastián in front of 2,000 fully charged rock fans, and responded immediately with an endorphin rush of pure excitement. With Señor Coverdale leading the battle charge, the band was firing on all cylinders when, during the fourth or fifth number, there was a power cut that reduced us to an impotent force. Only the drums could be heard acoustically, which, after the initial shock, was enough to rouse the band's camaraderie and ever-present sense of humour. Various onstage shouts of 'Drum solo!' and 'Take it, Duck!' managed to convey to the audience that we were still in charge and remained where we stood. Suddenly, the power was restored much to the delight of the crowd. Thirty seconds later, it cut out again, and Dave Dowle's expression was, by now, one of resignation regarding unamplified drum solos. There was a groan from the crowd, followed seconds later by a cheer as the power was once again restored. At last, the status quo was renewed and the gig was a resounding success.

We found out later that the second power cut was caused by the house electrician – a decrepit man of no determinate age – who responded to the first power cut and subsequent rebooting by pulling the main plug from its socket and staring gormlessly at it until our head technician removed it from his gnarled grasp and shoved it firmly back into the socket.

On the way back to the hotel, we heard what sounded like gunshots. The following morning, we were informed that three policemen had been shot dead by Basque Separatists.

CHAPTER 25

MUSIC, MIRTH AND MADNESS

Clearwell Castle is a mock Gothic mansion in the Forest of Dean, Gloucestershire, which was built in 1728 for Thomas Wyndham. It eventually went into disrepair until it was bought and restored in the 1960s and opened to the public. In the 1970s, it was used as a rehearsal and makeshift recording studio by such bands as Led Zeppelin, Bad Company, Deep Purple, Black Sabbath, Mott the Hoople, the Sweet and Peter Frampton. Although both David and Jon had experienced the luxuries of Clearwell's on-site amenities during the recording of the *Burn* album, the rest of us were in seventh heaven when confronted with four-poster beds, suits of armour and heraldic crests. The large dining room was dominated by a huge table from where we would be served first-class food and choice drinks by suitably attired nubile serving wenches! We also had the freedom to treat the place as our own for the designated period. The sudden realisation that our recording location had progressed from a claustrophobic cellar in Tin Pan Alley to a stately home in one of the most beautiful parts of Britain was as inspiring as it was exciting.

One of the rooms in the lower part of the building had, at some point, been turned into a tearoom for the tourists, but now served as the band's studio. Following the microphone cables under the door and out into a side entrance, one was confronted by the Rolling Stones Mobile, a large converted van that had started out as the Stones' personal location recording unit but now earned even more coffers for the Glimmer Twins et al. as a commercial entity in its own right. The Who, the Faces, Deep Purple, Frank Zappa and Led Zeppelin had all climbed the steps and entered the small space which was not occupied by the 24-track/32-output technical wonder on wheels (though, judging by the limited space, probably only two at a time) to listen back to their efforts. And there, in the captain's chair, sat our very own sonic architect, Martin Birch, with the mobile's manager and resident technician, Mick McKenna, never far away.

The serving wenches were impressive, offering us the kind of food and drink that had 'gout' written all over it. We'd accept graciously (the band would end up with the bill after all) and consume a calorific feast of Henry the Eighth proportions before staggering down the stairs to the crypt with every intention of laying down a new backing track. Alas, such over-indulgence is not a good prescription for energetic rock music, and, after a few bloated attempts, we'd either down tools and find a friendly pub or else deviate into periods of silliness. It took a couple of days of gastric and alcoholic indulgence to conclude that it was wise to pass on the sweet course and the port and brandy until a track or two had been recorded, *then* party!

I'd brought along an idea for a song that had been inspired, primarily, by the quirky slide guitar and vocal scat peculiar to some of the old country-blues recordings. Furthermore, I'd scribbled down a vocal hookline to complement the guitar lick, which read, 'I'm a Love Hunter baby, sneakin' up on you.' Spurred on by this sudden ability to wax lyrical, I attempted to write a verse, but soon curtailed my efforts when the developing vocal sentiment began to veer towards an oblique coupling of Blind Willie Johnson and the Venerable Bede. Back-pedalling to the more agreeable position of guitarist, I played the idea to David, who wasted no time in expanding the original chorus text into something more acceptable to the masses. Bernie latched on to the proceedings and, hey presto, we had a tune which would eventually become a staple fixture in the definitive Whitesnake song book.

By now, the mobile studio had been furnished with a small coffee table (complete with ashtray and paper rose) and was always referred to thereafter as the Café Mobile in the worst possible French accent that we could muster.

'Shall we go to ze Cafay Mobeelay?'

'Naturalmonty, monsoower!'

'Bon, bon. Birchie should be donz la shaise by mantenoh!'

And when Birchie did arrive, it was business as usual. With Martin, it was easy to see why the Deep Purple camp held him in such esteem. Having entered the fray in 1969 engineering the live *Concert for Group and Orchestra*, he continued twiddling the knobs for Purple through to 1974 when he celebrated his first assignment as producer/engineer. He held this position until *Last Concert in Japan* in 1977. Along the way, he engineered for Jeff Beck, the original Fleetwood Mac, Wishbone Ash, the Faces, the Groundhogs, Canned Heat and

John Lee Hooker, Stackridge, Flash and many more. He also produced Rainbow and Gary Moore. Right then, that was his CV at the time, now the character reference: talented, strong-minded, funny, diplomatic, athletic and . . . oh, that's enough!

We were booked into Clearwell Castle for most of May and set aside the first week to routine the new songs in the crypt-turned-studio. After a predictably late rise, we would emerge from our individually furnished bedrooms – several of us could boast a four-poster bed – and head for the breakfast room. Here, a meal of individual choice would be prepared by a local lady, who could well have been the grandmother of one of the serving nubes. Perhaps she'd waited at the big table herself in her younger days, dishing up rations to George Formby, Vera Lynn or Ambrose and his Orchestra. Now resigned to reviving pasty-faced musicians, she was, nevertheless, a cheery soul who could provide sustenance of cheek-colouring possibilities while keeping us all up to scratch with the local gossip. By now, the long-suffering Neil Murray, having read a selection of newly procured newspapers and magazines, would be contemplating his second breakfast. Neil was the sensible one who would retire from the nocturnal activities at a reasonable hour and, consequently, be up and raring to go at a time when the rest of us had just entered that period of non-rapid eye movement often referred to as 'deep sleep'. One morning, after a particularly late session, Bernie was negotiating the stairs in the direction of his bed when he encountered Neil on his way down.

'Ah-ha, the early bird!' mused Bernie.

'Oh no, not again!' replied Neil, with the sudden realisation that another trip to the newsagents and, in all likelihood, the local library, was now on the cards.

The new songs began to take shape: 'Walking in the Shadow of the Blues' stood out as a powerful testimony to blues-rock at its rockiest, while our only cover, Leon Russell's 'Help Me Through the Day', seemed to reprise our other respectful tribute, 'Ain't No Love in the Heart of the City'. 'Medicine Man' had an underlying sense of menace about it, and the twin-guitar breaks sounded suspiciously like something Lenny Kravitz would put out some years later! The lively ones: a musical Red Bull in the form of 'Mean Business' and good-time rock 'n' roll in the form of 'You 'n' Me' and 'Rock 'n' Roll Women'. The aforementioned 'Love Hunter' turned out to be a right ol' foot stomper, while 'Outlaw' was nurtured from a basic theme to a full-blown tune. David's heartfelt 'We Wish You Well' would, of course, progress to being played through the PA system at the end of Whitesnake's concerts as a sincere thank you, good night and safe journey home – Whitesnake's very own 'We'll Meet Again'.

COLLECTIVE THOUGHT PROCESSES INVADING THE CRYPT AIR SPACE:

'Oy, basic theme features, wake up!'

'Are you talking to me, big mouth?'

'Yes. How long before we get to the full-blown bit so I can get ready for the wave of achievement and satisfaction that will surely permeate the air?'

'Another thirty minutes at this rate.'

'Righto, keep your cells open.'

'Oh, you do go on!'

High jinks and mischievous pranks were never far away, and the Moody-Marsden partnership was beginning to extend far beyond the realms of mere musicianship. We were quickly becoming the chief practitioners of schoolboy behaviour, specialising in wind-ups, set-ups, practical jokes and general horseplay. Even those other devotees of fun and frolics, Messrs Coverdale and Fyffe, were sometimes taken aback by the often relentless pursuits of the guitar section.

Fishing line was always a good bet: here, tailored lengths of it were cut and strategically placed to achieve maximum effect. A regular ploy was to make some sort of excuse to leave the rehearsal or recording session in order to sneak upstairs to where the bedrooms and breakfast room were situated. Once the location was chosen, the almost invisible nylon wire was tied to an object, then unwound to a favourable distance before being cut. The end was then knotted and fitted with a position marker (in this case, a small piece of card). Metal coat hangers gave optimum results:

Step 1. Enter room of unsuspecting victim while unoccupied and affix line to one or more metal coat hangers in a wardrobe (ideal, as its powers of reverberation are second only to the bathroom). Thread line through doors of said receptacle and out along the margins of the skirting board and underside of door. Mark and tuck beneath hallway carpet.

Step 2. Wait until subject is asleep, then give almighty tug. The sudden racket from the screeching and scraping of metal on metal should be enough to wake said subject, who may reciprocate by yelling, screaming or crapping the bed. Perpetrators may now leg it, laughing hysterically.

High marks were given to the Rising Toilet Brush Method. Here, the chosen member of the Special Farces unit would attach the line to the vertical toilet brush, lead it up behind the water-supply pipe and cistern, along the top of the wall, then down along the door frame, under the door and out into the hallway. The marker would then be hidden under the carpet. Those in the know waited for the big moment, which finally arrived in the shape of a visiting girlfriend or wife. As we gathered quietly outside of the loo door, we listened intently for the sound of bare arse on seat then, at the first sound of pee on water, the custodian of the wire gave a hefty yank on the line and we heard the rush of brush on wall. A scream of shock and surprise echoed noisily around the bathroom followed by a further cry of anguish as the brush gave in to the law of gravity and landed on the poor girl's shoulder. This was enough to send the lot of us scampering back to the television lounge and our pre-production session on the ever-present acoustic guitars.

Although Jon appreciated a good laugh, he was not particularly pleased when he entered his room one afternoon to find one half of the Moody-Marsden alliance placing various objects onto the canopy of his four-poster bed.

'Can I help you?' he enquired with a disapproving look. Balancing on his bedside table, the scoundrel held a rictus grin as his brain mechanisms fast-tracked through to the 'desperately pathetic excuses' section.

'Er, could you pass that waste paper basket, please,' he replied meekly.

Jon didn't even bother to respond; his expression said it all. Well, what it actually said was, 'Get out of here now and leave me in peace!'

Wind-ups aside, it was an honour to be in the same band as Jon, one of the greatest keyboard players in the business.

Making apple-pie beds was great fun when pissed, especially when party to the fact that the intended victim was in another room getting even more rat-arsed. For the uninitiated, making an apple-pie bed involved folding back the top sheet on itself so that the intended's legs cannot be extended beyond the halfway mark. Dave Dowle got the full treatment one night when we added a few tablespoons of honey to the proceedings. The next morning at breakfast, he said absolutely nothing regarding his disturbed bed, though he was walking with a slight stoop and seemed to be having trouble with his socks.

One morning, I woke up in an adventurous mood and, after the usual ablutions, breakfasted on egg and tinned tomatoes on toast, then spoke in tongues with some of the guys and smoked a couple of Marlboro Reds. Neil had decided to stay up a little later in order to adjust his body clock to loony time and indulged in a couple of brandies, which may have interfered with his usual walk to the newsagents. He settled for a dog-eared *Readers Digest* instead. As usual, Dave Dowle had already undertaken a healthy stroll around the grounds and was raring to go. Instead of heading for the Café Mobile, I was taken with a large artist's sketch pad that was lying around and was at once impelled to do something out of the ordinary. With a large felt-tipped pen, I carefully marked out a poster, which read,

THE CASTLE GROUNDS ARE CLOSED TO THE PUBLIC OWING TO
THE FILMING OF THE NEW JOHN TRAVOLTA MOVIE.

I showed my handiwork to the others and, amid guffaws and giggles, placed it on an artist's trestle, positioned it by the front gates, and then headed back to the crypt where we recorded an inspired backing track to 'Medicine Man'. We'd just retired to the mobile to listen to the playback when, suddenly, the estate manager Bernard Yeates appeared and informed us that a reporter from the local newspaper had telephoned regarding the presence of John Travolta. There was synchronised lip-biting and muffled laughs: the game was up! I owned up and headed for the gates to remove the evidence. There were dozens of teenagers waiting with autograph books and I had to inform them that Mr Travolta had postponed the project indefinitely. They were not impressed.

It is to our credit that we could drink, smoke, satiate in general *and* write and record some great music in the process. The camaraderie went from strength to strength, though it sometimes felt like there was a collective split personality at work, albeit not in the dissociative sense. Let's just say we often 'departed from moderation', as did a lot of rock 'n' rollers; psychotic behaviour was for the real head cases. In recent times, there has been talk of people in their late twenties suffering from 'quarter-life crisis'; well, the only crisis a lot of 1970s rock musicians in the same age group fell prey to was being loaded at the end of the night and ending up in a lonely or maudlin state of mind. Alternatively, one could end up in a situation where the company was good and, quite possibly, euphoric. You can make what you like of that! In order to alleviate the possibilities of the former, Willy would sometimes make trips to Bristol Parkway station to pick up wives and girlfriends.

One Sunday afternoon – and for reasons long forgotten – we took charge of a firkin of scrumpy (very strong cider) and, as recommended in the brewer's guidelines, a batch of half-pint glasses. I'd drunk this stuff before and was aware of its potency, as were the other imbibers, but it didn't stop us knocking back 'a few halves' of the stuff during the recording session. As expected, a bout of silliness ensued, including an improvised ditty about a milkman with a nasty streak and his opposite number, a friendly paraffin delivery man. How this occurred when we were working on a song called 'Outlaw' is unclear without the help of someone within the field of psychiatry, although some sort of subconscious perversion of a typical Benny Hill sketch may have been the reason.

Such lunacy rendered us incapable of further recording until normal brain functions could be resumed, so a period of instant sobriety was decided on.

In the stone passageway outside of the crypt, we encountered a slightly perplexed Bernard Yeates, who informed us that the singer Donovan and a small group of fellow astral travellers were wandering around the castle grounds. Why they were there was unclear, though there was always a possibility that they'd been searching the land by Glastonbury Tor for the remains of King Arthur, or possibly Arthur Brown. I was heading towards my room to try to clear my head of cider and farcical songs when I came face to face with an attractive young lady who, judging by her general countenance and unhurried manner, was either as tipsy as me, stoned, or just a very free spirit.

'Hello, are you lost?' I asked with an application of maximum eye contact.

'Oh, no,' she answered, with a voice that put me in mind of Miranda Richardson's Queen Elizabeth in *Blackadder 2*. 'Just exploring.' My predatory instincts kicked in.

'Would you like to see my room? It's very nice,' I suggested from within a miasma of steadily mounting pheromone.

The ensuing whiff of genetic make-up must have prevailed because, in no time at all, we were lying on my bed in a passionate embrace, albeit fully clothed. Suddenly, from another part of the building, a man's voice bellowed out a woman's name in a tone that could be described as 'agitated'.

'Who the hell's that?' I asked.

'My husband, I think,' countered the Miranda Richardson voice.

Although the thought of being caught in a compromising position by some bloke and Donovan appealed to my love of the bizarre, a confrontation could have produced an emotional response by the offended party – a response that could well have resulted in a surfeit of pain and blood in and around that part of my anatomy known as my nose. Bat out of hell, shit off a shovel and rat up a drainpipe are all expressions that recount my reaction, and I was up off the bed and bundling the befuddled bird out of the door before you could say 'mellow yellow'.

And the moral of the story? Don't shit on your own doorstep – or in somebody's moat.

It wasn't all shenanigans at Clearwell Castle. We did actually spend a lot of time making good music, potting snooker balls and genuinely enjoying each other's company, even when one of Bernard Yeates's pre-booked old-age pensioners' day trips turned up for a pot of tea, a scone and a quick mooch around. One such party arrived a little earlier than planned one day while Bernie was still sound asleep in his room.

'Eh, Gladys, shall we have a look in this room? It's probably full of historical artefacts.'

'Yes, Maude, no one will know.'

'It's a bit dark in here. Ooh, look – a four-poster bed.'

'Oh, yes. Aaagh! There's somebody in it!'

Exit two nosey old birds and, within half an hour, the whole lot of them – the blue-rinse brigade and their mostly bored husbands whom David would refer to as the Moody Blues fan club!

CHAPTER 26

TROUSERS TO BE DROPPED, TORN AND DANCED IN

It was, indeed, a rare day when there wasn't something of a toxic nature mounting a reasonable challenge on my internal organs and bloodstream. And throughout all this indulgence, I did have the odd pang of conscience regarding my general health, which sometimes fell prey to ailments such as 'buckling knee syndrome', 'inner ear problems' or – and I wasn't alone here – 'completely knackereditis'. So when a drinking buddy suggested a round of golf as the answer ('There's always a drink in the clubhouse at the end of it!'), I decided to give it a go, bearing in mind the experience of another drinking partner whose friend had suggested the very same thing. It was a pastime for which he held no interest whatsoever; he could never understand why anyone would want to spoil a good walk by stopping every few hundred yards to hit a very small ball with a stick. On the course itself, it soon became apparent that he was not a natural, and his friend's initial enthusiasm suddenly began to wane. His strokes began to take on a more desperate stance, which resulted in him having to shout 'Fore!' before he attempted a putt into the cup. The end came when he was asked to fetch a sand wedge and returned fifteen minutes later with a ham-and-cheese baguette.

In June 1979 Rhodesia took power of its first black government in ninety years, Pope John Paul II became the first ever Pontiff to visit a communist country, there was a catastrophic oil spill in the Gulf of Mexico, Jimmy Carter and Leonard Brezhnev signed the Salt 11 agreement, NATO Supreme Commander Alexander Haig escaped an assassination attempt by the Baader-Meinhof terrorist organisation and there was a military coup in Ghana. All of these events (and more) were blithely ignored by the politically disinterested members of Whitesnake and their road crew, who spent the whole of that month touring Germany. My archive itinerary shows that we spent exactly thirty-one days there, though we only played nineteen shows: that's a lot of days off. As the majority of us adhered to a lifestyle of wine, women and song, that was no big deal, especially with a band supplement of characters such as tour manager Ossie Hoppe, Willy Fyffe, and our road crew – Jack, Steve, Stuart, Louis and Gary – for company. Fun times for the lads! Jack McGill was the archetypal roadie and true champion of the rock 'n' roll lifestyle: a fearless competitor in the game of 'live now, pay later'. And eventually, he did. Some mornings, he'd look like he'd spent the night in the reactor core at Chernobyl, but it never affected his ability to do his job well. A staunch bunch, which Jack would sometimes refer to in his classic Glaswegian dialect as 'Guid lads – nae poofters!'

TROUSERS TO BE DROPPED, TORN AND DANCED IN

Although the attendances at the gigs for this, our first headline tour, were relatively small in numbers – five hundred a night on average – the band would rip through a selection of songs from *Snakebite* and *Trouble*, a couple of Deep Purple classics, one or two solo spots and a sneak preview from the forthcoming album. After the shows, amid a rush of high spirits, we'd attempt to rip the back pockets off each other's jeans before going out on the town to imbibe for our country. There was never a dull moment and, as they say, there's always one! Our truck driver earned himself a place in the Rock 'n' Roll Hall of On-the-Road Stories when, on discovering the physical proof of a dose of gonorrhoea, he decided on an immediate course of action. Scouring the streets near the hotel, he espied a building that boasted a handful of brass name plaques by the front door. Among them was one that read Doktor Erich Schmidt. Once inside, he asked the lady on the reception desk if the doctor was available to assist him with an urgent matter. As luck would have it, the doctor was free and, a few minutes later, he was face to face with the impeccably dressed and well-groomed Dr Schmidt.

'Good afternoon, *mein Herr*. I believe that you require my assistance. What is the problem?' he enquired.

Without hesitation, our man of the road dropped his trousers and beheld his viscid member in his hand. 'This,' he replied.

Dr Schmidt's eyes widened at the sight of the stricken member, then, in a flat voice, he responded: 'I sympathise with your problem but I cannot help you.'

'Why not?' enquired the infected one.

'Because I am a doctor of law,' he concluded.

Playing to relatively small crowds must have been

something of a comedown for Jon and David but, to their credit, they never once mentioned it. And probably for one simple reason: they were having too much bloody fun to really care! After shows, we'd head to a recommended club or disco and party with the locals. It wasn't unusual to find some of us up on the dancefloor, a place of fun routinely ignored by most musicians. Due to our youthful enthusiasm and irrepressible dance moves, Bernie and I were soon nicknamed the Disco Kid and Pancho. For those readers of a certain age, this title refers to the *Cisco Kid*, a popular series on 1950s television in which our hero, along with his jovial sidekick Pancho, rode from town to town, boulder to boulder and cactus to cactus to help the needy and the downtrodden. Although the sombrero-hatted twosome were, apparently, desperados with a dubious past, their intentions were honourable and their intolerance towards baddies, matched by a kindness towards the downtrodden and abused, was commendable. I had some of the best nights of my life in those clubs – a far, far better alternative to sitting in a hotel bar full of blokes, or retiring to your room to get stoned and watch *The Waltons* in German.

Towards the end of our German tour, we performed at a number of festivals as part of a package supporting the Police, Dr. Feelgood , Dire Straits and Barclay James Harvest. Both the Police and Dire Straits were at the beginning of a meteoric rise to huge success. Backstage at the Sportshalle in Dortmund, I bumped into Mark Knopfler and his manager Ed Bicknell. Ed was a friend of Bob Young, but I had never met Mark before. To my surprise, Mark told me that he had seen me a couple of weeks earlier trying out a Dobro in Denmark Street (a guitar which I had subsequently bought).

Both the Police and Dire Straits put on a fantastic

performance and afterwards in the hotel bar the three blond Gods that were Sting, Summers and Copeland sat quietly amused as the Whitesnake entourage entertained them with their usual antics. They were especially taken by a cassette of an outtake from the Lovehunter sessions which we had put on behind the bar. This featured the inebriated Coverdale, Marsden and Moody improvising a song about an obnoxious milkman. There was special emphasis on the chorus which went:

'He's a c**t!
He's a c**t!
He's a c**t!'

The high jinks continued, and a ten out of ten was awarded to Ossie and Willy for all their efforts in modifying the welcoming sign outside of a Holiday Inn somewhere in the Rhineland. Enjoying the usual post-gig session in the bar, we were suddenly interrupted by an animated roadie who urged us to check out the amendments to the large, brightly lit billboard outside. The hotel's literary salutation to honour an instantly forgettable gathering of suits under some corporate name or other had been transformed into 'HER CLIT IS HOT MAN'. Where they found a ladder to undertake such a task was never revealed but, given Ossie's association with the famous Hoppe circus family, there was always the chance that some sort of acrobatic feat or unicycle spectacular had taken place.

Another high-spirited piece of tomfoolery was to catch each other unawares by attempting to tear off the back pockets of each other's jeans, often with interesting results. While the objective was to remove a single pocket in one concerted tug, Willy's black needle-cords were, in a collective effort, stripped of the whole back section. The image from the front afforded the trousers what appeared to be a pair of drover's chaps, while the rear view yielded plain, albeit functional briefs and a pair of pale legs. To his credit, he kept them on for the rest of the evening and was central to the ensuing lunacy at Munich's coolest disco, the Sugar Shack.

Alcohol figured highly as a social, day-to-day occurrence. In one particular *bierkeller*, I tried a local brew that reminded me of the pint of 'heavy' I once drank in Glasgow. This one was so strong and dense it had silt in the bottom of the glass! Other Teutonic tipples that we approached with extreme caution were Jägermeister (an evil-looking tincture that smelled suspiciously like syrup of figs); cut brandy from East Germany, which, though not high in alcohol content, tasted like it'd been distilled in Erich Honecker's cycling pants; and Bärenfang, a liqueur developed by fifteenth-century East Prussian masochists and reputed to have been made from vodka and unexploded bombs. Rumour had it that we could lessen the assault on our taste buds by eating a pretzel, a strangely-shaped leavened bread that could well have been manufactured by blind bakers in order to cover up severe cracks in walls. And the large variety of schnapps on offer was commendable, though too much indulgence in this *feuerwasser* could hasten the compulsion to pull on a pair of boots and march off in the direction of the Sudetenland. In a small bar in Ludwigsburg, one inebriated local insisted that songs send out the same message in any language.

'Ze songs, zay all send out ze same message in any language.'

Oh, really? Then try singing 'McNamara's Band' to a family of oppressed cockle-pickers from the Xinjiang Province and see what happens.

We were nearing the end of our tour/leisure break when we learned that Ian Paice was set to join the band. Although it was fantastic news, you had to have some sympathy for Dave Dowle, who was a great drummer, but at the end of the day business is business. And having half of Deep Purple in Whitesnake was definitely good for business.

When the philanthropist Thomas Holloway moved into the seventy-two acre Georgian manor house Tittenhurst Park in Sunningdale, Berkshire, in 1869, he could never have imagined that, a hundred years later, a hirsute man and his Japanese concubine would be living a bohemian existence under the very same roof. John Lennon and Yoko Ono were to put this attractive house on the world map by filming the video to 'Imagine' in the virgin-white confines of its sitting room. Not long after, they transmigrated from the sublime to the ridiculous by selling up and moving into a loft conversion in the Greenwich Village area of New York City. Although their tenure at Tittenhurst had been short, Lennon had the wherewithal to build a studio in the house. The new buyer, one Ringo Starr, lived there with his family for a while before transforming the house into a residential studio under the name Startling Studios. Blissfully unaware of most of the above, I arrived one sunny day to add slide guitar and Dobro to Roger Chapman's first solo album.

In the early 1970s, a fraternity of 'looners' – including the Patto band and other related madmen – had developed and utilised a greeting call that was a concise adaptation of a Tyrolean yodel. Chappo was an enthusiastic advocate of this form of greeting, and it was not unusual in those days to hear a condensed version of an Alpine cry resounding from a bar, a studio or a dressing room. Yoh-ooow! In between such sonorous activity, he was crafting an LP that would excel in both quality and individuality, featuring, among others, musicians of the calibre of Geoff Whitehorn, Billy Livsey, Ray Cooper and Poli Palmer, as well as good old boys Henry Spinetti, Dave Markee and Ron Aspery. It would mark the start of a long and successful solo career, especially in Germany, where Roger would soon emerge as a people's champion. It's often been said that Roger Chapman is one of the great characters of rock, and having worked with him many times since – both live and in the studio – I entirely agree.

Around this time, we were informed that Britain's first official nudist beach had opened in Brighton. For heaven's sake! Let's face it, it takes only one choppy morning to diminish the attributes of any exhibitionist, which, excluding young gays and voyeurs, generally amounts to middle-aged *Guardian* readers, raddled hippies and pensioners with pendulous tits or scrotums. Nurse – the screens! Resisting any temptation to take off our clothes and look like twats, we gathered at E-Zee Hire to begin rehearsals with Ian Paice, and it's no exaggeration to say that the difference his playing made to Whitesnake's sound was obvious from the first song we ran through. With due respect to Dave Dowle, this man rocked with a positivity that bordered on the unrelenting, and his involvement initiated the line-up that Tommy Vance would later refer to as the 'definitive' Whitesnake. Afterwards, we took Ian to the White Horse pub to meet Joe Hitchcock, who may or may not have led him to the dartboard before placing a nail into his mouth.

Impressed by Paicey's immeasurable physical effort, and inspired by a newspaper article on healthy living, I sought to improve my general health by speed-walking. I deduced that this could be achieved by walking quickly to the pub and back up to three times a day. Sadly, my self-denial regarding the alcohol-related calorie count soon put the mockers on that little scheme. It was easier and much more adventurous to get wasted, so that was that.

Ian made his debut at a festival in Bilzen, a small Belgian town close to the Dutch border. Also on the bill was Uriah Heep, featuring the seemingly ever-cheerful Mick Box, though his buoyant demeanour seemed somewhat restrained that night. Onstage, the 'Heep' riffed their way through a well-received set of heavy prog-rock favourites, but backstage there seemed to be an air of discontentment within the band. A few days later, singer John Lawton joined David Byron in the 'ex-Uriah Heep singer' department after alleged 'differences of opinion' with keyboard player Ken Hensley. Afterwards, we chatted with some fans who'd travelled from their homes on the Dutch-German border and who spoke in a language which seemed to have been developed solely for the clearing of the throat. They were drinking a type of beer unfamiliar to the rest of us, and further enquiries revealed that it was very strong, brewed by Trappist monks and would 'maikhhhh qhhuuu pisshht'.

CHAPTER 27

LOVE HUNTERS READY AND WILLING

It would not be inaccurate to say that, in those heady days of the 1970s, overindulged rock stars were charging from gig to gig like lascivious centaurs in the relentless pursuit of girls. Fired up on booze or (and) stimulants, good fortune and self-esteem, the rampant rocker soon deduced that casual sex was, in many cases, a healthy alternative to absolute stupefaction, although care had to be taken to ensure the two didn't cross. For some, winding down after an adrenalin-induced, euphoric, high-energy stage performance usually required more than a cup of tea and a Kit Kat. It was often the prelude to the kind of cavalier behaviour often associated with . . . er, supercilious cavaliers and hyped-up rock stars. If accounts in the many biographies and memoirs chronicling the heydays of Hollywood are true, history was simply repeating itself – entertainers will be entertainers. Allegedly, those particular shenanigans went mostly unreported as the powers that be considered accounts of inappropriate conduct damaging to the star's profile. How times have changed! For those of us who regularly yielded to temptation throughout the 1970s, hedonism was par for the course, if only in a nudge, nudge, wink, wink fashion.

Nowadays, it seems that promiscuous and even lurid behaviour are acceptable forms of tabloid reporting. However, most rock nutters pale into insignificance in comparison to the great violinist Niccolo Paganini, a genius of the first order and, arguably, music's first ever superstar. His virtuosity remains unsurpassed and, if all that's written about him is true, Keith Richards' personal history seems rather run of the mill by comparison.

Regardless of the above and bereft of any preconceived thoughts pertaining to the trials and tribulations of Signor Paganini – i.e. genetic defects, alcoholism, tuberculosis, syphilis, depression, cancer of the larynx, narcotics usage, gambling addiction, bankruptcy and death from haemorrhaging – we set forth on our travels. Our record company thought it fitting that Whitesnake should expose its fangs to the biggest record market in the world, and arranged a short trip to the United States in order to meet their counterparts in Los Angeles. Also on the itinerary was a single live performance, which would take place in the Royce Hall at UCLA (University of California Los Angeles), but, before we jetted off to the West Coast, I had the opportunity to meet one of my guitar heroes.

Eric Clapton had created a big impression on me back in 1964 when I first heard the wild yet tastefully controlled guitar solo on the Yardbirds' 'Good Morning Little School Girl' and the atmospheric *Five Live Yardbirds* album. He'd come a long way since then, and the Cranleigh Village Hall in Surrey was a rather surreal setting in which to catch EC along with his mates and undoubted partners in alcohol – Chas and Dave et al. Of course, this wasn't an official gig, just a local lad having a 'knees-up' with his mates, playing to a couple of hundred lucky souls who'd managed to get a ticket and some of us lucky liggers who managed to get into the backstage area!

Once aboard the plane to L.A., we settled in en masse with the usual laddish enthusiasm for the good time that surely awaited us, like a stag do without the impending wedding. Before our plane had even taken off, we undertook our first prank of the day – score cards for the air hostess. This particular caper had two fundamental requirements: that there were at least six of us sitting together in a row and that all of us were in possession of ready-made score cards with numbers ranging from one to ten. The panel was in sitting and judgement was forthcoming, young lady! Halfway through the stewardess's safety-procedure demonstration (and at a given signal), we held our score cards up high to the complete surprise of the stewardess and most of the passengers. Individual scores varied and, although encouraging scores were often given, one and a half points and even the occasional zero were sometimes offered up. Needless to say, the poor girl in question struggled to suppress her mirth!

Sleep was rarely an option, even on long-haul flights such as this, as having a good time with the lads just came naturally. Not a big drinker, Neil eventually found a relatively quiet spot and got some shut-eye while the rest of us ordered vodkas and tonic before visiting the galley section to chat to the crew. Another passenger – an individual with the personal magnetism of a depressed Ewok – asked us to keep the noise down, as he wanted to sleep. We apologised but within minutes we reverted back, quite naturally, to our collective role as party animals and in-house jokers. Later, we hit some turbulence, which gave rise to shouts of, 'Abandon ship . . . women and roadies first!'

In Los Angeles, the band and crew found themselves booked into the Sunset Marquee: a groovy hotel catering mostly to music and entertainment people, where we were presented with self-contained suites. Very nice! After the check-in, there was a gradual shift to the pool area, where we were pleasantly surprised to see all four members of ABBA frolicking by the pool – an interesting sight considering Björn and Agnetha's very public separation. Swedish professionalism at its best!

Later on, we headed for the offices of United Artists for a press call where, due to a lack of sleep, I crashed out under the boardroom table and missed the whole bloody thing.

If ever I'm asked by airport immigration if my visit is 'business or pleasure', I often think back to that particular visit to L.A. with nostalgia and a certain amount of yearning. I can best describe it in one very long sentence: after a few days dodging the Californian sunshine in the company of a disco singer I'd met in the United Artists office, performing at UCLA (where we all trouped back out to the stage area after the show to watch an emergency crew trying to free an obese girl fan from the confines of her seat), hanging out at the renowned Rainbow Bar and Grill, being taken to an expensive Japanese restaurant by our record company, attending a party in our honour and watching Monty Python's *Life of Brian* at George Grauman's celebrated Chinese Theatre, we headed for LAX and our skyward chariot of delight.

Due to the somewhat 'raunchy' nature of our new album,

Lovehunter, the band was obliged to face the press. One of the first to broach the subject of naked ladies straddling snakes was Phil Sutcliffe in the *Sounds* publication of 20 October 1979, where he expressed his views in an interview with David and Bernie: 'I opined the design was atrocious because it was brutally sexist, reinforcing the idea that woman is an object for man's pleasure and implying the right of domination by violence (rape/battery).' He then stated that the band was doing itself a disservice as 'most of the songs were not *sexist* but *sexy*'.

Another opinion soon followed: 'That cover certainly insults women but I reckon it also makes Whitesnake out to be a bunch of libidinous half-wits rather than the intelligent and sensitive men they are.' Bernie took a more ambivalent view: 'It is sexist, I have to admit that. Maybe we have done a wrong 'un. I don't know.'

David, though, was having none of it:

We're exercising the male fantasy of being peacock and strutting. We are playing cock rock. We are bathing in innuendo. In America the sleeve has been banned for sexism and the album is going out in a brown paper bag. I suggested stick-on panties for the boiler in the picture but they seemed to think that would make it worse.

The *Lovehunter* tour kicked off at the Portsmouth Guildhall, that grand neo-classical establishment of Victorian opulence which now reverberated to the stomping strains of 'I'm a lovehunter, baby, sneaking up on you.' What would old Queen Vic have said?

'Ship them to an Australasian penal colony, the immoral,

lascivious little feckers. Husband – time for the Prince Albert ring, if you please!'

Relaxing in the dressing room after the soundcheck, we were distracted from our inspection of the dressing-room food-and-drink rider by the hall manager who, in a state of mild irritation, informed us that there was a lady on the phone complaining about the album cover and using biblical quotes to render us sons of evil who will be cast forever into a state of perdition.

'What should I say?' he asked, somewhat perplexed.

'Tell her that white is the symbol of purity and that the evil serpent will be crushed forever to rise as a dove. We will be known as Whitedove,' replied Jon with tongue firmly in cheek.

'Er . . . right,' responded the voice of the tweed jacket and cavalry twills before scurrying back to his office to face the wrath of Maud.

During this tour, an early form of what is nowadays referred to as a 'meet and greet' would take place after we'd dried off, quaffed a beer/brandy/vodka and made ourselves relatively respectable. Willy Fyffe would find as large a room as possible and, once we were seated, the fans would snake through holding their programmes, albums and autograph books. Then, after their brief confrontation, they were encouraged by Willy to move along and make room for the next. It was an excellent idea and an ideal way to meet women, and, as I said earlier, this band attracted its fair share of them. Continuing our south-coast trek, we entertained a sea-sprayed audience at that wonderful example of British architecture, regal dominance and imperialistic excess, the Brighton Dome. Midway through the after-show meet and greet, I locked eyes with a dark-haired, good-looking young lady, and the pheromones kicked in from both sides of the table. I came straight to the point and asked her if she was on her own and, if so, would she like to wait a while until we'd finished our up-close and relatively personal interlude with the fans. Half an hour later, we were heading off to the Holiday Inn in Brighton, swathed in afterglow (plus a few vodkas), to nurture the beginnings of what would become an oft-repeated companionship.

I awoke later that morning and thought, 'God, this is good isn't it? A fantastic band led by a talented singer and frontman that attracts a great rock 'n' roll crowd which includes a rather nice woman.' Once again, Mel Brookes's self-satisfied affirmation rang clear: 'It's good to be the King!' How many twenty-eight-year-olds wouldn't have dropped everything to be in my shoes? Not many, Benny! And I guessed that any other young guy who'd been in a steaming rock 'n' roll band would have been entitled to feel just a little bit smug too.

The *Lovehunter* tour took in twenty-two dates in major towns and cities that included two nights at the Hammersmith Odeon. The camaraderie continued and we played and partied as you'd expect a bunch of blissfully happy young blokes to do.

They say that rooms have eyes; if so, hotel rooms are the luckiest voyeurs in the world. In rare moments of relative peace, the TV was, by today's standards, limited, but still a welcome break. *Coronation Street* was a must-see. How could you not get involved when Ray Langton found out about his wife Deidre's affair with Ken Barlow, and Alf Roberts had thoughtfully furnished his corner shop with a chair to aid the infirm? Sometimes, the excitement was too much and we'd have to change channel to BBC2 and watch the snooker, or, if feeling whimsical or suffering the effects of hedonistic indulgence, *Butterflies* starring Wendy Craig. One to avoid was *Panorama*, which was far too serious and often as interesting as trying to host a conference call for introverts.

An end-of-tour party was held at Jon and Vicky Lord's house, where someone, in their wisdom, had hired a stripper to 'get her tits out for the lads'. One of the lads that night was neighbour George Harrison, who soon pulled up a chair close to the hired exhibitionist. His presence was noted immediately and the naughty lady wasted no time in plonking herself in George's lap, much to his pleasure. Spearheaded by Bernie, a chorus of 'She Loves You' soon rang out!

A good review from Steve Gett was at odds with Paul De Noyer's piece in hard rock-haters' mouthpiece *New Musical Express*, which dealt with the continued popularity of 'dog-eared nostalgia' and the sustainability of certain acts, which included Whitesnake. In Mr De Noyer's view, Whitesnake valued their proficiency, which they used to crowd-pleasing effect. This was a winning formula apparently lost on the critics: 'They point this out to me as courteously as their low opinion of *NME* will allow.'

LOVEHUNTER UK TOUR-RELATED SNIPPETS
Robert Plant turned up at the Birmingham Odeon, as did one of Jon and Ian's neighbours, Mick Ralphs.

At Hammersmith Odeon, Mick Ralphs joined us for the encore of 'Rock Me Baby'. Afterwards, we talked about

Gibson Les Pauls and he informed me that he had a 1958 'sunburst' model for sale. I bought it – one happy lad!

After the show at the De Montfort Hall in Leicester, a teenage couple consummated their relationship – I know this to be true because a bloke came up to me in a pub fifteen years later, shook my hand and informed me that I was partly responsible for his first sexual encounter!

The Victoria Hall in Hanley had a sprung floor which, when pounded upon by fifteen hundred pairs of feet, caused the PA system to wobble precariously. Members of the road crew carried out running repairs using gaffer tape, rope and a pair of tights, which resulted in much mirth on stage.

Having ordered a burger on room service at a Holiday Inn in Liverpool, Bernie asked what it came with. A scouse voice at the other end of the phone replied, 'It doan cum wi' noh'n.'

During the final performance of the tour, at the Fairfield Halls in Croydon, somebody threw a blow-up doll on stage. It landed in David's outstretched arms, which resulted in much laughter. Great fun!

Pet names for people either professionally linked or personally affiliated to the band or band members on this tour included 'Squit' Wickes, 'Skid' Marks, Cathay, Z.Z. Magill, the Victim, Paine's Moaning Company, Morocco Mole, 'Fifi' Fyffe, 'Dustin' Patterson, Leopard

LOVE HUNTERS READY AND WILLING

Skin Woman, 'Percy' Peacock, Billiard Table Legs, 'Tony' Hoppe and Tina Beans.

Attending to one's personal responsibilities is never easy when you're globe-trotting, especially when you have mouths to feed and bills to pay. Whitesnake was not a cheap band to run, with management and agency fees (rather a lot), retainers for band and crew (negotiable in some cases), transport and catering for crew, plus the existence of various and sundry outgoings. I'm not going to go into the whys and wherefores, because that would be inappropriate here, but let's just say that, throughout my period with Whitesnake, both myself and my dependents lived a fairly modest lifestyle. Now on with the show.

A week after the Croydon gig, we turned up at a studio in London's Soho district to feature in a promotional video for the chosen single, 'A Long Way from Home', and were somewhat mystified as to the presence of plaster columns similar in style to those used in the construction of classic Greek and Roman architecture. After a short period of setting up and camera-angling – which included the customary bouts of schoolboy behaviour – we took up our positions for the shoot. It was only then that somebody enquired about the columns.

'The columns?' responded the director. 'Well, so it's in keeping with the song title – 'A Long Way from Rome.'

Meanwhile, back in the Young and Moody camp, producer Stuart Taylor had spoken enthusiastically about a song somebody had sent him from the States, which he thought might be suitable for Bob and me. It was called 'The Devil Went Down to Georgia' – a cotton-pickin' novelty song about a fiddle player who is challenged to a duel by the devil. If he wins, he gets a solid gold fiddle, but if he loses, Satan gets his soul. Thankfully, the devil is no Paganini and Johnny gets his prize. We were swiftly booked into a studio to record a slide-guitar-driven alternative, with Bob as the storyteller and yours truly acting out both parts. As a nice touch before the final mix, Francis Rossi joined in on the backing vocals. Just before we put it out, the original version by the Charlie Daniels Band was released in the UK. It was far superior. And to make matters worse, the wonderful Jerry Reed recorded *his* version, which, guitar-wise, made me feel like a complete inadequate. Asking British rock players to emulate 'good ol' boys' like Charlie Daniels and Jerry Reed is a bit like asking Ted Nugent to cover a Pentangle song. Lesson learned – best leave it to the experts.

On 3 December 1979 we arrived at Ridge Farm Studios, a residential recording facility built on the site of a medieval farm in the village of Capel on the Surrey-Sussex border. Armed with ideas and arrangements for new songs and a sense of excitement, we took a quick peek at the studio before retiring to our allocated rooms. Although the majority of the rooms were situated in the main house, a small cottage was commandeered by David and yours truly, with Willy Fyffe allocated a bed-settee in its small lounge. Bernie was still en route from a holiday in Africa and, on arrival, would find himself ensconced in a former stable stall, which had been converted into a rather nice bedsit! Apart from the occasional rook's 'caw-caw' or, if the wind changed, the low rumble of an airliner departing a distant Gatwick airport, this place was *quiet*. However, if a mere mortal wished to escape this scene of rustic solitude, there was always the option of a social divine intervention.

'We're in the back-arse of beyond!'

'Fear ye not, for there is a pub. God has graced us with The Plough in Rusper!'

'Marvellous – it's only nine forty-five. We might just be in time for the last supper!'

Ridge Farm's previous clients had included Bad Company, Queen, Jethro Tull, Thin Lizzy and Roxy Music, and some of these visiting artists may well have been seen locally sporting bumps and bruises on their upper foreheads courtesy of the sixteenth-century Plough Inn's implausibly low-beamed ceilings and doorways. Consequently, the dull thud of head on wood would occasionally resound, accompanied by the inevitable 'Ow!' As expected, most of us would visit the pub during our sojourn at Ridge Farm and, during one of these visits, the subject of the dwarfed interior was broached. It was judged accordingly by one of the locals: 'Ooh aar, peoples was small in them days.'

The fresh air obviously did us good. From day one, rehearsals for the new songs seemed to flow effortlessly, with ideas for arrangements coming thick and fast, and one new tune in particular – 'Fool for Your Loving' – had instant appeal. Prior to the recording, I'd worked on an idea for an acoustic-based tune in an open-C guitar tuning: an unusual configuration I'd figured out from listening to a Blind Willie McTell song called 'Statesboro Blues'. Sitting before a coal fire in the snug confines of our cottage, I played it to David, who took an instant liking to the tune and suggested that we record it onto his portable Sony cassette player. He would soon produce a set of lyrics, which I personally consider to be among his best, and the fireside tune evolved into a Whitesnake classic, the dynamic and atmospheric 'Ain't Gonna Cry No More'. My recently acquired 1958 Les Paul made its studio debut and, once we started running through the new stuff in the studio, it soon became apparent that other new titles such as 'Sweet Talker', 'Ready and Willing' and 'Black and Blue' were bristling with character. Ian's drumming had made such a difference to Whitesnake's sound; it really was the icing on the cake. And talking of cakes, Bernie had arrived back from his holiday a day late, thus missing the rehearsal and recording of the title track and, ultimately, a writing credit for the song itself.

From within this hub of creativity and free-spirited camaraderie, distraction was never far from reach and almost always possible to attain. My lady friend from Brighton came to visit me with provision for some 'quality time', though her lack of experience within the confines of the studio control room left a lot to be desired. While we were listening to one of David's demo tapes, she remarked, 'It sounds like "Don't Fear the Reaper" by Blue Öyster Cult.' The look on David's face said it all really, and I heard him mutter, 'Get her out of here!' which I duly did.

On a cold day just prior to our return home, Neil became an unexpected superhero when, aware that one of our road crew was about to head back to London, called out, 'Watch out for the black ice!' Within minutes, the silliness began and cries of 'Watch out for the black ice!' rang out from vantage points in and around Ridge Farm, firmly establishing our mild-mannered bass player's forthcoming (and unexpected) role as Captain Black Ice! A legend was born – and all due to an oversight by the local council. They should have been prudent enough to have painted the roads white so motorists could have seen the afflicted areas and driven around them, thus avoiding accidents.

LOVE HUNTERS READY AND WILLING

By now, Ossie Hoppe had decided to devote more time to managerial activities and handed over the title of tour manager to John 'Magnet' Ward, a former crew member for Led Zeppelin and Deep Purple. A down-to-earth and friendly man from the Midlands, he was reputedly a good man to have on your side (especially if trouble raised its ugly head), and was alleged to have attained his unusual moniker through his ability to attract women. And so, mindful of such notable competition, we packed our bags and headed home for Christmas.

CHAPTER 28

IT'S GOOD TO BE THE EMPEROR

woke up late on 1 January 1980 feeling no different than I had back in the 1970s. And as for the people who say that if you can remember the 1970s, you weren't really there, well, I probably had a hangover from the New Year's Eve celebrations but I can remember exactly where I was – the Sun Inn in Barnes, south-west London, as I often was in those days. The beginning of a new year is often a time for retrospection, a time to reflect on the past before resuming that outward journey into the future. Back then, we were young, bold and frequently reckless, part of a habitual professional and social maelstrom, whereas nowadays I often find myself at odds with the majority. And with that in mind, I shall now head back to the past!

John Coghlan's Diesel Band took to the road during the second half of March for a short tour of selected venues, including the Channel Islands, which would be a first for me.

Neil Murray joined John, Bob Young, Andy Bown, Jackie Lynton and yours truly for what promised to be ten days of fun under a self-proclaimed banner of good-time rock 'n' roll. Of course, there was never a dull moment with Jackie (a former student at Woking College of Further Wind-Ups) and, if precedence was to be regarded as a pointer of things to come, the customary laddish behaviour would never be far away!

We arrived on the island of Guernsey on a blustery night, checked in at our hotel and made for the bar, where a local group was murdering the hits of the day. The manager, who bore more than a passing resemblance to singer Jack Jones, was more than happy to accommodate a bunch of characters with a little more spirit than his usual clientele, and was ecstatic when we leaped onto the small stage for a blow. Jackie led us through 'Lucille' before Andy struck up the intro for Chuck Berry's Christmas song 'Run, Run, Rudolf', an odd choice for a windswept night in March. A mounting gale howled around our cliff-top abode, the drinks flowed and John Coghlan announced, 'We're called the Diesel Band 'cause it's cheaper than petrol!' Er, right. John was immensely proud of his band of musos and, although it was essentially a covers band, he put his heart and soul into it. Back at the bar, 'one for the road' turned into 'one for the storm', which in turn became 'another one' and so on.

Jack Jones looked on gleefully as his annual March bar profits soared by approximately seven thousand per cent.

The following morning, the squally weather was still in evidence as we gathered in the foyer to down cups of coffee in the hope of reducing the turbulence on our battered frontal systems. And, if I may milk the meteorological puns for a moment longer, our roadie – a Scotsman with a taste for

Guinness and whiskey – certainly looked under the weather. He'd been sailing close to the wind during our stationary high at the bar, and now presented a physiognomy that indicated a deep depression and a possible storm warning in his underpants.

Stimulated by the coffee and Marlboro Reds, we headed to a local church hall for the first of two rehearsals prior to our brace of shows in St Peter Port. On the way, Jackie spoke quite openly, albeit tongue in cheek (I think), about the benefits of self-gratification and household sinks, a subject which is probably best left to the imagination. Hoping to raise the bar a tad in the conversation stakes, Neil informed us that people from St Peter Port were nicknamed Les Villais or 'townspeople', a fact which aroused mild curiosity but was possibly a bit too far removed from Jackie's personal relationship with plumbing fixtures to stir up any genuine interest. The social talk turned swiftly to the set list – a subject much closer to our hearts.

The hall, set next to the church of St Philippe in the village of Torteval, was warm and appealing, though the inclement weather continued to hound us with more than the occasional rattle and roar. Our stage backline was noticeably increased by the somewhat unusual presence of a timpani drum, that large bowl-shaped percussion instrument more commonly referred to as a kettledrum, and which was greeted with a measure of excitement by John. We soon found out why. During our rendition of 'Who Do You Love', John leaped up from his drum kit, grabbed a pair of beater sticks and began to belt out a primitive rhythm on it, paying particular attention to the instrument's foot pedal, which, when pressed, raised the pitch of the drum. Although this particular effect was quite dramatic (a sort of ascending 'boinngg!'), the effort required seemed to affect John's facial expression every time he attacked the drum head, which resulted in a wide-eyed look of surprise not unlike that of the long suffering, moustachioed James Finlayson in one of those old Laurel and Hardy films. Dooooh!

After a second night of drink-inspired contributions to the newly founded Jack Jones- Lookalike Caribbean Holiday Fund, we headed back to the church hall for our second and final rehearsal. Due to the incessant stormy weather and the thought of another disturbed night due to unacceptably draughty windows, Bob sent our tour manager out to purchase a small tent, which he intended to erect in his hotel room!

The question on everybody's lips: 'How are you going to stabilise it, or do you intend to hammer steel pegs into the floor?'

The answer from Bob's lips: 'No, fuckwits. I intend to tie the guy ropes to a door knob and a radiator and, at floor level, employ anything heavy enough to hold down the sides. This may include wall bricks, cases, bedroom furniture or you.'

That evening, the tent – rendered almost firmly in place with all of the above, plus a selection of potted plants borrowed from the bar – was open for viewing and received favourable comments. We trooped off to a local club and, in the spirit of rock 'n' roll, a few of the local women were invited back to the hotel bar to help us top up Jack's profits. A couple of them ended up upstairs and one even spent the night in the tent. Its *raison d'être* was never questioned; I suppose a bunk-up's a bunk-up at the end of the day.

Both of our shows at St Peter Port's Little Theatre were well received and fortified by the presence of Rick Parfitt, who joined us on stage for a couple of songs. Being in the Channel

Islands evoked mixed feelings for Rick: 'Me and Youngie wrote 'Living on an Island' here when I was a tax exile,' he would inform Jack Jones later in the hotel bar. 'It was bloody boring – I couldn't wait to move back home.'

The following day, the Diesel Band and crew boarded a couple of very small propeller-driven planes to island-hop over to Jersey for a show at the Hotel Lido de France. I can honestly say that this was the noisiest plane I've ever been on, before or since; I couldn't hear a thing for the next few hours. That night we rocked Jersey, and Rick Parfitt once again joined us onstage for a finale that inspired the air guitarists to lower their hair to the floor and go for it. For the final beat of the final tune, Neil decided to accentuate the musical full stop with a sweeping gesture of his bass, but this downward curve was cut short by the unexpected interception of my head. Within minutes, I was in the promoter's car on my way to the hospital, clutching a towel which was helping to staunch the flow of blood from a machine-head-sized laceration on my forehead. The staff in the emergency department soon cleaned and dressed the wound before discharging me with a good old-fashioned bandage around the head and a strong painkiller. I emerged looking like an extra from *Carry On Nurse* and, in need of a local anaesthetic, made my way straight to the hotel bar where my bandmates ordered brandy for my condition. The drinks flowed and Jackie made us laugh, while at a quiet, windswept hotel in Guernsey, a Jack Jones-lookalike bemoaned his modest night's takings.

Prior to Whitesnake's first Japanese tour, we played a one-off concert at the Rainbow Theatre in London, from which I have a press clipping of the following review by one John

Orme. It's such an entertaining piece of journalism that I just had to reproduce it in its entirety:

In the beginning there was an Audience. And the Audience did seek a Sound so total that nothing would matter ever again. And the audience did take themselves to the Rainbow in search. And behold, they did find the Sound and the Word. And the Word was Whitesnake.

So devout is the following and fanaticism inspired by man-in-black David Coverdale and his get-down crew that sound quality, clarity and diversity mean nothing – quantity is the only criterion, and Whitesnake wheel it out in mega-watts.

No problem – heavy metal has always been a baptism by total immersion at the point where sound and feeling merge into bombastic ritual – but on Wednesday night the sound was over-cranked to the point where Ian Paice's drums sounded like he was driving heavy earth-moving equipment; he collided with the jarring bass to form a blanket compression of sound so solid that the guitars of Micky Moody and Bernie Marsden, the staple of a band like 'Snake', bounced off into the stratosphere. For all the flying fingers and heroic poses they would have been just as effective with their leads out.

Working with their personal Big Bang theory, the Whites wrung out the decibels on tracks from the 'Lovebites' album plus material from the new offering, 'Ready and Willing'.

No changes there; it's all 'Me man, you lie down' lyrical delicacy, the riffs as solid and sterile as ever, except the title cut does have an almost funky interplay between Jon Lord's clarinet and Paice's rattling drums. Progressive, huh?

Coverdale himself is a man of few words, most of them 'Waaahgghh' or 'Rrrigghhtt', but he can do no wrong with the devoted, who responded to every piece of throat with the uniformity of string puppets. Mick Moody, bless him, researched the blues for his slide solo feature, lulling some nodding heads to sleep for the rest of the show, but managing to slightly boost the evening's crass count. The Whitesnake home for retired rockers is now open, visiting hours 8 to 10.30pm.

Memo: Fair enough John, but I'm mystified by the reference to Jon Lord's clarinet; it was a long time ago but I have no recollection of us playing any Acker Bilk tunes. And the *Lovebites* album? Surely *Lovehunter*.

PS. I'd been researching the blues for at least fifteen years prior to the gig!

A few hours before the Rainbow show, we recorded a promotional video for the chosen single (for it was the One, and the Audience liketh it). 'Fool for Your Loving' would turn out to be a firm favourite with fans across the globe, and has evolved into a bit of a rock classic. Hanging around the backstage area between the video and the show while awaiting the arrival of 2,000 rock fans and John Orme, I chatted to a lady who was old enough to know better than hang around backstage areas. What transpired was par for course those days and, I have to admit, my extracurricular socialising sometimes took precedence over the show itself. However, it wasn't all hedonism and selfish indulgence; we did manage to write and perform a few good tunes as well. There was quite often an acoustic guitar at hand to thrash out a few new ideas, plus elongated soundchecks to put some of these into practice.

By this time, the set list consisted of tracks from the *Snakebite* EP, *Trouble*, *Lovehunter* and the soon to be released *Ready an' Willing*, plus Deep Purple's 'Mistreated' and, as an encore, 'Breakdown' from David's first solo album. Quite an entertaining set really, disregarding Johnny O's personalised critique.

Job done; next gig – the Yubin Chokin Hall, Tokyo!

Although I still meet people from the past who claim to be young at heart, they tend to look slightly older in other places. And in other places, they tend to look slightly different. Take Japan, for instance. When Whitesnake first visited Japan, it was virgin territory for me, though, in the literal sense, I would quickly discover that it wasn't. And when Paul McCartney arrived at Tokyo's Narita airport on 16 January 1980 and was promptly busted for possession of half an ounce of marijuana, it left us with a slight advantage in the popularity stakes: Macca 0 – Whitesnake anything from 1 upwards.

We finished off the new album at Central Recorders during the first half of February, and then took six weeks off to do what rock 'n' rollers do in their spare time.

Our manager had decided that the most economical way for Whitesnake to travel to Japan was to fly tourist class for something like twenty-two hours courtesy of Pan Am Clipper flight 002. This particular transport of delight traversed the world heading east from London and calling at Frankfurt, Beirut, New Delhi and Hong Kong before landing at Tokyo. A hell of a journey or, more appropriately, a journey from hell, especially for nervous fliers like myself who found themselves clutching the arm rests and monitoring their palpitations during lift-offs and landings. Between these uneasy interruptions, we continued to operate in the manner to which we had become accustomed: drinking, smoking, joking, acquainting ourselves with the crew and discussing music – both our own and of others.

As a possible means of introducing the hapless air passenger to the sights and smells of the Orient, the Hong Kong authorities kindly provided us with a welcoming belt of raw sewage, which permeated the cabin of the plane via the fresh air ducts as we landed. 'Hong Kong? More like bloody Hong Pong!'

We left the plane for a brief wander around the duty-free area and a beer, but were soon back on board and ready for yet another lift-off. The long journey was beginning to take its toll and, due to an ever-increasing combination of tiredness and boredom, I found myself bereft of conscious travelling companions, so I ordered another drink in the vain hope that I'd be able to influence my erratic circadian rhythms. It took a few more large ones before the influence became total. The next thing I knew, I was being roused from my slumbers by the hostess, who was informing everybody that we'd be landing at Tokyo's Narita Airport in half an hour. Groan.

After a longer than anticipated immigration and customs check (thanks, Mr McCartney), our travel-weary retinue headed off into the early-evening Tokyo rush-hour traffic in the hope of grabbing a couple of hours' sleep prior to our first social engagement – a traditional Japanese meal, courtesy of our record company.

Incredibly, we all made it to the restaurant on time, citing hunger pangs and mounting excitement due to the anticipation of a night on the town. For some of us, this was our first time in Japan, so eyes down for a full house! The restaurant – very traditional in style and complete with serving geisha girls – offered us a private room in which to enjoy the welcoming feast. The first course was a small bowl of raw fish chopped up into bodily segments, which, in my case, was presented with the former fish's head pointing directly at me, its expressionless face devoid of all emotion. Unsure of the exact procedure regarding fish refusal, I looked about me for an unwanted-fish deposit box but, alas, there were none present. I executed a quick room scan for a suitable receptacle but, apart from the jacket pocket of the man from the record company, no opportunity was forthcoming. I had no option but to bide my time toying with the ex-fish until the opportunity presented itself. Once the geisha girls had returned to the kitchen and everybody was deep in conversation, I seized the day and tipped it down the back of a nearby radiator.

In retrospect – and now somewhat guilt-ridden – I regret my actions and sincerely hope the restaurant owners eventually found it! Just imagine if it's still there in a dark, silent room that the owners have been unable to let for over thirty years due to an inexplicably vile stench of death, its services no longer required except for a grisly scene in one of Takashi Shimizu's horror films. To the best of my recollection, the remainder of the fare was mostly edible and the drink totally acceptable (there's always malarkey with beer and sake).

As I sipped my after-dinner digestive, I tried to imagine the Japanese equivalent of a pie and a pint being served at the local pub, The Shogun's Head:

Meal Deals

Choose from our 'dicing with death' platter – Poisonous Fugu Puffer Fish Pasty with a bottle of Sapporo Lager (sake top) – or, for a longer life, good ol' Raw Cod and Rice with Mushy Peas washed down with a large Shochu on the rocks. Already eaten? Then knock back half a gallon of Stella Artois geisha-beater – you know it makes senseless!

The next port of call was a highly recommended club called the Byblos – a place which, over the next ten days, we would come to regard as almost a second home. On our initial visit, we were shown to the VIP section: a seated area with panoramic views of the dancefloor and bar which David immediately christened the Snake Pit. Within minutes, our table was surrounded by a bevy of female admirers awaiting attention; within seconds, they had it. It was Mel Brooks time again, cue self-assured voices: 'It's good to be the king!'

The following day, a number of self-assured and gratified young men joined the rest of the entourage at the Yubin Chokin Hall for the first of five shows in Tokyo. This run of gigs would incorporate three different venues across the city: odd, though possibly a tradition in Japanese rock promotion. In the backstage area, I was introduced to a representative from the Ibanez guitar company while Bernie spoke to a rep from Roland, the company responsible for the production of the groundbreaking G-303 guitar synthesiser. The amiable man from Ibanez offered me one of their Artist models in an endorsement deal, which I approved.

'I also like the look of the blonde semi-acoustic model in your brochure,' I ventured. 'Could I have one of those too?'

'Ahh, sooo, should be possible,' he replied. He bowed slightly, and then readied himself for the journey back to head office.

'Er, and that lovely George Benson model, you know, the top of the range one,' I continued. He shot me a worried look.

'Oh, this expensive. You pray jazz too?' came the response to match the worried look. 'I make other call.'

'Oh, and you know that George Benson signature logo between the last two frets?' I added.

'Yes?' he answered uneasily.

'Could you replace that with *my* name, please?' I asked somewhat sheepishly. He cast me a jaundiced eye before beating a hasty retreat. Well, if you don't ask. . .

To be honest, I thought I'd pushed my luck with that request but not so. Prior to our return to England, I was presented with a full complement of free guitars and am still the proud owner of the only known Ibanez George Benson GB 10 signature model in existence with my name inscribed upon it!

This was Magnet's first assignment on the road in his capacity as Whitesnake's tour manager and, though he'd already been acquainted with David and Jon in Deep Purple, and Bernie in Paice Ashton Lord, it took no time at all for the rest of us to appreciate his professionalism, leadership qualities and an ability to see the funny side of things. Perfect! His tactical skills were soon put to good use during the show at Nagoya, when, in their determination to hang on to a towel thrown from the stage, two over-enthusiastic souvenir hunters were about to engage in hand-to-hand combat. Magnet suddenly appeared from the darkened periphery of the auditorium, wearing an orange gilet, and made his way to the centre block in the stalls. Arriving at the scene of dissent and administering the art of gentle persuasion, he removed the towel from the tenacious grip of the warring factions before applying an unorthodox technique, which involved the use of both hands *and* teeth to tear it into two pieces. Job done: now sit down and behave.

After the show, we retired to our customary gathering

in the hotel bar and I was approached by an intense young woman who presented me with a hand-knitted doll. Closer inspection revealed it to have been made in my image (complete with fedora and moustache), which I found to be both complimentary and a bit strange. I bought her a coke and sat at the bar while she surveyed me with the piercing stare of a psychopath. After twenty minutes of her extreme scrutiny, I began to feel uneasy and moved to another table, which, thankfully, was occupied by young women with less alarming demeanours. The staring continued until I suggested to my immediate company that we move. Thankfully, she didn't pursue her own personal goggle-fest and left, mumbling, soon after. The following day, I half-expected a package to arrive at the soundcheck that, once unwrapped, would reveal another, identical doll, this time with pins stuck in it.

Following a show in Osaka (a city to which we travelled on the famed Bullet train), we had a night off in Kanazawa. After dinner, I went with Jon and Bernie to a club across the road from our hotel with the sole intention of having a couple of beers with the indigenous. Once outside, we encountered the usual fixture: a poised, fit-looking man in a tracksuit who looked like he was no stranger to the noble art of karate.

'Good evening,' said Jon in his usual genial manner. 'What is the admission charge?'

'Orrr, caha come in. Is couples night – must have woman,' explained the doorman.

'We don't have women with us,' replied Jon. 'We're working here tomorrow night.'

'Sorry, but caha come in,' he countered.

'We're with Whitesnake,' clarified an optimistic Bernie,

who, pointing towards Jon, proudly announced, 'This is Jon Lord from Deep Purple.'

The expression on the doorman's face was a picture of absolute surprise. 'Jon Ror? Dee Purper? Orrrr!' He turned and ran into the club and, from our vantage point at the door, we could make out his excited cries of 'Jon Ror . . . Dee Purper! Jon Ror . . . Dee Purper!' Thirty seconds later, the door burst open and a dozen of his friends and colleagues emerged wide-eyed and in a state of manifest excitement. They proceeded to run around like headless chickens, spreading the word to no one in particular. 'Jon Ror . . . Dee Purper! Jon Ror . . . Dee Purper!'

Confident that we'd made an impression and that free entrance and VIP treatment was now a mere formality, we strode towards the door. Suddenly, the commotion stopped as the doorman held up his arm, showing us the palm of his hand. His facial expression changed quickly into a mask of unadulterated seriousness and, in a grave voice, he announced, 'Still caha come in.'

The promoters were an odd couple – a shifty middle-aged Korean and a nebulous Dane – who kept a fairly low profile. They gave the distinct impression that they were new to the business or, perhaps, just new to each other. Mmm. To their credit, they did make an effort on a personal level by taking us to a fish restaurant where we were given the opportunity to choose our dinner while it was still alive and swimming about in a glass tank. I can't recall if any of us accepted the offer, but I do remember the Korean insisting on us joining him for a starter of live prawns, which were duly fried to death on a hotplate in the middle of our table. The sound of their agonised screeching as they slowly expired was as disturbing as it was unnecessary. If we'd wanted to familiarise ourselves with the sound of living creatures verbalising the embodiment of extreme pain, we could have listened to Wayne County and the Electric Chairs, or that singer from Any Trouble.

A few days into the tour, I woke up with a sore head and looked about me. I was alone in bed in a small, neat apartment and had absolutely no idea where I was. The young lady I had left the Byblos with had no doubt gone to work, leaving me with the task of finding my hotel, the name of which I couldn't remember and the address of which I had no recollection. I found this quite worrying, though you're never quite alone with a personality disorder. ('Where am I?' 'I don't know.' 'Well, find out then.' 'Fuck off, you do it!') I glanced at my watch and suddenly realised that we were due to leave for a soundcheck in forty-five minutes, and mobile phones were a fairly unknown commodity. Ignoring the urge to shower, I found my clothes, donned my underpants, shirt and trousers, then entered into some kind of involuntary hopping-and-falling-over dance as I attempted to put on my socks while standing up. Once outside, I managed to hail a taxi manned by a driver wearing a suit, a peaked cap and just one white glove. He spoke in Japanese; I answered in English and then quickly deduced that it was going nowhere.

'Hotel – tall, many western people,' I blurted out. 'And do you have anything for a headache?' He stared at me like I was some out-of-it rock musician and said something indecipherable. I racked my brain for recently embedded place names, and reeled off 'Ginza . . . Shinjuku . . . Shibuya, er, Akihabara'. Something struck a chord and his eyes turned Tic Tac Toe.

'Orrrr,' he said, before putting his foot down.

This guy was on the ball, and his powers of perception were incredibly welcome. We headed downtown, and then drove around searching for landmarks. After fifteen minutes of head-thumping, scrutinised searching, I recognised the hotel facade.

'Stop!' I yelled.

'Orrrrr!' responded One White Glove with a sudden stomp on the brake.

Seconds later, the glove in question was holding quite a lot of my yen, but I was grateful for his efforts.

Magnet was pacing the foyer as my legs raced through the door followed breathlessly by the rest of me. Regarding me with those steady, coolly calculating eyes of his, in a rich Black Country accent laced with delightfully wry humour, he declared, 'Nice of you to join us, Mr Moody. Will you be requiring a truss later?'

This short yet hugely enjoyable tour climaxed with two nights at Tokyo's Shibuya Kokaido Hall where, prior to the penultimate show, Magnet led us into the dressing room and, with a mischievous grin, announced, 'The rider has been updated!' Then, with a sweeping gesture of his hand, he alerted our gaze to half a dozen carefully chopped-out lines of white powder. Impartial to our looks of shock and surprise, he picked up a jar of coffee creamer and, pointing to the label, announced, 'Best quality Creap!' Creap? Yes, a commercial brand of powdered milk which had cunningly realised its personal appellation as a contraction of CREAming Powder. Interestingly, the official Japanese translation of 'creap' is 'to sneak up slowly' or 'generally unpleasant, weird individual'. Nice one, Magnet!

Disregarding the opportunity to snort powdered milk,

but fired up from another enthusiastically received gig and readily available vodka, we made our way once more to the Byblos where the Disco Kid and Pancho plus Willy not only boogied their way around the dancefloor but also took part, alongside David, in a yo-yo competition! Daft, admittedly, but it didn't seem to diminish our credibility in the eyes of our ever-present friends and admirers. And though the local champion hammered us, Neil assured us that he could 'pull a few strings' and get us free membership with the Tokyo Yo-Yo Club.

A real 'must-do' while in Tokyo was to pay a visit to the duty-free market, where a batch of the newly introduced Sony Walkman personal stereos surely awaited us. What a revelation: we can have music wherever we go! There would be less conversation on the plane journey home, that was for sure. I also invested in a wristwatch with an inbuilt calculator and a satin baseball jacket embroidered with a beautiful tiger motif. I wore it for a meal prior to our final show – a social event which promised a novel dining experience and one that Bernie had organised through the local Gibson guitars representative, a man proffering complementary Larry Carlton t-shirts and a company expense account. After a short cab ride, we met up at a discreet little restaurant specialising in a *sukiyaki*-style dish called *shabu shabu*. This noteworthy title was, we would soon learn, an onomatopoeia derived from the sound made when the ingredients were stirred in a cooking pot. To my recollection, the aural effect of this gastronomic disturbance was more of a 'ssshhwwiiisshhhwwoahaschwish' than a 'shabu shabu', unless the latter relates to the sound made by toothless *bon viveurs* eating this particular dish with greased chopsticks. Presented with the emphasis on fondue, it was delicious, especially when complemented with the ubiquitous sake!

Whitesnake bade farewell to Japan with a cracking gig and a firm promise to return. What with all that unsurpassed hospitality, state-of-the-art duty-free goods and the lovely little gifts from the lovely little fans, it was like all our birthdays had come at once.

During the encore, I was momentarily distracted by an object that suddenly appeared in front of me. Was it a bird? Was it a plane? Was it a young lady's *kamikaze* father on the lookout for a dishonourable Jack the Lad? No, it was a lone shoe I'd discovered under my bed at the Bristol Holiday Inn and which I'd decided to adopt as a sort of mascot. The roadies now kept it with the equipment and it would occasionally appear unexpectedly on top of amps or on Jon's organ. It was now suspended from the lighting truss by fishing wire, sporting cardboard wings, and hovered just inches from my face, much to the bemusement of the unsuspecting fans and the amusement of the suspected road crew. Though I'd been hoisted by my own petard, it was nice to know that the crew were in good spirits *and* taking care of the much-travelled Lone Shoe, which would, without doubt, appear again in the most unlikely of places.

On the plane home, in between the usual bonhomie, I amused myself by browsing through a bunch of fanzines written and illustrated by Japanese Whitesnake fans. I was especially charmed by the cartoon strips in which we appeared, looking like long-haired fourteen-year-old children (or in the case of both Jon and myself, fourteen-year-old children with moustaches).

CHAPTER 29

WIND-UPS AT RINGO'S

These days, we all live under the shadow of uncertainty in a world fraught with danger – namely the threat of a nuclear holocaust, terrorism and televised golf. In the spring of 1980, the last had yet to evolve into the global menace that now assaults our screens on an almost daily basis. It's something we have to live with, and death from boredom has become a worrying reality for sports-loving couch potatoes.

We'd only been back from Japan for a week or so when six terrorists burst into the Iranian embassy and took twenty-six people hostage. Terrorist acts involving middle-eastern countries were relatively scarce on British soil back then, and even my shock-proof watch was taken aback by such an abominable occurrence, which resulted in the deaths of five terrorists and one of the hostages. Thank God for the SAS, who we watched going into action from the comfort of our own living rooms. Or from the pub, where recreational drinking would often lead to recreational anything, and where one was never short of company!

My close friendship and musical adventures with Bob Young continued to flourish and happy times were in abundance. Bob's philosophy was simple: do it well and have a good laugh while you're doing it. And we did! This was a doctrine that I embraced wholeheartedly, as I suppose anybody would (except Victor Meldrew or Mick Wall, perhaps). And in the midst of all this horseplay, we managed to come up with a song that had commercial possibilities: a reggae-flavoured tune called 'All the Good Friends', which once again gave Francis Rossi an opportunity to put on his producer's hat. Fun prevailed, and, in between takes, we created a version of the Nolan Sisters' 'I'm In the Mood for Dancing' in the style of 'I'm In the Mood' by John Lee Hooker – i.e. with me doing an impersonation of John Lee Hooker singing the Nolans' hit and Bob providing the spoken voice of Howlin' Wolf. Although this might sound rather surreal, believe me, it comes quite naturally when you're daft.

At the end of May, as Whitesnake rehearsed at E-Zee Hire in preparation for the forthcoming UK tour, Nottingham Forest won the European Cup courtesy of a goal by the cigarette-smoking, pie-eating John Robertson – a true working-class hero. Oh, and our new album, *Ready an' Willing*, was released.

The first reviews for *Ready an' Willing* appeared a few days before the start of our UK tour, and were heralded by the interestingly named Mike Mercury from *New Musical Express* – though the name didn't fool me as I, too, was a fan of 1960s television puppet series, including *Supercar*! He presented a piece of such a constructive nature that, after Orme's literary onslaught, it was positively glowing. He even ended his review with, 'I believe, admirable though Rainbow and Gillan are, it's Whitesnake who'll prove, in the long run, to be the most productive branch of the Deep Purple family tree.' Geoff Barton was similarly heartening, awarding us four stars for our efforts, and *Record Mirror*'s Daniel Bonutto gave us reasons to be cheerful with a string of compliments. These examples are from the only related reviews that appear in my personal archives, so I can't offer any negative ones, though I'm sure not everyone agreed with the views expressed by these particular writers. Hopefully, they will be reproduced in the forthcoming publication, *Whitesnake: The Shit Reviews*, compiled by Mick Wall and John Orme.

The *Ready an' Willing* tour kicked off at the Liverpool Empire to an audience that was so enthusiastic it was impossible not to give your all. We worked our way up to Scotland (more uninhibited enthusiasm from the audience) and back down again. By the time our coach slipped into Birmingham, it was time to meet the press. Brian Harrigan from *New Music News* was one of the journalists invited to a show at the Odeon, and afterwards – having interviewed David in the bar – he was sitting in a room partying with a motley collection of Whitesnake members, crew and sundry hangers-on when there was a knock at the door. Brian Harrigan remembers:

> Someone opens the door and in strolls an elephant followed by a crocodile and, dear God, a giraffe. I look at my drink through one squinting eye and decide on the spot that this is obviously nature's way of introducing me to delirium tremens. As I'm resigning myself to never drinking again the elephant takes its head off and I can feel panic rolling round my veins. The head of Whitesnake

guitarist Bernie Marsden hovers into view on top of the elephant's body. The croc reveals itself as Magnet and the giraffe is guitarist Micky Moody.

I've heard of bands making sure that things don't get to tedious on the road but I've never come across any that's gone to the extent of buying pantomime costumes for a tour.

Later, Marsden and Moody dress up in a pantomime horse outfit and take a canter down to the hotel reception accompanied by Magnet. Magnet stands at the night porter's desk while the horse does a quiet but stylish soft shoe shuffle.

'Can I help you, sir?' asks the night porter.

'No, I'm with the horse,' says Magnet scarcely able to hold the giggles.

'Very good sir,' replies the porter and returns to his office without batting an eyelid.

He's either blind, unbelievably cool, or the Birmingham Holiday Inn regularly has pantomime horses dropping in at 3 in the morning. Whatever the reason, he receives Whitesnake's undying admiration.

Of course, you can't believe everything you read in the press, and I can state categorically that Bernie was not wearing an elephant costume – it was actually a panda.

During our two-day sojourn at the Birmingham Holiday Inn, we learned that the album had risen to No.6 in the LP charts. Hooray! Being in a top ten album-selling band was a personal first for Neil, Bernie and me, and we celebrated in style at our next house of temporary residence, the Sandpiper Hotel in Manchester. Following the second of our two shows at the Manchester Apollo, we headed back to the hotel, which certainly lived up to its reputation as a *real* rock 'n' roll hotel – i.e. one that actively encouraged late-night drinking and related revelry! We settled in front of the fireplace in the bar, the acoustic guitars appeared and, hey-ho, it was sing-song time! My overriding memory from this session – give or take a few pantomime-animal interruptions – is of a rousing version of the Small Faces hit 'All Or Nothing', notably inspired by the percussive obtrusions of Willie Dee, the singer from our tour support, Gary Moore's G-Force. This masterstroke (or rather master thump) of resounding proportions was enthusiastically delivered at precisely the right moment in each chorus by Mr Dee whacking the large brass overhang above the fireplace with his fist! Such expressionism not only added to the general ambience, it eventually created a fist-sized dimpled effect on the smooth brass finish: 'And it's BOOM BOOM, all or nothing!'

The chosen single, 'Fool for Your Loving', was selling well and would eventually reach No.13 in the charts. I think it was David who retitled it 'Fuel for Your Oven', which in retrospect probably deserves a mention, if only to amuse lovers of witty puns and nonsense verse.

You meet all types on the road. After the second show in Birmingham, I started chatting to a lady in the hotel bar who, it transpired, worked nearby at the ITV television studios. I asked her what brought her to a place like this, and she informed me that she was a boom swinger. My perception receptors swung swiftly into motion and, in my mind's eye, there appeared an image of a sexually permissive nymphomaniac with an explosives fetish. 'Oo-er,' I thought. Should I carry on with this chat-up? Thankfully, my concerns were allayed when she further explained that her job was to position the large boom microphones in the correct places so as not to impede the cameras' access or the performers' ability to move around freely. We were getting on rather well when our moment was interrupted by a laughing giraffe with a West Midlands accent, who wandered past with a pint in his manly hoof. Magnet – who was fooling nobody in that outfit – eventually settled next to Willy Fyffe, who was standing at the bar with some fans and wearing the back half of the pantomime horse. The front half was soon spotted walking towards the toilet, with the exposed part of the costume displaying the unmistakable hind parts of Bernie's blue Formula One driving suit.

At this point, more than one person must have begged the question: how does the front half of a pantomime horse take a piss?

Back in a world devoid of vaudevillian stunts and women's interesting job descriptions, Whitesnake's live performances were, as they say, ass-kicking, and it was indeed a sweaty bunch that left the stage to roars of approval each night. The critics would sometimes have a go at us for including too many solo spots in the show, but our take on this was, as the Americans say, 'If you've got it, flaunt it!' And we did. Slide guitar, keyboard and drums did indeed perform solos, and Bernie excelled in an extended solo during 'Mistreated'. Amid these somewhat diverse musical interludes, David would often leg it backstage for a lungful of oxygen. And who could blame him? He sang with such power and passion that he often didn't have time to breathe in.

During one performance, David introduced Jon with, 'This song features Jon Lord and his huge organ.' Jon responded with a two-fingered gesture.

'*Two* huge organs!' counteracted David.

Towards the end of this highly successful tour, we played two sell-out concerts at the Hammersmith Odeon, which were recorded under the watchful eye, ears and wit of Martin Birch, who took up his usual position in the producer/engineer's seat. The resulting double album would consist of highlights from these shows, plus a previous Odeon recording from 1978, which, until then, had only been available in Japan. *Live in the Heart of the City* would prove to be one of the band's most popular recordings and, soon after its release later that year, would rise to No.5 in the UK album charts, as well as generating respectable sales worldwide.

At that particular time, I lived close to the Odeon and, before one of our two sell-out shows, chose to make my way to the afternoon soundcheck on my bicycle. As I unwittingly overtook the band's limousine on the traffic-stalled Hammersmith Broadway, wearing, among other things, a beret and a parka, there were both groans and laughter from within. Image? What image?

On 6 July 1980 we assembled at Startling Studios, Tittenhurst Park to commence work on our new album. It was good to be back at Ringo's gaff with its cosy studio, welcoming bedrooms and a small, family-orientated staff who provided us with wholesome food and drinks as well as keeping the place clean and tidy. Although this arrangement was a far cry from the semi-decadent indulgences of Clearwell Castle, it was a pleasant environment, plus there was a pub within walking distance. Indeed, the bar staff at The Cannon public house were given a rare treat after we'd discovered some old orange curtains in an outhouse following a game of football in the Tittenhurst grounds. By the simple expedient of draping the lengths of material around us then cutting the white plastic football in half to produce two bowl-shaped head pieces, Bernie and myself were instantly transformed into a couple of shaven-headed Hare Krishna devotees! We entered the pub banging tambourines and chanting, 'Hare Krishna, Hare Rama, Hare Secombe, Harry Worth!' It soon became patently obvious that either John or George Harrison had already introduced some of the devotees to the area when a barmaid exclaimed, 'Oh no – they're back!'

There was a certain amount of 'import duty' going on, and Willy would assume the role of 'bird chauffer' and pick up the lady in question from a nearby railway station.

It was time for a wind-up! There was a gift shop in nearby Ascot that sold personalised tea mugs and I had a cunning plan, so I bought one with 'John' emblazoned on the side. Back at Tittenhurst Park, armed only with a small stone and a knife, I crafted a few chips and scrapes on the receptacle in question before rubbing a credible amount of dirt into the defaced areas, thus transforming the mug into a condition nowadays referred to as 'distressed'. Having gleefully alerted the others to my little scheme, I legged it up to David's room to inform him that I'd discovered a mug in a cupboard and that it must surely have belonged to the house's former owner, John Lennon. I then offered it to him as a present, much to his delight. The following day, he excitedly informed us that 'John's' mug had already inspired him to write a new song. Later that day, he decided to clean it up in the dishwasher; once removed, he was somewhat taken aback by the results. His muse now resembled a brand new mug with a few chips out of it. I'd been rumbled, but there was more to come!

Nicky Horne from Capital Radio was due to record an interview with David the following day, and the exchange would take place on a bench by the small man-made lake in the grounds. Bernie was now in cahoots and, a few hours before the expected arrival of Mr Horne, we sneaked down to the bench with a couple of sharp knives to carry out our dirty work. Ten minutes of inspired handiwork and schoolboy giggling produced carvings on the bench that proclaimed 'JL loves YO' and 'John and Yoko were here'. A couple of days later, we tuned into Capital Radio, where an enthusiastic Nicky Horne started his interview with, 'I'm at the famous Tittenhurst Park, the house were John and Yoko lived and where John recorded his *Imagine* album, and I'm sitting on a bench by a small lake with David Coverdale. And this is no ordinary bench!'

And so it continued until the two culprits had to leave the room due to an inability to suppress lip-biting and uncontrollable sniggering.

Of course, it wasn't all mischief and recklessness; there was some serious music being laid down. David had obviously spent a good deal of his time musing on new tunes, and some of his musical ideas were very inspired. 'Don't Break My Heart Again', 'Till the Day I Die' and 'Come and Get It' were solo offerings of a high quality, and joint efforts like 'Hit and Run' and 'Would I Lie to You' also stood out. In retrospect, the bluesy side of Whitesnake may have been overlooked and only 'Lonely Days and Lonely Nights' paid homage to that particular influence.

The recording room itself was quite small (after all, it was basically John Lennon's personal studio) so, to get that 'big' drum sound – often associated with John Bonham – Martin had Ian set up his kit under the stairwell in the main hallway of the house. This produced a natural reverberation, which was pivotal in the overall recorded sound, though if you wished to avoid the onset of premature tinnitus it was wise to avoid the hallway when he was playing!

After a short spell back at Central Recorders to edit and mix the live recordings from the Hammersmith Odeon dates, we packed our bags and readied ourselves for a trip to the United States.

CHAPTER 30

THANKS FOR THE SUPPORT: WE SHALL ALWAYS WEAR IT

Ian Anderson had established his frontman status by crafting an image of a long-haired, bearded, wild-eyed extrovert who played the flute while standing on one leg. And, believe me, it hadn't gone unnoticed! It was evident at the soundcheck of the first gig that Bernie and I were in a frolicsome frame of mind, and, before Jethro Tull had even finished their own soundcheck, a roadie had been despatched to the local music store to purchase a couple of flageolets. Although more a recorder than a flute, the flageolet was, nevertheless, symbolic enough in its appearance for the pair of us to demonstrate our powers of piss-taking. David, Jon and Magnet would react with glee to some of our antics, while Neil and Ian often looked on with a mixture of amusement and apprehension. The Disco Kid and Pancho could concoct the unpredictable at a moment's notice. Who would be next?!

Although the choice of Whitesnake as the opening act for

Jethro Tull was hardly on a par with the Snafu/ELP debacle, it was not an ideal pairing. Whitesnake was a kick-ass rock band and Jethro Tull was progressive rock, so, as well as a lack of both leather and denim jackets, there would be a surfeit of odd men, often with well-cultivated beards. Let's face it, JT was never going to attract many of the opposite sex, and throwing shapes at blokes who looked like Victorian labourers was never on my agenda, personally. Sure, I admit to some exaggeration there. Some of them looked like off-duty traffic wardens; others looked like the kind of people who liked to argue with off-duty traffic wardens.

At the soundcheck, we'd noticed that the front of the stage was flanked by two walkways – or 'ego-ramps' – and a white line divided the stage from the walkways. After our soundcheck, Magnet informed us that under no circumstances were we to step over the line – this was Ian Anderson's territory. Prior to the first show at the Wimico Civic Centre in Salisbury, Maryland, Bernie and I unveiled an example of things to come by hopping around one-footed backstage while blowing quite tunelessly on our flageolets. A quick, strangulated refrain from 'Living in the Past' followed, which brought appreciative giggles from within the Whitesnake camp and concerned looks from passing Jethro Tull roadies.

Standing at opposite sides of the stage, both Moody and Marsden were immediately confronted by the indisputable confines of the white lines. By the time we'd reached the first chorus of the second song, Bernie and his Les Paul were strutting their way down the ramp. A split-second later, I was heading, Les Paul in hand, swiftly along the other one, throwing shapes and casting baleful glares at the disconcerted throng. A few moments later, we scurried back. Mission accomplished!

Needless to say, Magnet had the last word: 'If it 'appens again, we'll be off.'

After our spot, and just before JT went on stage, I came across David, who was talking to somebody in a space suit, glass helmet and all.

'Micky, this is Eddie Jobson, Jethro Tull's keyboard player. He's from our neck of the woods originally.' I shook hands with him.

'Nice to meet you, Eddie,' I said, while casting a mischievous eye over his apparel. 'When are you on stage?'

'Oh, in a few minutes,' he replied.

'Aren't you going to get changed into your stage clothes then?' I concluded. And so it continued.

Bass player Dave Pegg had alerted us to the fact that Mr Anderson ran a tight ship and that late nights were frowned upon. Before the next show, we arranged to have members of our road crew positioned at various points backstage and, after an initial signal, courtroom-like shouts echoed throughout.

'Call Eddie Jobson!' ('Call Eddie Jobson! Call Eddie Jobson!')

'Call Dave Pegg!' ('Call Dave Pegg! Call Dave Pegg!')

'Set them free!' ('Set them free! Set them free!')

Bernie and I had genuine respect for the band's musicianship, especially guitarist Martin Barr, who could flit between progressive rock and blues quite effortlessly. However, the shenanigans continued.

As the tour went on, the white-line traversing was reduced to just an occasional 'dipping-a-toe-in-the-water' episode, and Neil and Eddie Jobson became quite pally. Cue another Moody and Marsden wind-up! Shopping at a department store in Cleveland, Ohio, we purchased a pair of cheap, pale blue

Y-fronts and headed back to our hotel, where, with the aid of a brown magic-marker pen, we inscribed the Y-fronts with an arrowed heart and the words 'Neil loves Eddie'. Naughty! Once ensconced in our dressing room prior to the show that evening, the underpants in question were secreted in Neil's bag, where at an opportune moment they would be removed and exposed by Bernie. I can only describe the opportune moment as unfortunate timing, for just as Bernie reached into Neil's bag, removed then held up the undergarment with a 'Neil, what's this then?' the unsuspecting Eddie walked in playing 'Ain't No Love' on a violin! After a second or two – which seemed to freeze in time – Bernie fell to the ground and wedged the defaced smalls under the nearest chair, leaving the slightly bewildered Eddie to contemplate the amused faces in the room.

A few days later, at the Holiday Inn in Kansas City, Magnet stepped into a lift where a redneck accused him of being 'a goddamned faggot', then moved towards him. It took only one well-aimed punch from our illustrious tour manager to flatten him against the lift wall, from which he slowly slid to the floor, unconscious.

Ian and Jon's families were based in Los Angeles for the duration, so they would fly back there as often as possible. Given that our forty-five-minute opening slot was early in the evening, they sometimes caught a late flight back to L.A. in order to enjoy a couple of days of family life. The intensity of this tight flight schedule sometimes meant that our set had to be cut short, which broke the contractual agreement and gave cause to a longer interval. Ian's personal mindset was to give the audience the full quota of songs, albeit played at increased tempos. This became painfully obvious one night when we found ourselves playing the blues ballad 'Ain't No Love' at a speed not dissimilar to Motörhead's 'Ace of Spades'.

As our final song, 'Take Me With You', thundered to its full stop, Ian threw his sticks aside and ran straight off stage to a waiting limo, followed by Jon, Marlboro in mouth, struggling to keep up with the drummer's Linford Christie impersonation.

David would keep us amused with his introductory bellow before the song 'Ready an' Willing'. What had started out as a precursory 'Are you ready an' willing?' began to vary from night to night. This in turn produced some classic malapropisms, the most memorable being 'Are you Freddie from Wigan?' and 'Are you Willy from Reading?' Another one of his regular participations was to accompany our opening power chord with a personalised greeting – e.g. 'Hello, Chicago!' This salutation peaked in the Oklahoman town of Norman when his 'Hello, Norman!' brought us to our knees with helpless laughter, causing Bernie to drop his Les Paul, which clanged with indignation through his Marshall stack. The image of Norman Wisdom stayed with us for a long time, as did the image of the fat bird at our table in the hotel bar afterwards, whose bottom was so massive that when she got up to go to the toilet the chair remained wedged to her arse.

Of course, it wasn't all rock 'n' roll crazies; sometimes you got tired, and sometimes the blues kicked in. My usual antidote to the latter was to go to my room, pick up my guitar and play it until dawn.

AC/DC had become a big draw, so when we were offered the support slot on their month-long German/French tour it was a no-brainer. The scene was set for a night of no-nonsense rock 'n' roll where Gibson guitars were in pole position: Angus

Young with his SG Standard, Bernie with his Les Paul and me with both (my SG being set up for slide). The shows turned out to be classic rock gigs, all stand-ups and all sold out. The Ack-Dacks (as David referred to them) were bona-fide rockers who liked a game of darts prior to going onstage; if their game overran then tough – the audience just had to wait. Quality!

A couple of weeks into the tour, we awoke to the news that John Lennon had been shot in New York. It was obviously a shock to us all, and that night we dedicated the gig to him then drank to his memory in the hotel bar afterwards. To make matters worse, David tore a ligament in his knee during the show and we had no choice but to cancel the remaining shows.

A few months later, we were back in Europe to promote the newly released *Come an' Get It* album. Slade were happy to support us, or at least some of them seemed to be. Bass player Jim Lea said very little and guitarist Dave Hill didn't say anything – or anything decipherable – even when we were good enough to invite them onto our tour coach. No, to be fair, Dave actually came up to me in the hotel bar after the final gig and mumbled something which may have alluded to enjoying the tour. He then offered something which may have alluded to a compliment.

'A loik all tha' Leadbelly stoof ya do on the bottleneck,' he ventured.

'Eh?' I responded. I was no expert on the concise works of Leadbelly, but he was certainly not known for playing slide guitar. End of conversation.

Noddy Holder and Don Powell were thankfully more at ease with the noble art of social etiquette, and we enjoyed a few bevvies together in various hotel bars. Cum on, reel the boyze!

Back in Britain, we played to houses of between three-and-a-half thousand and eight thousand and, according to the *Melody Maker* of 2 May 1981, *Come an' Get It* made the No.1 spot in the album chart, although other periodicals suggested one or two places lower. Whichever, it was still a fantastic achievement and coincided with the showing of a Levi jeans advert which I'd written with Bob Young, and which featured the magnificent voice of Graham Bonnett.

After a short headlining Japanese tour, we flew to the US as support to Judas Priest on a roadshow, which also featured Iron Maiden. It wasn't really an ideal scenario, as both Priest and the 'Irons' were disciples of heavy metal, which was not really our domain. The former was led by Rob Halford, a flamboyant biker with a thick Brummie accent. Backstage, the aroma of leather and studs was sometimes overwhelming. To be honest I had no real interest in Judas Priest, and, after catching the first ten minutes or so of their set on the first show, decided that from there on in I'd be heading off to some bar or other each night. After the gig in Memphis and a visit to some local dive for a beer, I headed back to the hotel, where I made myself comfortable at the bar. I started chatting to the guy next to me, and after a few seconds became aware that he had an English accent.

'You're a long way from home,' I said. 'What brings you here?'

He gave me a long, hard stare, then replied: 'I'm on tour with a rock band. The one that you're fucking supporting!' It was Rob Halford.

JP's guitarist K.K. Downing had extremely long hair, and one of his onstage poses required him to lean as far back as possible without falling over. Bernie suggested that he was actually trying to touch the stage area behind him with his lengthy locks. He also suggested that his full name was Keith Keith Downing, though I had reservations about that and recommended Kevin Keegan Downing as an alternative.

Whether we were only booked to play a selected number of dates or whether politics was involved escapes me, but we parted company with the tour after a couple of weeks. It had been reasonably active in the late-night-escapades department, plus we saw a bit of the country too, but it was good to get back to England and join AC/DC and Slade at the Castle Donnington Monsters of Rock festival. I also enjoyed some welcome leisure time, which enabled me to stay at home and play a selection of instruments supplied via an endorsement deal with the American company Washburn. These included not only electric and acoustic guitars but, at my request, a nylon-strung classical model and a five-string banjo. Yee-haw!

The advantage of being 'well connected' or 'knowing the right people' was highlighted when Young and Moody's management suggested that our next single could be something out of the ordinary. Further to confirmation, there was every chance of a one-off Young and Moody Band single featuring the Nolan Sisters and Lemmy! Apparently, they'd appeared on the same edition of *Top of the Pops* and had struck up an unlikely alliance. Furthermore, Cozy Powell was also on the cards to add method to the madness. Once we had the go ahead, Bob and I put our heads, guitars, pens and, most probably, spliffs together and came up with the Quo-esque 'Don't Do That'.

A week later, we gathered at Bronze Records' studio in Chalk Farm to lay down the track – an enjoyable experience marred only slightly by Lemmy's apparent inability to get the

CHAPTER 31

SNAKES AND DINNERS, BANJOS AND BREAK-UPS

The songwriting sessions for the next 'Snakes' album took place at Nomis rehearsal studios, and, after a somewhat uninspired start at a facility on the Shepperton film studios site, we settled in once more at Clearwell Castle. Nothing had changed: serving wenches, huge dinners, the odd coach full of old dears and dodderers, and a general air of tranquillity. The 'Cafay Mobeelay' was parked in its usual location and, once billeted among the four-posters, we were back in our element. Down in the basement, Martin Birch and Mick McKenna finalised the microphone positions and we were up and running.

The songs went from the sublime ('Here I Go Again' and 'Crying in the Rain') to the ridiculous ('Bloody Luxury' and 'Dancing Girls'), with a bunch of well-performed – albeit unremarkable – rockers hovering about in the middle. And the riff-laden title track, 'Saints and Sinners', seemed to just stroll off into no-man's land. To be fair, 'Rough an' Ready' and 'Victim of Love' would surface occasionally at future shows and, of course, 'Here I Go Again' would be remodelled in hair and spandex to re-emerge later in the decade as a massive hit.

Of course, the fun continued and, down in our basement den of a studio, David took on the dual role of northern working men's club master of ceremonies and resident singer, while Jon Lord acted out the perfect foil, the club piano player: 'I've worked with 'em all, y'know.' 'Yellow River' and 'You Are the Sunshine of My Life' were delivered with such authenticity that we could have been the resident combo at some salubrious dive off Stockton High Street.

'You are the apples of my aaayes!' Aaayes down for a full house!

I think many lovers of quality rock music would have been surprised and a little shocked had they been a fly on the wall at some of the sessions. Our asinine behaviour might have given them a good enough reason to feel concerned. However, within minutes of our portrayal as rock's answer to the Grumbleweeds, we would morph back into our true personas and deliver performances of a seriously rocking nature. To minimise sound leakage, poor Ian Paice was once again isolated from the rest of us, though this time it was only a curtain and not a kitchen, a hallway and a staircase that separated us. Sadly, he was not always privy to the studio antics, and cries of 'Come on!' and 'What's going on?' often rang out through our headphones.

Clearwell Castle's manager, Bernard Yeates, announced that a wedding reception had been booked well in advance and that the bride's parents had, with some reluctance, accepted the fact that a rock group would be lurking around the bar and general communal area during the festivities. We were delighted and pleasantly surprised to see Billy Connolly and his other half, sexy comedienne Pamela Stephenson, among the guests. David remarked that he would 'crawl over broken glass to get to that'. I assumed he meant Pamela, not Billy. And this was Billy before he took the pledge to abstain from his indulgences, namely booze.

I think he'd already had a few before his arrival, which he announced to a roomful of sober-suited guests who were sipping buck's fizz and enjoying the passive strains of a string quartet. 'Come on, yer bastards, liven up!' was probably not the subtlest of entrances but, hey, this was the Big Yin talking. We'd found a kindred spirit with alpha-hooligan tendencies!

From what I remember, Pamela didn't seem too shocked; she'd probably seen it all before.

As the night wore on, we ended up partying rather than recording. And why not, especially with the marching powder doing the rounds? In true rock 'n' roll fashion, some of us ended up in an anteroom waffling in a fashion peculiar to the combination of toot and booze. Enter Mr Connelly who, spying my recently acquired banjo, picked it up and proceeded to play some nifty picking piece. Of course – he'd played it with the Humblebums, the duo he appeared in with Gerry Rafferty. I was delighted, of course, and he even showed me a few tunings.

'Yay can gea o'er a hunred diff'run tunins on the five-string banjo, laddie!'

The following day, we were back in the makeshift basement studio and the banjo was back in its case. It still is.

After a month of late nights and creative effort, we packed away our Gibsons and gizmos and left Clearwell with tape boxes of backing tracks. A few days later, we were back on tour in Germany: a period scheduled to take us up to Christmas. Unfortunately, we didn't complete the full itinerary due to Ian Paice becoming infected with mumps – a condition that brought out Magnet's best old crone impersonation. 'Oh, it'll make his knackers swell up! He'll become impotent, y'know!' he intoned with a wicked grin. Sadly, the funny bits were less in evidence on that tour.

If people ever ask me why I quit a particular band – and bearing in mind that I've never been one to hang around if the feeling has gone for good – my stock reply is, 'There are only two reasons why musicians leave bands – ego clashes or money issues. Either one or the other and, occasionally, both.' In this case, it was definitely the latter; we just couldn't seem to make enough. Being in a band with three ex-members of Deep Purple constituted a financial 'pecking order' – Bernie, Neil and I were under no illusion about that. There were just too many people on the payroll, coupled with a general mistrust of the management. Once the overdubs were completed, I decided to go my own way.

Not long after, David decided that Whitesnake should take some time out to ponder its future.

Prior to Whitesnake's sojourn at Clearwell, I'd been enlisted as both guitarist and co-producer to Bob Young's interesting country-styled slant on songs he'd co-written for Status Quo. The songs, which included 'Caroline', 'Down Down' and 'Living on an Island', dovetailed nicely into this particular genre and were enriched by the country licks of guitarist Albert Lee and steel-guitarist B.J. Cole. Fun was never far away, and a touch of silly authenticity was added by the hiring of polystyrene cacti, which were dotted around the studio to excellent effect! Albert plugged in his Echoplex echo unit for 'Mean Girl' and stunned us all with his soloing before being picked up by Lonnie Donegan to play a gig later that evening. I had a chance to try out my new 'toy', the Roland GR-300 analogue guitar synthesiser, while the ubiquitous Graham Preskett was never far away with his fiddle – or anything else that might be lying around.

The recording would become *Bob Young in Quo Country* and, the following spring, Bob Young and the Double M Band found itself in one of the support spots at the annual Silk Cut Festival of country music at Wembley Arena, supporting the likes of Kris Kristofferson, Marty Robbins and Billy Swann. Somebody called Grandpa Jones was on the bill, and we learned that he'd earned his moniker by acting as a kindly elder statesman to young country artists. Boxcar Willie was also on the bill but offered no explanation as to the origin of his name. Somebody suggested it was a condition that was caused by sleeping around in too many freight trains.

Being an unknown commodity, we were greeted with a lukewarm response, though it was worth being there just to people-watch. Hell, y'all, did they like to dress up for the occasion, and Colin and June from Bromsgrove really *did* look the business in their cowboy hats and chaps.

The promoter, Mervyn Conn, had gained a reputation as somebody who was careful with his money and was averse to frittering it away on useless items such as aspiring country musicians. This was succinctly appraised by another backstage musician, who remarked, 'Conn? Con, more like.'

I was pleasantly surprised to receive a phone call from David Coverdale regarding the finishing touches to the recent recordings. More importantly, he'd thought long and hard about Whitesnake's future and had decided that changes were the way forward. Alas, Ian, Neil and Bernie didn't figure in the transformation, and their exclusion made way for Cozy Powell, former Trapeze guitarist and singer Mel Galley and, somewhat surprisingly, Colin Hodgkinson on bass. Colin, of course, was well known and respected by both of us but seemed an unusual choice for Whitesnake, until it transpired that Cozy had chosen him to play on his most recent solo album, been impressed and suggested him to David. Having worked with another former Trapeze man – Glenn Hughes – David was very familiar with Mel's talent, which was augmented by the addition of an underlying rock 'n' roll attitude!

Having busied myself with sessions for the likes of Roger Chapman, Sheena Easton and Mike Oldfield, I was pleased to be back in the studios with David to add a few guitar licks to the Clearwell recordings. Mel was also involved, albeit as a vocalist, and we shared the backing-vocal duties for the album, which would become *Saints and Sinners*. Although Mel was the only guy in the band I hadn't worked with previously, it was obvious from the start that, both personally and musically, we would get along fine. It was to be the start of a new era for Whitesnake.

Sadly, it would turn out to be the end of an old era for me: an era of great fun, fabulous music and unprecedented camaraderie. And sadder still, from this revised line-up, Jon, Cozy and Mel are no longer with us.

Due in no small measure to Cozy's extravagant drum solos, Whitesnake Mk II was an odd kettle of fish live. David had decided to retain the solo spots – those interludes of individual expression so often loathed by reviewers. There may have been three possible reasons for this: he admired the players' abilities and thought it only right that they should be endorsed; it was a way of winding up the reviewers; or he needed to leave the stage at set intervals for a blast of oxygen, a Marlboro Red or both. Jon's classically-enhanced organ and sound-effects showpiece, my own slide-guitar feature, Colin's brief yet extremely individual take on country-blues and Cozy's mammoth percussion-and-pyrotechnic spectacular were, indeed, strange bedfellows. Still, the crowds were growing in stature and *Come an' Get It* had proven to be Whitesnake's biggest success to date.

The band continued to headline throughout the early part of 1983 with continued success but, for me, it just wasn't the same. Although there had never been any doubt that David was the undisputed leader and main man in Whitesnake, there was now an uneasy feeling of 'him and us' within the ranks. Bonding with ex-paratroopers on Dartmoor was not my idea of rock 'n' roll and I'm pleased to say that most of the band agreed. Not that we were asked to take part in such manoeuvres, although Cozy, being the alpha man that he was, bless him, was only too happy to! I soon began to feel that I was a proverbial pawn in an increasingly high-powered game of ego-driven chess, and somewhat out of my depth.

The new line-up entered Musicland studios in Munich in the summer to record a new album. Between them, David and Mel had written the bulk of the album, but I was successful in persuading David to record a backing track I'd written. This turned out to be the stomping, slide guitar-led 'Slow and Easy', a track ideally suited to Cozy's brain-crunching drum fills. It's remained a popular live song ever since, both with Whitesnake and some of the line-ups I've been involved in since. Mel's melodic influence on the songwriting was obvious; the new songs were more commercial in style than on *Come an' Get It* and a long way from those on *Ready an' Willing*. There was little trace of the British-styled blues-rock that had roused my soul in the late 1960s and early 1970s, which was a big influence on the early Whitesnake sound.

After headlining at a bunch of festivals, including Castle Donnington, where Cozy spiced up his drums-and-flames routine with the presence of an army helicopter hovering overhead, we headed to Europe for a run of shows. Geffen Records was now involved, and there was a gradual realisation that its interest in moustachioed men in fedoras and mild-mannered, left-handed bass players was negligible. Any doubts I'd harboured about leaving Whitesnake were soon cast aside in a hotel bar after a show in Germany, where David suddenly turned on me and criticised my stage persona in front of Thin Lizzy's John Sykes. It was a cheap and nasty way of handing my mantle over to John, who was as embarrassed as I was humiliated by such petulant behaviour. It was a cunt's trick and I never forgave him for it.

As I said earlier, there are only two reasons for leaving a band and, believe me, they were very much in evidence on that tour. I quit after the last gig on the European jaunt and may well be the only person to have left Whitesnake twice! I never got to tour the new album, *Slide It In*, and, to be honest, with a title like that, I suppose I should count my blessings!

So that was that then. Although I'd been in the business professionally for over fifteen years, it was my first taste of the big time. It would also be my last. I'd just spent five years with one of the top rock acts in Europe and I had very little to show for it. I was never big on responsibilities or workaholism but, if this was the sum total of success as a rock star, I would sooner go back to what I was doing before – i.e. being a musician. And I did.

We all have our ups and downs during that constant journey known as life and I've had my fair share, both professionally and in my personal life. I've been lucky enough to have been able to pull into an emotional lay-by, pick up a guitar and soothe my soul. And a sense of humour, whether pie-in-the-face or wry in nature, is essential for one's mental well-being, as a young Chet Atkins learned in a heart-to-heart with his dad.

'Dad, when I grow up, I want to be a guitarist.'

'You can't do both, son.'

SPECIAL
THANKS

To my dad, whose encouragement and willingness to part with his hard-earned cash to help a penniless schoolboy will never be forgotten. To Neil Murray, for help with dates and photos and lasting friendship. And to Ali Maas for technical support, personal stress management and much more.